By Good and Necessary Consequence

By Good and Necessary Consequence

A Preliminary Genealogy
of Biblicist Foundationalism

CARLOS R. BOVELL

WIPF & STOCK · Eugene, Oregon

BY GOOD AND NECESSARY CONSEQUENCE
A Preliminary Genealogy of Biblicist Foundationalism

Wipf & Stock
A Division of Wipf and Stock Publishers
199 W. 8th Ave., Suite 3
Eugene, OR 97401
www.wipfandstock.com

ISBN: 978-1-4982-5295-9

Manufactured in the U.S.A.

"... in the context of evolutionary dynamics, religious beliefs are selected for their utility and not their veracity, the question of whether or not any particular religious belief is warranted or true is an entirely different matter ... Let all participants understand, however, that [an inquiry into warrant] must be performed in the full awareness of what ... has [been] learned about the general phenomenon of religious belief."

— HOWARD VAN TILL

"... the social source of an idea is usually construed to be relevant to its truth, regardless of the existence of a formal logical relationship: we tend to mistrust information that comes from demonstrably unreliable sources."

—DAN FRANK

Contents

Acknowledgments

A s with my first book, *Inerrancy and the Spiritual Formation of Younger Evangelicals*, a number of evangelical scholars have encouraged me privately in the publication of this book. I would like to thank them, the staff at Wipf and Stock, and the Reverend Harald Peeders. Thank you Jamie, Elena, and Mateo for eating all my pancakes, and Jen, the love of my life, for being such a good sport about all the crazy stuff I do.

Abbreviations

APo.	Aristotle, *Posterior Analytics*
Conf.	Augustine, *Confessions*
Cons. Phil.	Boethius, *Consolation of Philosophy*
De Trin	Augustine, *De Trintate*
Enn.	Plotinus, *Enneads*
Eth. Nic.	Aristotle, *Nicomachean Ethics*
Met.	Aristotle, *Metaphysics*
Rep.	Plato, *Republic*
Summa Th	Thomas Aquinas, *Summa Theologica*

"Concerning objects proposed for study, we ought to investigate what we can **clearly and evidently intuit or deduce with certainty**, and not *what other people have thought or what we ourselves conjecture.* For knowledge can be attained in no other way."

—Descartes

"The whole counsel of God concerning all things necessary for his own glory, man's salvation, faith and life, is either **expressly set down in Scripture, or by good and necessary consequence may be deduced from Scripture**: unto which nothing at any time is to be added, whether *by new revelations of the Spirit, or traditions of men.*"

—Westminster Confession of Faith

Introduction

THERE IS A CONTROVERSY underway over what might be regarded as theological innovation during post-Reformation Christianity. There are scholars who are convinced that some negative developments are discernable during this time period. However, they are still trying to provide a satisfactory description of what it is they see in post-Reformation Christianity that is unaligned with prior orthodox streams of Christianity. The idea that an inerrant Bible was introduced for the first time during this period has already been introduced. That post-Reformation Christianity took on a more "scholastic" approach to faith than earlier periods has also been submitted.[1] For various reasons, neither of these proposals has been accepted as altogether convincing.

In an effort to help keep the conversation going, I have attempted a genealogy for a particular mindset toward theology that seems to have its roots in seventeenth century Protestantism. I suggest a sense of cultural urgency marked seventeenth century theology, facilitating the decision among Protestants that all ecclesial practices and every Protestant dogma had to be either taken directly from scripture or necessarily deduced from scripture. In this book I trace out a preliminary genealogy of biblicist foundationalism in order to help identify what meta-theological *discontinuity* was introduced to Christianity during the course of seventeenth century Protestantism. The biblicist foundationalist mindset I have in mind is expressed well by the clause cited above from the Westminster Confession of Faith. In what follows I conduct a preliminary genealogy for this "good and necessary consequence" clause and attempt to make the following salient points.

First, I argue historical circumstances were such that religious leaders of the seventeenth century were expected to respond to a pervasive, cultural skepticism by showing their positions had proper epistemological foundations. Second, the most promising way for Protestant theologians

---

1. See, for example, Rogers and McKim, *Authority*, 185–88.

to fend off the cultural and epistemological skepticism of the time was to follow cultural trends and work toward the contrivance of a biblicist foundationalism. Third, I claim that the use to which this biblicist foundationalism was put during the seventeenth century—i.e., to shore up Reformed versions of the Christian faith against the triple threats of Catholic, enthusiast, and literary/rational forms of skepticism—is discontiguous with the classical invention, subsequent appropriation, and contemporary estimation of axiomatic and deductive methodology. Fourth, although such methodological developments may have been suitable for seventeenth century religious communities given their cultural context, they should not be welcomed today. Fifth, I illustrate an important consideration against biblicist foundationalism: when a believer's faith is epistemologically ordered in a foundationalist way with conservative biblicism at the center, once the biblicist foundations are irrecoverably questioned, the whole faith is seriously upset. Sixth, it is high time that alternate responses to biblicist foundationalism be expressly sought and articulated.

1

The Seventeenth Century Context

T<small>HE SEVENTEENTH CENTURY WAS</small> a time during which a number of profound cultural revolutions were underway. The present treatise attempts a preliminary genealogy for the revived interest in methodological deduction and its introduction to theology as the methodological ideal in the form of biblicist foundationalism. During the late Renaissance, "[s]keptical questions about the natural world were often stated in terms of whether one can deduce from one's representations alone that there exists a natural world outside ourselves that causes us to have these representations in the first place."[1] But not until 1637 would Rene Descartes publish the *Discourse on Method* where he proclaims that he has finally found a way to methodically inquire into the general principles of whatever is said to exist and also to determine what can properly be deduced from them. His third rule, composed several years earlier, reads:

> Concerning objects proposed for study, we ought to investigate *what we can clearly and evidently intuit or deduce with certainty*, and not what other people have thought or what we ourselves conjecture. For knowledge can be attained in no other way.[2]

By 1687, pressures regarding methodological procedure culminated in such a way that Isaac Newton writes:

> But hitherto I have not been able to discover the cause of those properties of gravity from phenomena, and I frame no hypotheses; for whatever is not deduced from the phenomena, is to be called an hypothesis; and hypotheses, whether metaphysical or physical,

---

1. Filosofiska Institutionen, "Skepticism."
2. Excerpt from Achinstein, *Science Rules* [italics mine].

whether of occult qualities or mechanical, have no place in experimental philosophy.[3]

Surely there is an important connection to be made between the seventeenth century's interest in methodological deductivism and how during the middle of the century the Westminster Confession of Faith introduces to Protestant confessionalism a deductivism of its own—a deductivism that requires that theology be done by deducing good and necessary consequences from statements expressly set forth in scripture. This chapter briefly describes the cultural context for the entrance of what I call biblicist foundationalism: the decision to restrict confessional theology to the deduction of good and necessary consequences from express biblical statements.

In the eighteenth century, the mathematician Maclaurin lectured on Newton's methods, promulgating its authority in establishing truth and encouraging its application in every discipline "in order to proceed with perfect security, and to put an end forever to disputes."[4] By claiming only to accept what has been deduced from phenomena, Newton is reassuring his readers that what he has adumbrated in the *Principia* can be regarded as more sure than the theories of Descartes or Leibniz. For in the *Principia*, Newton presents an argument *more geometrico* and wherever in his train of mathematical proofs he posits the existence of some entity as the cause of other phenomena, at some later stage in the investigation he also sets out to verify that entity's existence (except in the case of gravity) via a synthesis *a posteriori*.[5] Yet as Cohen observes:

> It is a feature of the Newtonian style that mathematics and not a series of experiments leads to a profound knowledge of the universe and its workings . . . He hoped that his readers would go along with him and would not reject the physics of the *Principia* on philosophical grounds without going through the mathematical development he had presented and then seeing how the physi-

---

3. Newton, *Principia*, 428. Although Newton was an empiricist, deductivism still played an important part in his natural philosophy. This scholium did not appear in earlier editions.

4. Grabiner, "Newton," 849.

5. An argument *more geometrico* refers here to an argument that patterns itself after the manner of geometric proofs. Geometric proofs have been looked upon as the exemplar for philosophical rigor throughout the history of western philosophy. See, for example, Lucas, *Conceptual Roots*, 68.

cal universe would prove to be an analogue of the mathematical system he had developed.[6]

In a similar way, Galileo appealed to mathematics in defense of his scientific proposals. Strong explains: "the strongest argument that Galileo can advance . . . is that the proposition can be demonstrated mathematically and that experiment will support the principles upon which the demonstration is based."[7] Galileo, before Newton, argued that mathematics procured the most certain knowledge humans can possibly achieve. In fact, he insisted that mathematical arguments brought one as close to divine knowledge as humans can get.[8]

Both Galileo and Newton are representative of a general trend taking place in seventeenth century thought. As Janiak points out, "Euclidean geometry and its methods were seen as a fundamental epistemic model for much of seventeenth-century philosophy . . . "[9] In fact, some English mathematicians had even gone so far as to look to mathematics to find "the distinct expression of all things and notions that fall under discourse" and in this way reduce *every* manner of discourse to just a few basic laws.[10] Yet the skepticism that plagued seventeenth century Europe was so thoroughgoing that even the foundations of mathematics were being called into question. As a result, many disciplines were under severe pressure (insofar as theoretically possible) to substantiate their claims via argumentation *more geometrico*.[11]

In due course, theologians, too, were expected to give a legitimating account of their discipline's foundational authority. Protestant theologians were not immune to mounting cultural pressures to propose an "analogy of science" for their theologies.[12] The certainty associated with mathematical method and knowledge was the only ray of hope. For example, a letter written in 1659 by mathematician John Wallis reveals the

6. Cohen, "Newton's Method," 140.

7. Strong, *Procedures*, 138.

8. See Remmert, "Galileo."

9. Janiak, "Introduction," xi.

10. Cohen, *Equations*, 26–27. Cohen's citation refers to the collected works of John Wilkins (1614–1672), mathematician and bishop of Chester.

11. See, for example, Floridi, "The Debate."

12. Phrase from Lonergan, *Method*, 3.

motivation behind his unlikely embroilment in a dispute with Thomas Hobbes:

> As if the Christian world knew nothing sound or nothing that was not ridiculous in philosophy or religion; and as if it has not understood religion because it does not understand philosophy, nor philosophy because it does not understand mathematics. And so it seemed necessary that now some mathematician, proceeding in the opposite direction, should show how little he understand this mathematics (from which he takes his courage).[13]

The looming skepticism was trenchant and an antidote desperately sought.

How were Protestants to respond to such a seething skeptical *ethos*? Guillory summarizes their strategy: "Needing to offer more than a rational basis for reformation, and at the same time fearing the probing that claims to divine inspiration might provoke, the original reformers restricted the *Wort Gottes* to the Bible, a finished revelation that is only extended into the present by the act of reading."[14] In a manner similar to Descartes, seventeenth century theologians began concentrating on two chief methodological aims: 1) To procure a sure basis for normativity in theology, and 2) To contrive an absolute certainty for theology, a certainty that would be capable of providing the psychological stability requisite for serious religious commitment, especially in the face of rampant skepticism.[15]

A retreat to origins as epistemological foundation is par for the course for seventeenth century thinking. As Snider remarks: "The seventeenth century's attempt to ground truth in a non-contingent absolute made the equation of knowledge with the recovery of origin a matter of 'common sense.'"[16] Stout says of the seventeenth century: "It was *reasonable* for Descartes, in a way that it could not be for us, to view the category of probable opinion with the gravest kind of suspicion and to turn instead to the quest for certainty, even as a prelude to empirical inquiry."[17] It was precisely this dual role—to provide theological normativity and psychological stability—that the Bible was gradually nominated to fill. Such a

---

13. As cited in Jesseph, "Geometry." Wallis was a Presbyterian minister, a doctor of divinity, and a professor of geometry at Oxford.

14. Guillory, *Poetic Authority*, 14.

15. Compare Bennett, "Infallibility," on Descartes.

16. Snider, *Origin*, 9.

17. Stout, *Flight*, 50, italics in original.

methodological development quickly culminated in the Protestant principle of *sola scriptura*.[18]

The emphasis on scripture as foundation came to a head during the course of the seventeenth century when various skeptical impulses had finally coalesced, cumulatively intensifying in cultural effect.[19] Stout has already recounted how the skeptical response to having a multiplicity of Catholic authorities could not be resolved by a Reformed emphasis on singular authority.[20] For it did not take long for the skeptical attitude directed towards Protestant enthusiasts to turn back upon authorized interpreters of the single Protestant authority (scripture).[21] As Abraham observes, in no time at all "the exegetical optimism which accompanied this revolution had clearly failed in practice."[22]

Protestant authorities held to an inordinate expectation that scripture could become *the* foundational ground for Protestant Christianity. Yet as history would have it, this methodological gambit was advanced precisely at a time when

> [o]rthodoxy had only polemic to oppose to that spirit of self-confident control of the world which was alive in Galileo, Descartes, Herbert of Cherbury, Hobbes or Spinoza, or in their pupils—that spirit which discussed the foundations of the physical and moral world and which put in question the basic positions of traditional faith . . . And while it was still working on the development of its doctrine of scripture, it was unaware that the very character of scripture as revelation was in dispute.[23]

18. For an account of this development in Anglican circles, see Greer, *Anglican Approaches*. For an account that describes Presbyterian developments, see Rogers, *Scripture*. See also Richard A. Muller, "Inspired," who vigorously disputes Rogers' claim that the English theologians were "insulated" from their continental counterparts. In my view, the most incisive account of these developments is Abraham, *Canon and Criterion*.

19. The skeptical onslaught was pervasive and manifested itself in every area of European inquiry. For illustrations, one might consult any number of studies, for example: Saracino, "Hobbes"; Lennon, "Jansenism"; Del Prete, "Against Descartes"; Gregory, "Libertinisme Erudit"; Russell, "Skepticism"; Rogers, "Basis"; Southgate, "Philosophical Divinity." For a smattering of primary sources, see Popkin and J. R. Maia Neto, *Skepticism*.

20. Stout, *Flight*, 44.

21. Guillory, *Poetic Authority*, 14.

22. Abraham, *Canon*, 163.

23. Scholder, *Birth*, 5.

A more sympathetic description of the decision to ground Protestant Christianity in scripture is given by McGowan:

> The Reformers and those who followed in their tradition wanted to emphasize that all of their teaching was drawn from Scripture; hence they began with a strong statement on the authority, sufficiency and perspicuity of Scripture before dealing with any other doctrine. In this way, they were underlining the fact that when they came to speak about God, salvation, the church or any other matter, everything they said would be drawn from the Scripture principle.[24]

Yet skeptical thinkers such as Montaigne had already decried the methodological effects of this type of epistemological ploy: "It is very easy, upon accepted foundations, to build what you please . . . For our masters occupy and win beforehand as much room in our belief as they need in order to conclude afterward whatever they wish, in the manner of the geometricians with their axioms."[25] The observation to make is that Protestant thinkers in the seventeenth century were trying to find a way to derive all of their theology from scripture alone precisely when every discipline was expected to trace their bodies of knowledge to an original source. Within this very context was the Westminster Confession devised.

During the course of his account of the evolution of Reformed confessions, Richard Muller writes: "Westminster is undoubtedly the greatest confessional document written during the age of Protestant Scholasticism."[26] Germane to the present study is his observation that in the Westminster Confession "[t]he sufficiency and fullness of the biblical revelation for the salvation of the world is stated and qualified with more precision and clarity than can be found in any earlier Reformed confession."[27] Muller specifically has in mind the following clause:

---

24. McGowan, *Divine Spiration*, 27–28.

25. "Apology," 403.

26. *Post-Reformation*, 87.

27 *Post-Reformation*, 97. Compare B. B. Warfield, "There is certainly in the whole mass of confessional literature no more nobly conceived or ably wrought-out statement of doctrine than the chapter 'Of the Holy Scripture,' which the Westminster Divines placed at the head of their Confession and laid at the foundation of their system of doctrine." See *Westminster Assembly and Its Work*, 6.3.

> The whole counsel of God concerning all things necessary for his own glory, man's salvation, faith and life, is either expressly set down in Scripture, or by good and necessary consequence may be deduced from Scripture: unto which nothing at any time is to be added, whether by new revelations of the Spirit, or traditions of men.[28]

The upshot of what I believe is a seventeenth century innovation is summarized by Robert Shaw:

> "All Scripture" is declared to be "profitable for doctrine, for reproof, for correction, for instruction in righteousness"; but all these ends cannot be obtained, unless by the deduction of consequences. Legitimate consequences, indeed, only bring out the full meaning of the words of Scripture; and as we are endued with the faculty of reason, and commanded to search the Scriptures, it was manifestly intended that we should draw conclusions from what is therein set down in express words.[29]

Shaw contends that the Westminster Confession mandates that "we hold that conclusions fairly deduced from the declarations of the Word of God are as truly parts of divine revelation as if they were expressly taught in the Sacred Volume." Or as a contemporary Presbyterian theologian has written: "If we deny the implications of Scripture, we are denying Scripture."[30]

The methodological claim is that theology is only properly done by axiomatizing whatever divine precepts are expressly set down in scripture and then proceeding by deduction to achieve its fullest sense for the purpose of subsequent systematic and discursive presentations. According to Richard Muller, "[T]he assumption . . . that the text of scripture provided principial or axiomatic truths from which right conclusions could be drawn for the sake of the formulation of Christian teaching . . . [can also be] found in both late Medieval and Reformation-era theology."[31]

---

28. Westminster Confession, 1.6.

29. "Exposition."

30. John Frame, *Doctrine*, 253. Frame qualifies that human deductions are fallible, yet to many, this qualification is disclaimed only in principle. An actual qualification is rarely tolerated, for that might nullify the sufficiency of Scripture. One problem is that the Bible is said not to need anything added to it, but at the same time it requires that good and necessary deductions be made. See, for example, Brownson, "Presbyterianism."

31. See Muller, "Inspired," 58. The ordering of the words in this sentence (namely the phrase coming after the last ellipsis) has been inverted for a smoother read in the context

Although this is true, the epistemological priority given to biblicist deductivism in the seventeenth century is unprecedented.

For example, consider how an experimenting with Cartesian logic had become fashionable in England (and specifically at Cambridge) during the middle of the seventeenth century. "Aristotelian and Ramist logical strategies," explains Kennedy, "tended to confirm and systematize static knowledge, while Cartesianism emphasized the method of geometry which was open-ended and expansive . . . Cartesian logic was more comprehensive and unifying, purporting that knowledge was an upside-down pyramid rising from a storehouse of a few axioms expanding to who-knew-where."[32] This particular logical strategy had been specifically adapted during the seventeenth century for religious purposes. In this way, knowledge could be "accepted from outside of the mind, then brought into the art or process of logic as the equivalent of axioms . . . The most important doctrines of Christianity are testimonies in the Bible or passed through time in the community of the church; therefore, dogmatically-inclined logics had to define and find ways to incorporate these inartificial, external arguments into logic."[33] By composing the good and necessary consequence clause, the Westminster divines are following epistemological conventions of their times, searching for origins and establishing what principles can be found there.

The innovative step taken in the Westminster Confession is its cultural adaptation of a Cartesian-like foundationalism, "[we seek] what we can [either] clearly and evidently intuit or deduce certainly; for in no other way is knowledge acquired," into a biblicist foundationalism, "The whole counsel of God . . . is either expressly set down in Scripture, or by good and necessary consequence may be deduced from Scripture." What's more, the Westminster Confession of Faith arranges its procedural negative axioms in precise correspondence to Descartes', replacing "what others have thought" and "what we conjecture" with "traditions of men" and "new revelations of the Spirit" respectively.[34]

---

of the present paragraph.

32. Kennedy, *Cartesian Logic*, 49. On Descartes' dissatisfaction with Aristotelian scholasticism, see Secada, *Cartesian Metaphysics*, 27–54.

33. Kennedy, *Cartesian Logic*, 21.

34. Referring to the enthusiasts and Catholics respectively. Descartes: "Concerning objects proposed for study, we ought to investigate what we can clearly and evidently intuit or deduce with certainty, and not what other people have thought or what we our-

In this way, it was hoped that during times of dispute scripture, along with all that can be deduced from scripture, would collectively serve as an elaborate set of laws by which Presbyterian churches might be made to abide. In fact, one of the framers of the Westminster Confession of Faith considered a legal metaphor apt enough to describe the clause in question:

> When the Earle of Strafford was impeached for high treason, one of his defences was, that no Law of the Land had determined any of those particulars, which were proved against him to be high treason. Which defence of his was not confuted by any Law, which literally and syllabically made many of those severall Lawes, and severall matters of fact, and by drawing of necessary consequences from one thing to another, which made up against him a constructive treason. If there be constructive or consequentiall *jus humanum*, there must be much more (for the considerations before mentioned) a constructive of consequentiall *jus divinum*.[35]

Be that as it may, epistemological developments were such that, in matters of theology, the clarity of scripture became "absolutely essential to [the Reformers'] epistemology of divine revelation. Once the clarity of Scripture, in the terms in which they framed it, was called into question, then their whole proposal about canon was in serious trouble."[36] The rhetoric used to communicate authority within seventeenth century Protestantism began emphasizing scripture as the only epistemological foundation in ways never seen before in the history of Christianity.[37] Why did certain strands of Reformed theology begin taking an active interest in whether deductions drawn by reasoning upon scriptural statements are just as sure and certain as those things that are expressly set forth in Scripture? What precipitated this epistemological turn in theology?[38] And more importantly, is it *desirable* that Protestant theology has

---

selves conjecture. For knowledge can be attained in no other way."

35. Gillespie, *Treatise*, 245.

36. Abraham, *Canon*, 152.

37. Theo Hobson goes so far as to argue that the role of authoritative rhetoric in Protestantism "can hardly be overstated . . . a rhetorical performance of authority is what Protestant Christianity essentially *is*." See Hobson, *Rhetorical Word*, 1, italics in original.

38. Several contemporary writers have had the cultural wherewithal to undertake such inquiries. See, for example, Abraham, *Canon*; Vickers, "Canonical Theism"; Grenz and Franke, *Beyond Foundationalism*; Webster, *Holy Scripture*; and McGowan, *Divine Spiration*.

taken such a turn?[39] One might begin taking steps toward a preliminary set of answers to such questions by observing, as we already have, that this new interest in inferring doctrines from those expressly set down in Scripture was not a privileged Presbyterian maneuver. It was rather a part of a historically-conditioned decision within Protestantism to participate in the broader cultural response to the literary and philosophical skepticism that was permeating late Renaissance Europe. To offer two specific examples, the Lutheran Johannes Andreas Quenstedt, when enthralled in debate against Cardinal Bellarmine, professed:

> This is our position: all things necessary to a saving knowledge and worship of God and to an attainment of everlasting blessedness are sufficiently contained in the written Word of God, either expressly and in so many words . . . in words with the same meaning and taken from that same fountain of holy Scripture through good, legitimate, necessary and certain consequences.[40]

And according to Preus, the Lutheran Johann Gerhard likewise insisted that "[t]he Lutheran position is this: of those things necessary for doctrine and Christian life certain things are taught in Scripture explicitly (*secundam literam*) and other things are taught only implicitly (*secundum rem*) and must be drawn from Scripture through legitimate deduction."[41]

This methodological expectation of seventeenth century Protestant theology—that all ecclesial practices and all Christian dogma should either be taken directly from scripture or carefully deduced from scripture—should not be understood merely as the culmination of the *sola scriptura* principle. The move to *sola scriptura* is not an isolated development within Protestant theology. If one steps back to consider historical context, the move to *sola scriptura* is very much in line with the wider contemporary political, philosophical, and cultural matrices of the time. Formulating orthodox boundaries for a Reformed doctrine of the Word and distinguishing Reformed Christians from their Catholic counterparts (not to mention the Enthusiasts)—these were matters of great concern

---

39. The title of Frame's first volume of his multi-volume systematic theology illustrates how important epistemological concerns have programmatically become for Reformed theology in particular. "The doctrine of the knowledge of God" had already earned the right of first locus for theological inquiry by the time the Westminster Confession of Faith was written.

40. Cited in Preus, *Inspiration*, 149.

41. Ibid.

for many seventeenth century Protestant dogmaticians, but there was also the very important matter of articulating a public confession that could withstand the rational and literary skepticisms that characterized later Renaissance thought generally.[42] As Brown points out, in every social quarter, *especially* religious ones, skeptical pressures had been progressively mounting for leaders to model all discourse according to argumentation *more geometrico* as far as methodologically possible.[43]

Accordingly, a preliminary genealogical exploration of the "good and necessary consequence" heritage of Reformed and evangelical theology may provide contemporary Christians with a more critical estimation of the decidedly epistemological turn taken in Reformed theology since the late Renaissance. For, as the present study sets out to illustrate, the impetus behind biblicist foundationalism—to shore up Reformed versions of the Christian faith against the triple threats of Catholicism, religious enthusiasts, and the rational and literary skeptics—is not at all commensurate with the classical invention and subsequent philosophical appropriations of axiomatic and deductive methodologies, not to mention contemporary estimations of axiomatic procedure. If this is right, then the Protestant expectation that good and necessary consequences should be drawn strictly from Scripture—and that these should be allotted the same authority as Scripture—will have little to no philosophical pedigree and should appear to readers, even if for the first time, *as a historically-conditioned innovation that was naturally elicited from Protestants by the prevailing intellectual milieu of the seventeenth century.* The point is not that Christian dogmatics should never experiment with biblicist deductivist approaches, but rather that theology *more geometrico*, exclusively based on scriptural axioms, should not appeal to conservative dogmaticians today in the same way

---

42. The "crisis" brought about by European religious disputes transpired precisely at the time that Greek skepticism was being rediscovered and other economic uncertainties had begun to set in. See Popkin, *History of Scepticism*; Dooley, *Skepticism*.

43. See, for example, Brown, *Edwards*, 30–35. Although the time period that is the focus of Brown's book happens to be slightly later than the time of the Westminster Confession, we can surely say the same thing for seventeenth century Protestantism. For the *quaestio de certitudine mathematicarum*, for example, as well as other related controversies across Europe were already well underway by the time the Westminster divines convened for deliberations. See Jardine, "Epistemology"; Wallace, "Certitude"; Mancosu, "Aristotelian Logic"; Lukacs and Cosentino, *Church*. For the humanities, see David Quint, *Origin* and Guillory, *Poetic Authority*. See also Popkin, *History of Scepticism*.

that it did to seventeenth century theologians—at least not in the same way in terms of gaining an epistemological advantage.

To help readers see this, the opening chapters present an episodic study of deductivism in ancient and early medieval philosophy. The point to be taken is that epistemology was not the motivation behind its usage or development and that epistemology's rise to ascendancy during the late Renaissance should not be mistaken for an inherently Christian (or even biblical) preoccupation with epistemic justification. The inspiration for the Westminster Confession of Faith's good and necessary consequence clause is the same cultural skepticism facing Descartes, not scripture (as its adherents insist). William Abraham reminds Protestants in his canonical theistic manifesto that "[t]he canonical heritage through which canonical theism is mediated is not in and of itself an epistemology, nor is it meant to serve as an epistemology. It is not a handbook on how to resolve disputes about rationality, justification, warrant, knowledge, and truth."[44] But in the face of enveloping skepticism, an epistemological sourcebook is precisely what seventeenth century Protestants thought the Bible could be.

The present study is offered to readers as a preliminary effort toward a deeper appreciation for the purposes to which the deductive method has historically been set. Its principal aim is to encourage readers to look anew at the conservative attitude toward constructing Protestant faith. The reader is invited to reconsider the desirability of a good-and-necessary-consequence mindset toward Reformed and evangelical theology. The phrase, "biblicist foundationalism," found in the subtitle, refers to an approach to theology that posits that the Christian Bible contains an exclusive, divinely revealed body of religious precepts, the core of which has been plainly expressed by God, and that by good and necessary consequence readers can deduce the whole counsel of God. The present volume attempts and reflects upon a preliminary genealogy of this self-conscious, deductivist practice in Reformed and evangelical theology. For it was commonplace during the English Renaissance to expect those paramount truths that all humans must grasp should by their very nature be "plain."[45] Yet there seems to be the additional understanding in our case that the body of precepts revealed in scripture is to be the *only* normative resource that can and should be used when contriving theological systems. That

44. Abraham, "Canonical Theism," 3
45. See Graham, *Performance*.

is, if one wants to be certain that the Christian theological system one is constructing is *really* of God then it is to be strictly constructed by good and necessary consequence, beginning with those express truths articulated in the Bible. The conclusions that are drawn from scripture as well as those that are drawn from the conclusions that have already been drawn from scripture are all to be construed as divinely revealed (without, of course, implying that the initial body of precepts is somehow lacking or insufficient).

Historically, the only discipline that even comes close to the methodological rigor imagined by biblicist foundationalism is mathematics.[46] Accordingly, after rounding out this introductory discussion about the cultural milieu within which the Westminster Confession was conceived, the book will occupy itself with the history and philosophy of ancient mathematics and especially the extension of these discussions to later exemplars of presentation *more geometrico*. Among these are the early efforts of the Pythagoreans, the mathematical compendium of Euclid, and also the metaphysical treatises of Proclus and Boethius (along with Aquinas' commentary on Boethius).

Readers should understand that it is *not* the aim of the present work to suggest that the Westminster divines (or any of the Reformers for that matter) were explicitly aware of the genealogy proposed here or that a direct genealogical influence can be definitively established. This book does take seriously, however, the results of earlier studies that have shown the wide ranging effects of skepticism on religious thinkers of the time in question. In other words, the Westminster methodological clause, "by good and necessary consequence," is understood to be indicative of fundamental shifts in Reformed theology, (*a shift that now must be confessed in a confession!*), toward things epistemological—a shift, one might add, that misunderstands deduction as an epistemologically superior, scientific *methodus*. To illustrate this, earlier uses of deduction in mathematics and uses of mathematical examples of deduction in philosophy are brought to bear upon the Westminster Confession's good-and-necessary-consequence innovation. For throughout the history of Western philosophy, and especially during the seventeenth century, mathematics was often considered as having a method *par excellence*.

46. Compare, for example, Stout, *Flight*, 49; Buckley, *Origins*, 77–85; Carson, "Locke." For developments in axiomatic genre, see Serene, "Demonstrative."

That mathematics had been officially recognized as a vital part of the *Ratio studiorum* at the Collegio Romano by the end of the sixteenth century has already been shown by Cosentino.[47] That the mathematical discipline of algebra was making revolutionary cultural advances in sixteenth and seventeenth century England has been thoroughly documented by Pycior.[48] Gilbert, for his part, keenly observes that humanists of the time were showing less and less interest in the insoluble disputations that characterized late medieval scholasticism. The study of Euclidean geometry was widely suggested as its foil and was promoted as a powerful vehicle for better understanding Aristotelian demonstration.[49] In literary circles, Snider illustrates how "a desire to establish the legitimacy of the present through the recovery and representation of origins figured prominently in the writing of both philosophy and epic poetry. Establishing truth at an absolute beginning that conditioned and controlled the emergent present, they regarded the pursuit of origins as a basic philosophical activity."[50]

Within Christianity itself bitter rivalries ensued between Protestants and Catholics and amongst Protestants and Catholics themselves. Without, wider cultural developments pitted committed religionists against skeptical humanists. Pressures mounted on all fronts for Protestant Christians to methodologically legitimate their own version of the theological enterprise and biblical deductivism was the response. In retrospect, there is some irony in the Reformed decision for axiomatic and deductive method, for contemporary historians of science have become "atheists" with regard to method. In other words, *historians of science have found that the structure of method discourses is not sufficient for accomplishing what they promise to deliver.*[51]

During the late Renaissance, the exemplary means of legitimating a scholarly discipline was for one to set out to establish its foundations (again, insofar as possible) on 1) indisputable, original source(s) in the humanities, or 2) primitive, first principles via argumentation *more geometrico* in the sciences. Insofar as theologians began to follow suit, it would appear that theology was perceived more or less in innovative ways. In

47. See, for example, Cosentino's contributions to Lukacs and Cosentino, Church. See also Sasaki, *Thought*, 19–44.

48. See Pycior, *Symbols*.

49. See Gilbert, *Renaissance*, 27.

50. Snider, *Origin*, 3.

51. See, for example, Schuster, "What."

Reformed circles, the innovation of biblical deductivism is expounded by Heinrich Heppe:

> By virtue of this the Holy Scriptures are the principle of the whole of theology, the exclusive norm of Christian doctrine, and the infallible judge of all controversies; and that in such a manner that all that is contained in the language (Wortlaut) of Scripture, or follows by indubitable consequence from it, is dogma, while what is contrary to it is error, and everything else, even if it does not contradict Holy Scripture, is indifferent for the soul's welfare.[52]

The preliminary genealogy of biblicist foundationalism attempted here involves an investigation of various methodological considerations associated with Greek mathematics. Greek mathematics was the ideal epistemic model for every discipline during the seventeenth century. The observation to make is the same made by Snider in *Origin and Authority in Seventeenth Century England*:

> The Aristotelian tradition recognized a paradox that the seventeenth century strove to repress: establishing the sources from which knowledge derives proceeds through an impossible process. If demonstrated truths necessarily follow from true premises, the premises themselves remain indemonstrable, or at least not susceptible to ordinary forms of demonstration.[53]

Yet an important observation to make is that the Greek deductive genre of argumentation *more geometrico* was formulated *prior* to the onset of formidable skepticism led by Sextus Empiricus. Popkin outlines the development of skepticism in his magisterial *The History of Scepticism: From Savonarola to Bayle* and explains that "[w]ith the rediscovery in the fifteenth and sixteenth centuries of writings of the Greek Pyrrhonist Sextus Empiricus, the arguments and views of the Greek skeptics became part of the philosophical core of the religious struggles then taking place."[54] Whereas skepticism was neither here nor there for the early development of axiomatic deductivism, it was a major catalyst for its seventeenth century revival.

During this time, skepticism infiltrated religion and theology. Cultural expectations were such that Protestant theology—the Westminster

52. Cited in Warfield, *The Westminster Assembly and Its Work*.

53. Snider, *Origin*, 5–6.

54. Popkin, *History of Scepticism*, 3.

Confession serving as a good illustrative case—had to give the appearance, insofar as possible, of deducing its distinctive theological tenets from scripture alone. Although biblicist foundationalism may have been a proper and natural response to the intellectual climate of seventeenth century Europe, it does not appear that it makes much sense now. Perhaps an investigation into the origin and early development and appropriation of deductive mathematics will provide some useful data with which to critically assess the good-and-necessary-consequence mentality that still characterizes much of conservative Protestant theology today.

2

A Preliminary Genealogy Outlined

I

N THIS CHAPTER, I shall provide an outline of my preliminary gene-
alogy. The next several chapters are devoted to the genealogy proper.
It is not until chapter ten that I return to the topic of the Westminster
Confession.

According to Howard Stein, ". . . the birth of mathematics can also
be regarded as the discovery of a capacity of the human mind, or of human thought—hence its tremendous importance to philosophy . . . "[1]
He explains that he is "taking the word *mathematics* to refer, not merely
to a body of knowledge, or lore, such as existed for example among the
Babylonians many centuries earlier . . . but rather to a systematic discipline with clearly defined concepts and with theorems rigorously demonstrated." Although it has become fashionable for some historians to insist
that various "procedures and checks in the mathematics of [Egypt and
Babylonia] . . . as a form of 'proof' in the broader sense" demand equal
attention,[2] the spirit behind Stein's remark that "it is surely significant that
. . . Thales is named both as the earliest of the philosophers and the first
prover of geometric theorems"[3] continues to compel and so will remain a
background commitment of the present genealogy.

In this context, one should recall how Koetsier has gone a long way
toward vindicating the hypothesis (put forth by Szabó and others) that
ancient Greek mathematics slowly developed through stages of mathematical rigor that culminated in what he calls the "Euclidean tradition." To

1. Stein, "*Logos*," 238.

2. Joseph, *Crest*, 128.

3. Stein, "*Logos*," 238. According to Szabo and others it is not clear whether Greek and
Oriental mathematics even "knew how to formulate" a general theorem, much less prove
one. See Szabó, *Beginnings*, 186–87.

what extent and by what means earlier stages of mathematical thinking were influenced by non-Greek mathematical communities is a topic of ongoing debate.[4] However, that a deductive approach to mathematical argument is an original Greek development cannot be disputed.[5] McKirahan and others have proposed that Aristotle's axiomatic method was an initial attempt to generalize ancient geometric method for all of the sciences by 1) offering more rigorous bounds that might help better define a given discipline; 2) drawing attention to the accepted starting points of a given discipline (perhaps via the composition of "Elements"); 3) furnishing recognizably coherent arguments that were logically justified by the dialectical licenses that have been accepted (at least by "experts") as starting points; and 4) further refining the analytic method by which the discipline under consideration might be continually and systematically developed.[6]

In some analytic circles, the axiomatic method is still considered the paragon for philosophical method. The ancient intentions behind upholding axiomatic geometry as the formal paradigm for all science are understandable; however, its historical depiction is sometimes confused. At least since the writing of Aristotle's *APo.*, there has been a considerable disparity between the ideal methodological program set out there and the actual practice of both philosophers and mathematicians. Yet it seems to be the case that even Euclid set forth his five postulates as hypotheses that propelled a certain trajectory of inquiry into how one might tackle various geometric and arithmetic problems.

McKirahan, Wians, Mueller and others have examined the tension that persists between Aristotle's axiomatic proposal and Greek mathematics by way of favorable and not so favorable comparisons between Aristotle's *Analytics* and Euclid's *Elements*.[7] Harari's interpretation of *APo*, by contrast, proffers, among other things, a resolution of the disparity between Aristotle's theory of demonstrative science and ancient scientific practice by ultimately disputing the traditional view that Aristotle was delineating the ideal strictures of demonstrative science in *APo*.[8] Of the recent treatments, however, Leszl's considerations seem the most histori-

---

4. For a brief summary of the historical developments, see Kleiner, "Rigor," 291–94.

5. Compare Teun Koetsier, *Philosophy*; Szabó, *Beginnings*; Kleiner, "Rigor."

6. See McKirahan, *Principles*.

7. See, for example, McKirahan, *Principles*; Wians, "Scientific"; Wians, "Aristotle"; Mueller, "Greek Mathematics"; Mueller, "Euclid's Elements."

8. Harari, *Knowledge*.

cally sensitive as well as the most theoretically informed.[9] Regarding *APo.*, Leszl claims that Aristotle should not be interpreted as having in mind a set of undeniably veritable postulates that a mathematician or philosopher happens upon from which a science will naturally follow. He argues rather that axioms are understood by Aristotle as preliminary points of entry that are carefully posited by the axiomatizer. The axiomatizer would thus have at least one eye always on the axiomatic arrangement of the given body of knowledge when deciding upon the hypotheses. In ancient Greek axiomatics, then, the hypotheses that are posited as axioms are subsequently "proven" by the consequences contained in the axiomatic system that follows. Such an understanding of axiomatics shows considerable continuity with arguments from hypotheses as they appear in *Phaedo*, *Meno* and other works.[10]

Subsequent chapters illustrate specific uses of axiomatics in metaphysics, i.e., "theology," in the context of ancient and medieval philosophical method. Chapters seven and eight, for example, examine how argumentation *more geometrico* was seized upon by Proclus and Boethius for pedagogical gain in two respective metaphysical works. Proclus' *Elements of Theology* and Boethius' *De Hebdomadibus* appear to have certain affinities with Euclid's *Elements* and these semblances seem to have affected anagogical growth.[11] In chapter ten, I argue that, based upon the case studies presented in the genealogy, Protestant theology should only proceed "by good and necessary consequence" for anagogical purposes, not epistemological ones. Otherwise it may not only lose a historic perspective on what deduction can methodologically accomplish, but also refuse to gain historical consciousness altogether. For as Boucher observes, "[i]t was in the course of seeking the authoritative origins of the present in the past that the people of the Renaissance were forced to confront their own historicity."[12]

For various reasons, seventeenth century English thinkers managed to forestall this development. Snider explains: "In the course of the seventeenth-century, once the discourse of originary language established itself

9. Leszl, "Mathematics."

10. See chapter four.

11. For other medieval Christian commentaries on Boethius and the influence of the *more geometrico* in medieval theology generally, see Evans, "Boethian," and Evans, "*More Geometrico.*"

12. Boucher, "Ambiguity," 29.

as an alternative to 'error,' origins underwent a decisive transformation."[13] My argument in a nutshell is that the good-and-necessary-consequence approach to Reformed and evangelical theology is not one that should be emulated by contemporary Protestants if what they hope to gain is the same perceived epistemological advantage that the seventeenth century hoped to gain. For as Schuster observes:

> [T]he history of method doctrines is in large measure the history of various and competing attempts to dress [the] notions [of knowledge acquisition] in conceptual vestments deemed appropriate to each methodologist's perception of the context of debate and structure of socio-cognitive relevances holding in his time and place.[14]

In short, what I attempt in this book is a preliminary genealogy of biblicist foundationalism. The genealogy is comprised of a provisional compilation of evidence that speaks, each in its own way, of the theoretical development of the axiomatic method in the context of sustained philosophical reflections upon mathematical practice and the potential for a geometric method as a viable means of doing philosophy and theology. In fact, certain strands of ancient and medieval philosophy might even be viewed as intermittent attempts to harness the perceived success of geometric problem solving for philosophy, enlisting presentation *more geometrico* for philosophy. Yet axiomatics and its forerunners were not generally perceived as fruitful methods for pursuing philosophical and theological topics. Quasi-axiomatic procedures were sometimes employed for the purposes of philosophic inquiry and presentation, but these were never for epistemological reasons. At least one mode of discourse evidenced here is inquisitive; but the others are didactic and pedagogical, serving primarily anagogical ends.

Chapter Three begins the genealogy by outlining a contribution made to the beginnings of deductive argument by early Pythagoreans[15] during the course of their religio-mathematical inquiries. An early Pythagorean proof of even and odd generating properties is proffered based upon a cluster of number theoretic theorems contained in Book VII of Euclid's

---

13. Snider, *Origin*, 4.

14. Schuster, "What," 204.

15. Traditionally, historians begin with Thales, but I begin with the early Pythagoreans.

Elements. The proof was first proposed by Becker and corroborated by Knorr, Mueller and others.[16]

Chapter four illustrates some of the methodological development that had taken place by the time the Platonic dialogues were composed. A comparison is made between what was perceived as argumentation *more geometrico*—what Plato calls the "hypothetical method"—and dialectic, Plato's own preferred approach to fleshing out philosophic problems. After comparing the various methodological discussions presented in the *Republic*, *Meno* and *Phaedo*, it is noted that although Socrates recommends the hypothetical method as the best method to use to search out answers to philosophical questions, in practice, he actually prefers the use of dialectic.[17]

The fifth chapter addresses Aristotle's attempt at a systematic presentation of axiomatics and why he so frequently employs mathematical examples during the course of *APo*. This chapter argues that *APo*. is a methodological prescription for all sciences, a prescription loosely modeled after Aristotle's perception of how ancient geometers went about their business. The chapter observes that there remain appreciable disparities between how *APo*. envisions the sciences might ideally proceed and how they are carried out in practice. Aristotle seems to have allowed for more than one kind of "demonstration," each depending on the nature of the discipline under consideration. The latter half of the chapter suggests that the axiomatic proposal of *APo*. was not one that even geometry pretended to live up to.[18]

The next four chapters survey adaptations of axiomatic approaches in Euclid, Proclus, Boethius and Aquinas' commentary on Boethius with an eye toward what it is that each author is attempting to do when opting for a deductive approach. The sixth chapter suggests that the Euclidian tradition stipulated five postulates as geometric hypotheses that delimited strict theoretical parameters for guided inquiry into various geometric properties and constructions. The hypothetical way as practiced by Plato assumed that if a dialectical link can be made between a proposed hypoth-

16. Chapter Three is a modified version of a paper that was presented at a conference on Boethius at the Franciscan University of Steubenville, Ohio in April 2007.

17. A condensed form of the fourth chapter was presented at the 2007 annual joint meeting of the Mathematical Association of America and the American Mathematical Society in New Orleans.

18. Portions of the fifth chapter were presented at the spring 2006 meeting of the New Jersey section of the Mathematical Association of America in Lakewood, New Jersey.

esis and a well-established truth then the validity of the hypothesis gains credence. This chapter argues that the Euclidian tradition also proceeded from hypotheses. It was hoped that others would accept five postulates once they saw that they could "discover" the Pythagorean theorem after a train of forty-plus propositions.[19]

The seventh and eighth chapters comprise a study of Proclus' propositional presentation in *Elements of Theology* and Boethius' appeal to axiomatic method in *De Hebdomadibus*. Proclus' work is explored for how his deductive sequence contributes to the reception of his work by student readers. He seems to have expected the presentation of ordered propositions to allow readers to approach via argument the necessarily intuitive grasp of the procession of all things from the One. In the eighth chapter, I go on to treat Boethius' work in a bit more detail since he explicitly states that he is employing a method taken from mathematicians. I explain how his practice appears to be other than he claims for 1) Boethius only sparingly incorporates his metaphysical axioms into the actual argument at hand, and 2) Boethius neglects to explicitly delineate crucial lemmas upon which his argument ultimately depends. Support for these observations is found in Aquinas' commentary on Boethius where he respectfully exposes 2) and remains silent regarding 1). The conclusion that begs to be drawn in each case is that argumentation *more geometrico* is utilized for the main purpose of helping persuade readers that the writer in question has procured certain metaphysical hypotheses from which a number of generally accepted principles follow. By so doing, each author sets out to charitably dispose students and other readers toward a deeper appreciation of profound matters of faith.[20]

Chapter ten concisely recaps some of the more important observations made in chapters three through ten. In this summative chapter, I remark on the historic usefulness of axiomatics for philosophical and theological inquiry and presentation. I critically examine some of the arguments given in favor of a good-and-necessary-consequence approach to scripture and elaborate more fully my opinion that alternatives to such

19. An earlier draft of this chapter was presented at the 2006 annual meeting of the Canadian Society for the History and Philosophy of Mathematics in Toronto and was included in its *Proceedings*.

20. Some of the material on Boethius' fourth tractate and Aquinas' commentary upon it was presented at the 2005 national meeting of the American Philosophical Association—Eastern Division in New York City.

an approach in conservative Reformed and evangelical theology are long overdue.

The eleventh chapter tells a cautionary tale regarding a possible consequence of biblicist foundationalism. In this chapter, I offer a conservative evangelical interpretation of Bart Ehrman's loss of faith, suggesting that, for Ehrman, once the axiomatic tenet regarding scripture's inerrant authority was called into question, it was only a matter of time that his entire faith system would come crashing down.

As an alternative to biblicist foundationalism, I propose in chapter 12 a robust, phenomenological perspective on theological method. A phenomenological approach has the benefit of deliberately disrupting the comfort gained from the good-and-necessary-consequence mindset: a conservative practical rationality. The alternate phenomenological perspective presented in this final chapter seeks to capitalize instead on the originary genesis of the apostolic corpora by curtailing the progressive transformations of meaning that befall the Christian faith when one does theology deductively.[21]

---

21. Portions of an earlier version of this last chapter were presented at the University of Washington World and Comparative Literature Graduate Conference, held in Seattle in May, 2006.

3

The Pythagoreans and the Beginnings of Deduction

OF PYTHAGORAS' PHILOSOPHY, JOHN Marshall made the following observations over one hundred years ago:

> Returning to the philosophy of Pythagoras, in its relation to the general development of Greek theory, we may note, to begin with, that it is not necessary, or perhaps impossible, to disentangle the theory of Pythagoras himself from that of his followers, Philolaus and others. The teaching was largely oral, and was developed by successive leaders of the school. The doctrine, therefore, is generally spoken of as that, not of Pythagoras, but of the Pythagoreans.[1]

The passage of time does not seem to have changed the situation much. Writing only twenty years ago, Jonathan Barnes makes a very similar observation:

> Pythagoras himself did not set down his notions in writing, nor did his early followers. (This is the orthodox modern view; but . . . there is disagreement among the ancients on the point.) . . . Later in the fourth century, the histories of Pythagoreanism and of Platonism became closely connected, and as a result accounts of Pythagorean philosophy became contaminated with Platonic material. Later still, various Pythagorean documents were produced and circulated, projecting back on to Pythagoras himself philosophical ideas of a more recent age. It is difficult to cut through this jungle and discover the original Pythagoras.[2]

The precise nature of the historiographical problem can be illustrated by considering some of the extant writings on the subject. For example, the

---

1. *History*, 23.
2. *Early Greek Philosophy*, 81.

opening remarks regarding Pythagoras made by Nicomachus of Gerasa in his *Introduction to Arithmetic* (first century C.E.) read as follows:

> [Pythagoras] is more worthy of credence than those who have given other definitions [of 'wisdom'], since he makes clear the sense of the term and the thing defined. This 'wisdom' he defined as the knowledge, or science, of the truth in real things, conceiving 'science' to be a steadfast and firm apprehension of the underlying substance, and 'real things' to be those which continue uniformly and the same in the universe and never depart even briefly from their existence; these real things would be things immaterial, by sharing in the substance of which everything else that exists under the same name and is so called is said to be 'this particular thing,' and exists.[3]

Obviously, the description of what were otherwise known as 'forms' along with an explicit mention of 'substance' belies a conflation of the teachings of Plato and Aristotle which postdate Pythagoras by over one hundred years. Thus later philosophical thinking is presented in descriptions of Pythagoras' own philosophy.

An anonymous *Life of Pythagoras* preserved by Photius (ninth century C. E.) explains that "Plato was the pupil of Archytas, and thus the ninth in succession from Pythagoras; the tenth was Aristotle."[4] The eleventh century Muslim historian Said ad-Andalusi similarly relates that "Socrates was one of the students of Pythagoras," that "Plato, like Socrates, adopted the philosophy of Pythagoras" and that "Aristotle is the son of Nicomachus al-Gehrashni, the Pythagorean."[5] Perhaps the conflation is due in large part to what Porphyry (third century C. E.) reports in his *The Life of Pythagoras*: "The Pythagoreans affirm that Plato, Aristotle, (and their followers) Speusippus, Aristoxenus and Xenocrates appropriated the best of [their teachings], making but minor changes, but later collected and delivered as characteristic Pythagorean doctrines whatever had been invented by envious and malicious persons, to cast contempt on Pythagoreanism."[6] It thus comes as no surprise that Guthrie would lament

---

3. *Introduction*, 181.

4. Fideler, *Sourcebook*, 137.

5. *Science*, 22–23.

6. Fideler, *Sourcebook*, 134.

that "[t]he history of Pythagoreanism is perhaps the most controversial subject in all Greek philosophy."[7]

The concern among historians is that, as Huffman puts it, the writings on Pythagoras by Diogenes Laertius, Porphyry and Iamblichus "arose in a spiritual climate in which there was a need to identify a divine man to whom all truth had been revealed."[8] In other words, many scholars have become convinced that much was attributed to Pythagoras that actually stemmed from within later neo-Pythagorean contexts.[9] Accordingly, Raven's dictum is oft invoked: "Since any account of Pythagoreanism that ignores the testimony of Aristotle is a house built upon sand, I shall examine first what Aristotle tells us about the Pythagoreans."[10] If what is reported in a later source is not also attested in an earlier one, like Aristotle, then the later report is to be discounted. Iamblichus specifically is accused of "projecting into the times of Pythagoras the methods of the philosophical schools of the third century."[11] But it should be noted that by portraying Pythagoras as a wonder-worker and a divine man, neo-Pythagorean writers were merely following a prevalent practice that certainly began before the time in question, a practice not restricted to shamanistic philosophers.[12] In addition, as Zhmud points out, "[w]e do not know of a *single* Pythagorean who ascribed his own discovery to Pythagoras. There is no reliable evidence that this tendency even existed in the Pythagorean school."[13] Motivations for writing pseudo-Pythagorean writings "simply showed a widespread fashion of the time," yet, besides Iamblichus, "none of the classical scholars mentions the tendency of Pythagoreans to attribute their scientific discoveries to the founder of the school."[14] And again, "it is clear that only later authors associated Pythagoras with *someone else's*

7. Guthrie, *History*, 146.

8. Huffman, "Pythagorean Tradition," 67.

9. For example, Morrow makes the extreme claim that "all the discoveries of the school are credited to him [Pythagoras]." See Proclus, *Commentary*, 53, n. 27.

10. Raven, *Pythagoreans*, 6. Compare Huffman, "Pythagorean Tradition," 69. Against this line of thinking, see de Santillana and Pitts, "Philolaos."

11. Phillip, "Biographical Tradition," 192, agreeing with Festugiere, *Revelation*, 2.33, 35, 38, 41–47.

12. Most, "Philosophy and Religion," 318–19.

13. Zhmud, "Pythagoras," 253, italics in original.

14. Zhmud, "Pythagoras," 254. According to Zhmud, Iamblichus inferred from the fact that since neoPythagoreans attributed spurious writings to Pythagoras that they also attributed to him scientific discoveries that he did not make.

discoveries and not early Pythagoreans with their own."[15] In any event, all that is required for the present study is the reasonable assumption that what many historians tend to describe as the mathematical discoveries of Pythagoras be ascribed to early Pythagoreans and not be entirely fictive, even if ultimately conjectural.[16]

A history of the development of Greek geometry appears to have been composed by Eudemus of Rhodes (early third century B. C. E.[?]). Scholars have identified a relevant passage from Proclus as being largely based upon Eudemus' work.[17] The passage reads as follows:

> Thales, who traveled to Egypt, was the first to introduce this science into Greece. He made many discoveries himself and taught the principles for many others to his successors, attacking some problems in a general way and others more empirically. Next after him Mamercus . . . and Hippias of Elis . . . Following upon these men, Pythagoras transformed mathematical philosophy into a scheme of liberal education, surveying its principles from the highest downwards and investigating its theorems in an immaterial and intellectual manner.[18]

Though some scholars have been eager to point out that the first sentence mentioning Pythagoras "is taken word for word from Iamblichus' *De communi mathematica scientia*—a work that Proclus copies sometimes by the page in his commentary on Euclid,"[19] others, such as Zhmud, point out that Proclus and Iamblichus more likely had a common earlier source.[20]

15. Zhmud, "Pythagoras," 257, italics in original.

16. Heidel claims that "we have no dependable evidence of mathematical achievements of Pythagoras himself" after surveying the extant classical references; however, his readings, at times, seem overly cautious. See Heidel, "Pythagoreans," 378. Zhmud clarifies that "[w]ith Pythagorean philosophy the picture is very different: its founder was credited with ideas that in no circumstances could have belonged to him . . . . Fortunately, the situation in the history of science is quite different." See Zhmud, "Pythagoras," 259. Netz, for his part, confidently asserts that "Pythagoras the mathematician perished finally" with the German publication of Burkert's monograph in Netz, *Shaping*, 272.

17. This, too, is disputed. See Heidel, "Pythagoreans"; Burkert, *Lore*, 409–12; and van der Waerden, *Science*, 91. For doubts about a Eudemian *History* in the first place, see Mejer, "Eudemus."

18. *Commentary*, 52–53.

19. Burkert, *Lore*, 410.

20. In a footnote, Zhmud mentions that by 1980 van der Waerden was able to report that Burkert abandoned his original suggestion that Proclus inserted the Pythagorean sentence into Eudemus' catalogue. See Zhmud, "Pythagoras," 266, n. 7.

In any event, some historians, such as Heath, have taken the Eudemian summary to indicate that "Pythagoras explored the first principles, starting with definitions, and built upon them a logically connected system."[21] Although Heath likely overstates the case, it does appear that by at least the fifth century B.C.E. some theorems were being proved in an immaterial and intellectual manner as opposed to empirically. The Pythagorean discovery of incommensurability, for example, contributed to the development of an already existing theory of proportions.[22] As a matter of fact, many authors introduce a discussion of the discovery and proof of the incommensurability of $\sqrt{2}$ precisely in order to contrast what might be called empirical and abstract investigations.[23] Before proceeding further, it will also prove helpful for us to do the same; however, we shall take our example of abstract argumentation from basic high school algebra.

Many schoolchildren learn to indicate that some number is "greater than five" by employing the notation: $x > 5$. During the course of learning how to manipulate such inequalities algebraically, students are usually taught that when one divides each side of the inequality by a negative number the inequality must be reversed. Although this is commonly taught in schools, its proof is seldom presented. Even more thoughtful students who ponder why this must be done tend to approach the question empirically. Suppose $6 > 5$. If both sides are divided by -1, for example, then the inequality becomes $-6 > -5$, which is false. Therefore, in order to maintain the inequality, its direction must be reversed. This empirical line of reasoning is obviously as good as any, but it does not constitute a general and abstract proof. Unless all possible combinations of values can somehow be tested, there can always lurk a host of counterexamples where it might not be necessary to reverse the inequality. Hence, this line of reasoning can only empirically strengthen the plausibility of an initial conjecture but can never serve as general proof. Compare the force of this empirical line of thinking with that of the following informal argument.

21. Heath, *Manual*, 110. Contrast Kline, *Mathematical Thought*, 1.34. There are others who, based on this and other references, understand Pythagoras to be the one who first, not discovered, but *introduced* and helped disseminate (with questionable [Schofield] or honorable [Huffman] intentions) others' mathematical achievements into the educational curricula of the time. See, for example, Schofield, "Presocratics," 51–56; and Huffman, "Pythagoras."

22. See von Fritz, "Discovery."

23 See, for example, Lloyd, *Early Science*, 32–34; and O. Neugebauer, *Exact Sciences*, 148-149; and in much more detail, Szabó, *Beginnings*, 199–213.

Suppose $-x > b$, during the course of rewriting the inequality so that x will be positive (by dividing by negative one, for example) one will inevitably have to reverse the inequality. To show this, add x to both sides: $0 > x + b$. Subtract b from both sides: $-b > x$. Thus $x < -b$ (and, of course, the same argument could be used for $-x < b$). Hence irrespective of what number is said to be greater than b, in order to maintain the inequality when dividing by a negative one, one will have to reverse the inequality in order to preserve it. This informal argument is certainly much more abstract than the above empirical one, but, more importantly, *it attempts to cover every case simultaneously.*[24] If valid, it consequently would duly be granted much greater argumentative force by arithmeticians and other practitioners.

The beginnings of such types of general proof are attributed by Proclus to Thales and Pythagoras.[25] Reconstructions of how Pythagoras may have proved the theorem that bears his name have been attempted elsewhere,[26] but as Knorr has remarked, emphasis on geometric contributions "betray the Pythagoreans' more fundamental interest in arithmetic relations, for which these geometric studies afforded an additional analytic instrument."[27] Lasserre helpfully distinguishes between an *ontological* arithmetic and an *axiomatic* arithmetic.[28] Whereas the latter kind of arithmetic "sees in every new truth the solution of a *problem*," the former "makes every truth an eternal truth and the object of a *theorem*."[29] Lasserre claims that by the time of Plato these two attitudes were irreconcilable but that earlier arithmeticians often pursued both concurrently. Thus for the purposes of the present discussion, we can restrict our attention to the reconstruction of a considerably less controversial claim for the early Pythagoreans than the Pythagorean theorem, namely that given their keen interest in even and odd numbers, the Pythagoreans had eventu-

24. Abstraction and generality are not necessarily the same thing. In the case of Pythagoras, it is the generality of proof that is germane.

25. As mentioned earlier, histories of the topic tend to begin with Thales. Our choice to begin with Pythagoras stems from the proposed facility of our chosen example.

26. See, for example, Howard Eves, *Introduction*, 80–81; and Heath, *History*, 147–49. That Pythagoras proved the theorem is, of course, debatable. Proclus is read by many to insinuate that even he himself had doubts that Pythagoras had ever actually done so. See Proclus, *Commentary*, 337–38.

27. Wilbur Knorr, *Evolution*, 132. Compare van der Waerden, *Science Awakening*, 109; Szabó, "Transformation," 117.

28. See Lasserre, *Birth*, 56–62.

29. Lasserre, *Birth*, 57.

ally stumbled upon proofs for some of the more mundane properties that pertain to them. The suggestion is that the Pythagoreans did so abstractly and not merely empirically during the course of contemplating the number generating properties of even and odd numbers. The observation that we are crediting the Pythagoreans with entails the simple realization that even and odd numbers can be regarded in various combinations as even and odd number generators, or put another way, that a few number generating properties regarding even and odd numbers can be gleaned from minimal reflection upon their definitions.

With regard to the controversies that surround the claim that Pythagoras was some type of mathematician, we might pause to remark that if he really did anything of the sort we are positing, we would not be crediting him with any great mathematical accomplishment. We would, however, be attributing to him a contribution toward the investigation of theorems "in an immaterial and intellectual manner." But is it really too much to believe that "[j]ust as Thales did in geometry, Pythagoras began in arithmetic with the simplest facts, which no one earlier had felt required proof"?[30] As we shall see, somebody did eventually prove these elementary properties; and for the purposes of the broader survey we are in the course of undertaking with regard to the early applications of axiomatics, it ultimately makes no difference at all whether Pythagoras is personally responsible for such proofs or not. The claim that matters is that these proofs, whoever composed them, were in the process of investigating even and odd number generators. We suppose these were conceived by the time fifth century Greek arithmeticians went about their mathematical business.[31]

According to Boethius, Pythagoras' definitions of even and odd numbers are as follows:

> An even number is that which at the same and single division is able to be divided into very large parts with small spaces or into a very small number of parts, with large spaces, according to the contrary properties of these two types. An odd number is one to

---

30. Zhmud, "Pythagoras," 261.

31. See Knorr, *Evolution*, 135–37. Knorr argues that the Epicharmus-fragment proves that the practices in question date at least to the mid-fifth century. Against this, see Netz, *Shaping*, 62–64 and 272.

which this cannot happen but whose separation into two uneven parts is natural.[32]

Boethius here builds upon a tradition that can be traced at least as far back as Nicomachus of Gerasa, who calls the definition "Pythagorean."[33] Another definition is also given by Boethius that is "according to a more ancient method":

> An even number is that which can be divided into two equal or two unequal parts, but in neither division is there an even number mixed with an odd number or an odd mixed with an even number, excepting alone the principal even binary number which cannot be divided into two unequal parts because it consists only of two unities ... An odd number is that which is divided into other odd numbers by means of any division; numbers always show both types and neither type of numbers is ever able to exist without the other, but one must be understood as even, the other as odd.[34]

Euclid treats a number of theorems that have to do with even and odd numbers in the ninth book of his *Elements*, Propositions 21-34 inclusive. A comparison of Boethius' "ancient" definition with these Euclidean propositions shows that number generating properties similar to the propositions proven in Euclid are simply mentioned in passing by Boethius as belonging to the definition.[35] In other words, Boethius, in order to help his readers better understand what even and odd numbers are, interpolates and appends provable theorems to the definitions of even and odd numbers as if they were part of the definition. Although Boethius does not here distinguish between a definition and a proposition, it is interesting to note that the relevant Euclidean propositions in Book Nine of the *Elements* do not appear to depend upon anything other than a few definitions enumerated

32. Michael Masi, *Number*, 77 (1.4).

33. *Introduction*, 181.

34. Masi, *Number*, 77–78 (1.5). Compare Nicomachus, *Introduction*, 191.

35. This seems to suggest that Boethius had very little interest in the mathematics about which he purported to comment and was only interested in preserving a tradition of mathematics that was thought to provide tools necessary for the conducting of other disciplinary inquiries. Masi suggests music theory. If this is correct, one can conclude that Boethius was not merely paraphrasing Nicomachus here but rather substantially filling in the text's definition. In other words, in an effort to help the reader understand the concepts being proffered, Boethius amends the definition with (apparently unbeknownst to him) proven properties of the evens and odds, a rare parenthetical interjection on Boethius' part.

at the beginning of Book Seven (and perhaps each other). Knorr, Zhmud, Mueller, and others (following an initial proposal by Becker), in fact, argue that this section of the *Elements* actually represents an early Pythagorean, self-contained theory of even and odd numbers.[36]

Regarding the Euclidean propositions, it is first worth mentioning that Heath, in his translation and commentary of the *Elements*, makes the following remarks immediately after Euclid's proof of Proposition 21:

> In this and the following propositions up to IX.34 inclusive we have a number of theorems about odd, even, "even-times even" and "even-times odd" numbers respectively. They are all simple and require no explanation in order to enable them to be followed easily.[37]

This is important to bear in mind because Burkert, among others, has complained that "[i]n Euclid, the theory unrolls in systematic fashion, and one proposition presupposes the preceding, in the strictly deductive manner, where as proof with [pebbles] is essentially inductive and pictorial."[38] He argues that in the proposed reconstruction "every set of facts is evident in itself" and "[t]here is no need for a systematic structure, which is of the essence of deductive mathematics." Burkert indeed raises a very good point here, but its relevance dissipates once it is realized that the beginning theorems in question do not strictly build upon preceding propositions but rather rely almost singularly upon the definitions only.[39] That is precisely what is so suggestive about the reconstruction in the first place. The steps taken to apply this basic knowledge to help establish additional mundane features regarding even and odd numbers and their ability to generate each other would require only the slightest deductive inclination (and even that overstates the case). And this we posit, the early Pythagoreans, if not Pythagoras himself, could have certainly

---

36. Knorr, *Evolution*, 137–42; Zhmud, "Pythagoras,"260–61; Ian Mueller, "Greek Arithmetic," 296–98; van der Waerden, *Science Awakening*, 108–10; all following (and in the case of Knorr, expanding upon) Becker, "Lehre." Van der Waerden concludes that "*Book VII was a textbook on the elements of the Theory of Numbers, in use in the Pythagorean school*" (*Science Awakening*, 115, italics in original). Compare Szabó, "Transformation."

37. Euclid, *Elements*, 2.413. This observation was apparently penned before Becker proposed his reconstruction.

38. *Lore*, 435.

39. Compare Artmann, "Euclid's *Elements* and Its Prehistory," 32. See also Mueller's remarks in "Greek Arithmetic," 297–98.

mustered during the course of their deliberations on the even and odd in the grander scheme of their esoteric philosophy. We should keep in mind that as Thales seems to have been the first to try deduction with the help of pictures,[40] Pythagoras may have tried his hand at deduction with the help of pebbles. The postulation bears scrutiny when we recall that "the difference between [Euclidean] deduction with its definitions, technical vocabulary, diagrams and formalistic descriptions, on the one hand, and informal manipulation designed to bring out general truths about numbers or rules for producing them is not great."[41] The present claim is that during the course of inquiring into the properties of even and odd numbers, the early Pythagoreans landed upon a general pattern that they were able to generalize with the aid of pebbles. The reconstruction proceeds as follows.

At the beginning of the seventh book of the *Elements*, Euclid lists the following two definitions among the several that he enumerates:

1) An even number is that which is divisible into two equal parts.

2) An odd number is that which is not divisible into two equal parts, or that which differs by an unit from an even number.[42]

Knorr condenses Propositions 21–29 of Book Nine in the following way:

Theorem 1. (a) The sum of any multitude of even numbers is even (IX,21); (b) the sum of an even multitude of odd numbers is even (IX,22); (c) the sum of an odd multitude of odd numbers is odd.

Theorem 2. (a) In subtraction, the difference between two numbers of the same parity is even (IX,24 26); (b) the difference of two numbers of opposite parity is odd (IX,25, 27).

Theorem 3. (a) The product of a number by an even number is even (cf. IX, 28); (b) the product of an odd number by an odd number is odd (IX,29).[43]

---

40. See Mueller, "Greek Arithmetic," 289–90.

41. Mueller, "Greek Arithmetic," 295. Szabó attempts to reconstruct some of the early developments that pertained to these specific theorems in "Transformation." But see Mueller, "Euclid's Elements."

42. Definitions 7 and 8. See Euclid, *Elements*, 2.277.

43. *Evolution*, 140. Knorr goes on to give the following corollary: "(a) The square of an even number is even; (b) the square of an odd number is odd." (141)

The clustering of nine propositions into three theorems (and especially the grouping of four propositions into a single theorem) highlights not only how closely related some of the propositions in question are but also how similar the proofs for each are. It takes no stretch of the imagination to believe that the early Pythagoreans stumbled upon deductive proofs for these properties of the even and odd numbers without having to incorporate them into a "logically connected system" as Heath suggested above. In fact, these types of even-odd theorems may be prime instances of theorems that were discovered *by being proved*. [44] The proofs are remarkably simple and qualify as abstract deductive proofs (employing pebbles as opposed to diagrams) that could easily have been discovered during the course of number generating investigations.

We shall present a version of Knorr's proof to Theorem 1a below; readers are referred to Knorr and Heath for comparative proofs of the others.[45]

Let even numbers A, B be arrayed as even numbers. Let their sum E be arrayed such that the left part of E consists of the left parts of A, B and the right part of E consists of the right parts of A, B. Since the parts of A, B are respectively equal, their sum will also be collectively equal. Therefore, E is also an even number.[46]

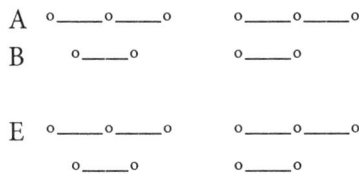

Knorr himself admits that there is no documentary evidence that this exact proof was ever actually done—a fact critics are very quick to point out—but as Zhmud remarks, "[s]ources in early Greek mathematics are so few that to expect evidence for each proof would be utterly utopian."[47] Of the oppositions listed on Aristotle's 'Table of Opposites' (*Met.* A5, 986a22ff), limited-unlimited and odd-even have been judged to be the

44. See Stenius, "Foundations," 256–60.

45. For a commentary on the differences see Szabó, *Beginnings*, 190–97.

46. Adapted from Knorr, *Evolution*, 141. Knorr follows Euclid and begins with four even numbers.

47. "Pythagoras," 261.

most ancient.[48] In fact, Pythagoras' suggestion of a duality of principles, according to Vlastos, "is something absolutely without parallel in antecedent or contemporary natural inquiry."[49] In other words, conceptual curiosity had been peaked by Pythagorean metaphysical speculations and the arithmetical tools were already present for these kinds of pedestrian mathematical inquiries.

It should be observed that there is no reason to conclude on the basis of a proof like the one presented above that a genuine interest in mathematical rule-generating deduction on the part of the Pythagoreans argues against an intense religious enthusiasm that is usually associated with Pythagoras. In fact, it might be suggested that the tendency among modern commentators to presume such a strict dichotomy is itself a bit misguided. Indeed, the belligerent skepticism that has attended recent treatments of Pythagoras' role in the history of mathematics almost seems reactionary.[50] A middle road approach will likely prove more to the point, something along the lines of Cornford's remarks made some time ago: "The Pythagorean philosophy was mathematical, but its inspiration was mystical and religious."[51] Surely it would be in keeping with this picture of Pythagoras to make the rather conservative claim that his followers extended his mystically motivated inquiry to formulate a generalization of this type when they realized that their minds were not playing tricks (as Rota puts it[52]) when it came to evens and odds, their relation to each other, and their capacity to generate one another.

A final observation is in order: even though Pythagorean mathematical thinking was philosophically motivated, the proposed discovery is primarily mathematical.[53] Granted, the Pythagorean discovery posited in this chapter must, in the final analysis, remain one of several possible reconstructions, but, whether we have Pythagoreans to thank for such

48. See, for example, Raven, *Pythagoreans*, 112–45; along with Vlastos, "Raven's Pythagoreans and Eleatics," 181.

49. Vlastos, "Theology," 18–19.

50. Even Netz sees a need to remind his readers that Pythagoras was a "real historical figure." See Netz, "Pythagoreans," 77.

51. Cornford, *Before and After Socrates*, 62. Compare Rutt, "Sources," 380–81.

52. Rota, "Complicating Mathematics," 154. In other words, he only needed a minimally convincing demonstration. Compare with remarks made regarding Euler's Theorem, $V - E + F = 2$, in Bundy, Jamnik and Fugard, "What."

53. Not to be confused with the claim that Pythagoras was more of a mathematician than a religionist.

proofs or not, a case can certainly be made that the foregoing material presents a very early contribution to the beginnings of "good and necessary consequence" reasoning, a deductive mathematical discourse based upon properties inherent in definitions, stumbled upon during the course of conducting empirical even and odd number-generating investigations. By the time of Plato, geometric method had developed considerably. The next chapter observes that the Platonic dialogues give some indications as to how philosophers felt about the method's prospects for philosophy.

4

Deduction and Dialectic in Plato

IT IS NOT AN accident of history that Platonic notions were eventually attributed to Pythagoras (as in the Nicomachus quote above). Plato did incorporate Pythagorean notions into his philosophical musings. Netz, speculating on the mystery-religion aspect of Pythagoreanism during the course of his "dogmatic statement" regarding "what made the Pythagoreans *Pythagorean*," provocatively suggests that

> [a] certain 'mystery' statement—or act—is meaningless on its own, but it does suggest a meaning which however is different from its surface meaning. If we call the statement P, then the form of the expression is 'P is not P'. By immersing yourself in a system of expressions of this kind, you are made to become non-yourself, and this is the basis for the transformative power of mystery practice.[1]

The object of Pythagoreanism, says Netz, is the rationalization of mystery and "the best starting point for the rationalization of mystery would be a thing that *literally is something else*: an object that is simultaneously two radically separate things, so that for which, the paradoxical statement 'X is not X' could be literally true."[2] For Pythagoreans, according to Netz, music and its mathematization serve this very purpose. But the latter would serve not only the Pythagoreans but also Plato himself. As Burnyeat remarks: "All they [i.e., Platonists] agree about is that the ultimate principles of explanation are to be derived from reflection on mathematics . . . The task of searching for the ultimate principles of explanation by reflecting on mathematics is the task set for dialectic in Plato's Republic."[3] Whereas the Pythagoreans are depicted as enchanted with *music* and its role as the

1. Netz, "Pythagoreans," 91, 94, italics in original.

2. Ibid., 94, italics in original.

3. Burnyeat, "Platonism," 216.

doorway to mathematics (possibly via a theory of proportions[4]), Plato decidedly targets *mathematics* as the doorway to knowledge of the eternal principles of sensible things.[5] An examination of the *Meno*, in light of parallels found in *Phaedo* and the *Republic*, shows that Plato adapts ancient mathematical method for his own dialectical purposes and develops the method in such a way that abandons deductive proof in favor of dialectical exposition.

In the *Republic* (510b), the two subdivisions of the Divided Line are set out as a proportion that, taken together, comprises the intelligible realm:

> In the lower one the soul's perception is restrained by a method of inquiry that reduces to images those things we defined as physical objects or models in the subdivision immediately below. Moreover, it operates with the kind of assumptions that lead to conclusions and not to first principles. But in the highest subdivision the soul makes no use of images. It also begins with assumptions and hypotheses but rises to a level where it relies exclusively on forms, a level of intellection that is free from all hypothetical thinking.

What do these subdivisions correspond to? The subject matter and methods of mathematics and dialectic respectively. Plato observes the following regarding mathematics (510c–d):

> Among those who work with geometry and arithmetic and related subjects you know that the odd and the even, the several geometrical figures, the three kinds of angles, and other things related to their inquiries are treated as givens. That is, having adopted them as assumptions, they see no purpose in giving any account of them to themselves or others. They perceive them as self-evident. These premises are for them the starting points of inquiries, which they pursue in all consistency until they arrive at the conclusions they originally set out to verify.

Most writers rightly consider Plato as being critical of mathematicians here.[6] Yet it is interesting to note that this is precisely how Socrates himself describes his own inquisitive procedure in an earlier dialogue.

---

4. Netz homes in on the potential for proportions to associate otherwise incommensurable domains.

5. Huffman suggests that there was also a specific method of inquiry illustrated in the *Philebus* that was adapted by Plato from the Pythagoreans. See Huffman, "Method."

6. A point taken for granted, for example, in Heinaman, "Plato," 377. See also

"There are few things that I should claim to know, but that at least is among them, whatever else is," declares Socrates in *Meno* 98b. Socrates refers here to a proposed distinction between knowledge and right opinion and the stance that knowledge is "more valuable" than right opinion since the former is "tethered" by "working out the reason".[7] Socrates makes the following methodological proposal (86e–87c) during the course of a discussion with Meno that seeks answers to two classic questions, "What is virtue?" and "Can virtue be taught?"

> [A]llow me, in considering whether or not it can be taught, to make use of a hypothesis—the sort of thing, I mean, that geometers often use in their inquiries . . . Since we don't know what it is or what it resembles, let us use a hypothesis in investigating whether it is teachable or not. We shall say: 'What attribute of the soul must virtue be, if it is to be teachable or otherwise?' Well, in the first place, if it is anything else but knowledge, is there a possibility of anyone teaching it—or, in the language we used just now, reminding someone of it? We needn't worry about which name we are to give to the process, but simply ask: will it be teachable? Isn't it plain to everyone that a man is not taught anything except knowledge?[8]

There is, of course, a good deal of disagreement over what these passages mean. In what follows, we shall assume that Socrates employs an argument from hypothesis "under an appearance of yielding to Meno's rule" (i.e., agreeing to answer Meno's question about whether virtue is teachable and not Socrates' own question, "What is virtue?") in order to "win [Meno's] participation over again in a joint dialectical search."[9] The emphasis will be placed upon the hypothetical method's origins in mathematics and how Plato adapts the method for his own purposes.[10] For now, we observe that Socrates prefers knowledge over right opinion and that—at least on the

---

Cornford's seminal article, "Mathematics."

7. For knowledge as a "species" of right opinion, see Fine, "Knowledge."

8. During the ellipses, Socrates gives a geometric example for which there is no consensual reconstruction. A few options are presented in Brumbaugh, *Imagination*, 32–38. See also Knorr, *Traditions*, 71–74.

9. Ionescu, *Meno*, 106. See further the discussion in Bedu-Addo, "Recollection."

10. See, for example, Mueller, "Mathematical Method"; Mueller, "Notion"; Cornford, "Mathematics"; Vlastos, "Elenchus"; Gonzalez, *Dialectic*; Burnyeat, "Platonism"; and the three essays by James H. Lesher, Hayden W. Ausland and Harold Tannant in Scott, *Socrates*.

face of it—he commends an adaptation of a method that mathematicians of the time often used in an effort to secure a knowledge that could claim to be worked out through reason. After surveying what transpires during the course of this dialogue, we shall set out to place it in the context of the foregoing episode in the *Republic*.

Socrates formulates the following conditionals to articulate what has been called the 'limiting conditions' of the inquiry, or as Socrates puts it in *Meno* 87c, "on what condition virtue would be teachable":

a) If virtue is teachable then it must be knowledge.

a´) If virtue is knowledge then it must be teachable.

This hypothesis is the most explicit declaration in the section.[11] Still, Socrates seems to repeat the same procedure of setting conditions for the ensuing discussion to the following effect by introducing a subsidiary assumption, namely, that virtue is good:

b) If knowledge does not exhaust every thing that is good, then virtue cannot be knowledge.

b´) If knowledge does exhaust everything that is good, then virtue can be knowledge.

He repeats the procedure again after introducing another assumption, that there are "spiritual qualities" other than knowledge that are potentially good:

c) Spiritual qualities accompanied by wisdom are beneficial.

c´) Spiritual qualities not accompanied by wisdom are detrimental.

Socrates accordingly links virtue with wisdom since virtue is inherently beneficial. He then appears to introduce a final assumption—that wisdom acts upon one's "spiritual character":

d) "The mind of the wise man" makes these qualities beneficial.

d´) "The mind of the foolish" makes these qualities detrimental.

Socrates again links virtue with wisdom and concludes that virtue cannot, therefore, be a natural quality (presumably since people are not

11. See, for example, Mueller, "Mathematical Method," 178–79. Furthermore, Meno says later that "it is obvious on our assumption that, if virtue is knowledge, it is teachable" and Socrates explains himself, saying, "I don't withdraw from the position that if is knowledge, it must be teachable."

born wise but rather become wise). Meno faithfully follows Socrates' lead and concludes that virtue must then be teachable, which would prove that virtue is, in fact, knowledge as they had implicitly assumed at the outset. The hypothetical approach to virtue has apparently been successfully executed.[12]

But then Socrates amazingly begins to question whether Meno's conclusion necessarily follows by bringing a) and a') under suspicion! Before reflecting upon this remarkable move, let us compare what Socrates does here in the *Meno* with a method of inquiry delineated in the *Phaedo* (99e–100a):

> . . . I was afraid that by observing objects with my eyes and trying to comprehend them with each of my other senses I might blind my soul altogether. So I decided that I must have recourse to theories, and use them in trying to discover the truth about things . . . and in every case I first lay down the theory which I judge to be soundest; and then whatever seems to agree with it . . . I assume to be true, and whatever does not I assume not to be true.

A more detailed description of the proposed method is picked up a little later (101c–d):

> You would dismiss these divisions and additions and other such niceties, leaving them for persons wiser than yourself to use in their explanations, while you, being nervous of your own shadow, as the saying is, and of your inexperience, would hold fast to the security of your hypothesis and make your answers accordingly. If anyone should fasten upon the hypothesis itself, you would disregard him and refuse to answer until you could consider whether its consequences were mutually consistent or not. And when you had to substantiate the hypothesis itself, you would proceed in the same way, assuming whatever more ultimate hypothesis commended itself most to you, until you reached one which was satisfactory. You would not mix the two things together by discussing both the principle and its consequences, like one of these destructive critics—that is, if you wanted to discover any part of the truth.

Perhaps now we are in a position to better understand Socrates' dialogical behavior in the *Meno*.

---

12. For the relation of the hypothetical method with the Socratic elenchus, see Benson, "Method of Hypothesis," along with Wolfsdorf's reply. See also Fine, "Inquiry"; and Brickhouse and Smith, "Vlastos." Vlastos, for his part, seems to have thought that the Socratic drive for elenchus had died by the time of the *Meno*. See Vlastos, "Elenchus."

In light of the above passages from the *Phaedo*, one could plausibly surmise that Plato was growing less and less comfortable with resorting to empirical evidences and began taking a preference for theoretical argumentation. After a life-long investigation into various theories, he had landed upon ones that seemed more plausible than others and would habitually set these down as hypotheses.[13] One can see the beginnings of this approach to virtue in particular as early as the *Protagoras*.[14] The discussion is far more developed in the *Meno*, to the point of following the proposed consequences of the hypothesis to a tentative set of conclusions. After diligently attending to the acceptability of the hypothesis' consequences, Plato redirects the dialogue back to Meno's understanding of the hypothesis: if virtue is knowledge if and only if it is teachable, then who in the world would be qualified to do the teaching and why are they not teaching now? The reduction of the initial hypothesis to related ones yielded no apparent contradiction.[15] Plato accordingly halts the inquiry in favor of a retrospective turn such that Meno is asked to consider whether his understanding of the hypothesis made for a less than secure starting point for the ensuing discussion.[16]

Such an outcome is programmatically problematized in the *Republic* (511a–b):

> The method of investigation I have just described certainly belongs to the realm of the intelligible, but we must recognize its limitations. First, the method is necessarily dependent upon hypotheses. Because it is unable to go beyond these hypotheses, it is also unable to attain the level of first principles and the new beginnings . . .
>
> Then let us go on to understand intelligibility at the highest level. This is the realm that reason masters with the power of dialectic. Assumptions are not treated as first principles but as real hypotheses. That is, they are not employed as beginnings but as ladders and springboards, used in order to reach that realm that requires no hypotheses and is therefore the true starting point for the attaining of unobstructed knowledge . . .

13. The precedence for this had possibly been set by the Eleatics. See Szabó, *Beginnings*.

14. See Politis, "*Aporia*," 100–1.

15. For the use of hypotheses in reduction, see Striker, "Aristotle," 217; and Wolfsdorf, "Method."

16. Compare Day, "Introduction," 3–4. Gooch views this as a superficial reading. He is so bothered by the unsoundness of the hypothesis that he suggests that the dialogue was written in "ironic mode." See Gooch, "Irony."

Unfortunately (once again) there is a good deal of disagreement over what is being described here, especially with respect to the passage's relation, if any, to ancient Greek geometric analysis.[17] For our part, we must guard against becoming all too easily bogged down with contemporary logical and mathematical comparisons between geometrical and dialectical analyses or being drawn into others' more general philosophical attempts to discern the answers to a host of related metaphysical questions.[18] Such discussions will take us too far afield. For better or for worse, it must suffice to simply note at the present juncture that one of the main questions of interest revolves around to what extent the hypothetical and dialectical methods are deductive *for Plato* and, if applicable, to what extent the hypotheses are convertible.

Unhappily, we are nowhere shown how Plato's dialectic, as described in the *Republic*, is actually to be carried out. This may be why so many writers have looked to roughly contemporary mathematical practice to exposit what Plato has in mind.[19] In fact, there is, in many ways, a palpable historiographical need for the claim that Plato himself was not only the director of mathematical instruction at the Academy but a formidable mathematician in his own right, fully conversant with current mathematical practice.[20] For our part, we shall say a few words on the relation between mathematics and dialectic.

In the *Republic*, Plato propounds that the more capable philosophers will require extensive training in mathematics. After all, it is the contemplation of abstract objects that mathematics encourages (albeit via diagrams) that is the preliminary act requisite for the more direct apperceptions of forms. As an illustration of this belief, Vlastos interprets Plato's choice of geometric example in the *Meno* as a "warning [to] his

17. See, for example, Cornford, "Mathematics"; Gulley, "Greek"; Mahoney, "Look"; Hintikka and Remes, *Method*; Marchi, "Method"; Popovich, "Concerning"; Suppes, "Limitations"; Knorr, *Traditions*; Behboud, "Greek Geometrical Analysis." Barbin briefly discusses analysis in the early modern period in curious isolation from its antecedent history. See Barbin, "Meanings."

18. Related studies abound. See, for example, Wedberg, *Plato's Philosophy*; Moravcsik, "Plato"; Fine, "Forms"; Fine, "Knowledge"; Burnyeat, "Platonism"; Bolton, "Discovery"; Mueller, "Divine"; Mueller, "Platonism"; Rowe, "Explanation."

19. Compare Annas, *Introduction*, 278: "Nearly everything about dialectic is disputable." Annas suggests that although Plato says nothing explicit about dialectic, readers can infer some things by following Plato's lead and contrasting it with mathematics. (277)

20. See, for example, Fowler, *Mathematics*, and compare Cherniss, "Plato."

readers that if they have not already done a lot of work in that science they will be unable to follow him . . . to keep up with the best [Plato] has to offer they must learn geometry."[21] By extension, then, mathematical method will also play an important role "along the way" to doing philosophy more capably. Accordingly, whatever methods Plato takes over from mathematics for the training of philosophers should not be seen in contradistinction over against how dialectical philosophy is ultimately done, but rather as a more preliminary phase of doing Platonic philosophic investigations.[22] Hypothetical and dialectical approaches are both to be constructively employed in the service of carrying out philosophical discourse through its various dialectical phases. We shall take the *Meno* as our example.[23]

According to M. V. Popovich, Platonic "analysis" consists of "accepting the unknown as known."[24] Some scholars have gone so far as to argue that this description also makes the best sense of Greek geometric analysis, *including Euclid's axiomatic Elements*.[25] M. Mahoney and several others schematize the progression of analysis as follows, where P represents the hypothesis proposed: $P \rightarrow P_1 \rightarrow P_2 \rightarrow \ldots \rightarrow P_n \rightarrow K$.[26] Others, such as Jaakko Hintikka and Unto Remes, assume that K (in our example) must be the hypothesis proposed and complain further that "[t]his schema leaves entirely unexplained the role of the desired theorem [K] in analysis."[27] Already we are faced with the problem of 'direction'. Both M. Mahoney and Hintikka and Remes base their opposite reconstructions on Pappus.[28] Even if the directions of the reconstructions are ultimately compatible,[29] in accord with the pattern shown in Plato's writings above, Mahoney's schema will prevail for the moment:

---

21. Vlastos, "Elenchus."

22. Compare Benson, "Plato's Rationalistic," and Benson, "Plato's Method."

23. Day, for example, is persuaded that a theory of Forms is, at the very least, "near the horizon" in the *Meno*. See Day, *Meno*, 12–14.

24. Popovich, "Concerning," 118.

25. Marchi, "Method," who follows Szabó.

26. Gulley, "Greek," 321.

27. Hintikka and Remes, *Method*, 33.

28. The problem holds for the Pappus text itself which seems, for all intents and purposes, hopelessly confused. The passage from Pappus' *Collections* can be found in Thomas, *Greek*, 2.597–99, as well as in Mahoney, "Look," 322.

29. See Hintikka and Remes, *Method*, 13; and Szabó, "Working," 122–24.

"[A] man is not taught anything except knowledge"[30] is the known fact with which Socrates and Meno would like to link their hypothesis. Thus the Socratic line of reasoning proceeds as follows:

Virtue is teachable if and only if virtue is knowledge. (Hypothesis)   P

    Virtue is good.

        If knowledge does not exhaust good things, then virtue cannot be
            knowledge.

        If knowledge does exhaust good things, then virtue can be knowledge.

            There are "spiritual qualities" other than knowledge that can be good.

                Spiritual qualities accompanied by wisdom are beneficial.

                Spiritual qualities not accompanied by wisdom are detrimental.

    Virtue must be all or part of wisdom since virtue is inherently beneficial.

    Wisdom acts upon one's "spiritual character":

        "The mind of the wise man" makes these qualities beneficial.

        "The mind of the foolish" makes these qualities detrimental.

    Virtue must be all or part of wisdom.

    Therefore virtue cannot be a natural quality.

Virtue must be teachable

Virtue is knowledge.   K

Socrates' argument progresses in a rational and generally convincing manner, but it is certainly not strictly deductive and by no means conclusive. Although its format is claimed to be taken from mathematics, it seems to lack the persuasive power of a geometric proof, for example. In fact, Socrates (*Meno* 89c–d) admits as much and reveals his reason why, in agreement with the *Republic* passages above:

> **Meno**: I don't see how we can escape the conclusion. Indeed it is obvious on our assumption that, if virtue is knowledge, it is teachable.

---

30. Mueller states that the following proposition presupposes the hypothesis-lemma: Virtue is knowledge. See Mueller, "Mathematical Method," 178–79. Formally, of course, he is correct; for a bi-conditional to be true, both sides have to be true. However, it seems *procedurally*, though, that "a man is not taught anything except knowledge" is what is presupposed. Virtue is knowledge is K here, not P.

Socrates: I suppose so. But I wonder if we were right to bind ourselves to that.

. . .

Meno: . . . But what has occurred to you to make you turn against
it and suspect that virtue may not be knowledge?

Socrates: . . . I don't withdraw from the position that if it is knowledge, it must be teachable; but as for its being knowledge . . .

It does not seem to be the case that Plato's Socrates is disappointed with
the cumulative persuasive effect of the steps (P_1, P_2, etc.)—or of any of the
steps individually—that the argument takes to finally arrive at K. It seems
rather that Socrates (as in the *Republic*) is not concerned with groping after an articulate Platonic philosophy of mathematics *per se* but rather for
a methodological philosophical mathematics, as it were.[31] In other words,
"[t]he only difference between Dialectic and mathematics which Socrates
explicitly recognizes is a twofold difference in method."[32] First, mathematicians sometimes employ visual aids during the course of their work, but
it is the second, and more important, facet of Anders Wedberg's twofold
difference that concerns us (since mathematicians are said not to *really*
concern themselves primarily with the visual): the one regarding method.[33]
This difference, of course, extends far beyond the Platonic corpus. Gábor
Kutrovátz, for example, makes the following observation in his remarks on
Szabó's reconstructive history of Eleatic philosophy:

> With regard to the actual relation between philosophy and any sci-
> entific, understood in a broad sense, enterprise like mathematics,
> the philosophical approach is dominated by the sceptical attitude
> to re-examine and criticize every basic theoretical and conceptual
> commitment of our culture, while the scientific enterprise on the
> other hand needs some commonly accepted foundations on which
> it can proceed further.[34]

The hypothesis would not necessarily have been subject to critical examination if Socrates had actually restricted himself to the procedure
outlined earlier in the *Meno* as that belonging to the geometers. For although geometers are known to inspect hypotheses, they never examine

31. Compare Brumbaugh, *Imagination*, 280 n.29.

32. Anders Wedberg, *Plato's Philosophy*, 103–4.

33. For a fuller discussion of these and related points, see Annas, *Introduction*, 272–93.

34. Kutrovátz, "Philosophical."

all. According to the procedure delineated in the *Phaedo*, a critical examination of initial hypotheses characterizes a subsequent phase of an
apparently widely prescribed protocol for philosophic investigation—one
belonging to a more mature facet of philosophy, or more to the point,
dialectic. Although geometers are impressively thorough in their quest
to prove propositions (and their converses in many cases), crucial early
hypotheses often remain unexamined. A philosophy that proceeds dialectically questions even the most initial hypotheses, making philosophy
far superior to mathematics in Plato's eyes, not merely by way of method,
but by way of metaphysical quality, as it were, by its potential to provide
philosophers with a more fundamental grasp of reality.

Socrates' hypothetical argument, then, is not strictly deductive, stem-
ming from basic definitions, common axioms, and previous deductively
proven theorems. Yet it is still understood that the argument will derive
whatever validity it possesses from the security of the initial hypothesis.
Since the hypothesis under discussion was explicitly formulated as a bi-
conditional, it seems entirely appropriate to inquire into whether, though
not strictly deductive, the main propositions of the argument are somehow convertible. Highlighting the bi-conditionality of the hypothesis,
however, suggests that rather than approaching even a loosely deductive
format, each round of argument is, in practice, introducing a new hypothesis, as it were. These invariably have some argumentation supporting them (whereas the initial hypothesis has none) and may or may not
be analogous to Jaakko Hintikka and Unto Remes' "auxiliary constructions".[35] In any event, the stated hypothesis again is:

Virtue is teachable if and only if virtue is knowledge. P ← → K

The plan of attack, obviously, is to attempt to find a way to derive P from
which K will immediately follow. Thus the conclusion:

Virtue is teachable; therefore, it is knowledge.   P → K

Note how Socrates immediately sets out to test the argument for
convertibility:

If virtue is knowledge, then it must be teachable.   K → P (?)

But, unfortunately, this test fails. If anything is teachable, there would be
teachers and students of the subject in question, but Socrates knows none

35. See Hintikka and Remes, *Method*.

and his subsequent interrogation of Anytus along these lines proves unsuccessful. Rather than deny the known fact with which they had hoped to eventually link K—that a man is not taught anything except knowledge—Socrates suggests that Meno abandon K. This is something that Plato thinks that mathematicians do not do enough, especially with respect to ultimate hypotheses. The dialectic approach demonstrates in his mind, among other things, the superordination of philosophy over mathematics.

Whether he is right or not on this count is neither here nor there for the present study. What does matter is that Plato incorporated into his philosophical inquiries a method putatively taken from geometers and adapted it to whatever degree for his own purposes. He then supplemented the inquisitive procedure with a summative evaluation of the starting hypothesis. The procedure might conceivably be called axiomatic insofar as it depends upon an "axiom" (or an "axioma medium"[36]) for its validity and purports to follow consistently, but not necessarily deductively, from this axiom to a conclusion. The dialectical "check" for the procedure might also be called axiomatic insofar as it similarly depends upon the conclusion as a starting point—at least in the *Meno* example above—for its validity and attempts to, in a consistent manner, arrive at the original hypothesis.

To what extent this dialectical procedure mirrors the actual Greek geometrical procedure of analysis is practically immaterial.[37] As Knorr observes: "[G]eometers' actual motives need not much have affected Plato's views of them."[38] One might wonder instead whether Plato utilized these methods for purposes of inquiry or pedagogical presentation. In light of our discussion so far, it would seem that Plato (at least in the *Meno*) attempts what might be called a guided axiomatic philosophical *inquiry* into the nature and properties of virtue. This particular inquiry in the *Meno* happens to dead end—even if a positive position is finally enunciated at the end of the *Meno*. Yet it, too, presumably must, in turn, be subjected to the same type of procedural examination: the procedure itself is never abandoned or evidently disparaged. It is important to mention that a necessary condition is placed by Plato on the continued em-

36. As Shorey calls it in Plato, *Republic II,* 110, n. b.

37. Mueller is content to see only a loose fit; he warns against forcing anything more. See Mueller, "Mathematical Method." He says elsewhere that "there is not a word of truth" in the standard account of geometric analysis (for example, those that follow Cherniss). See Mueller, "Review."

38. Knorr, *Traditions,* 74.

ployment of the cumulative dialectical process: that the security of initial hypotheses be established by a reverse axiomatic examination, as it were. The fact that this quasi-axiomatic procedure is presented as a method of inquiry suggests that the hypothetical method represents at least one way by which Plato seeks to initially strive to investigate the Forms.[39] As Annas explains, "[R]eason treats the hypotheses as literally hypothetical, as things laid down, to be treated as steps to reach the first principle which is unhypothetical [the Good]."[40]

The foregoing considerations have provided enough evidence to steer the present discussion toward agreement with Hans-Georg Gadamer's observations regarding Platonic argumentation:

> It seems clear that despite the inadequacy of [the *Phaedo's*] proofs they have a sort of logical order to them and display increasing cogency, but it is just as clear that ultimately these arguments must be thought of only as expositions of assumptions and not as conclusive demonstrations.[41]

Platonic "good and necessary consequences", as it were, are explored for their expository usefulness and never for some set of epistemological ramifications. As Gadamer surmises, "Thus the point of the demonstrations, it seems to me, is that they refute doubts and not that they justify belief."[42] Epistemological certainty was neither here nor there with regard to the adoption of arguments from hypotheses in the *Republic*, *Meno* or *Phaedo*. Much rather, the methodological legacy of Platonic arguments "from hypotheses" was much closer to a "hypothesis seeking understanding" approach to philosophical investigation, even if conducted under the cover of analogical imitation of a proto-Euclidean, Q.E.D. ideal.[43] The hypothetical gesture toward understanding is subsequently taken up by dialectic but never under the pretenses of achieving certainty.[44]

---

39. Huffman traces the history of a possible second in "Philolaic." See also Deslauriers, "Plato."

40. Annas, *Introduction*, 277.

41. Gadamer, *Dialogue*, 22

42. Ibid., 37.

43. An ideal kept alive, of course, by Peripatetic interests in demonstrative science and eventually put to auspicious use by Galilean science. See, for example, Wallace, *Galileo's Logic*.

44. Compare Annas, *An Introduction*, 281–84.

Aristotle, of whom we shall undertake a short study, sets out to improve upon Plato's insights. The next chapter briefly considers the development and systematization of Aristotle's axiomatic approach in *APo*.

5

The Use of Mathematics for Philosophy in Aristotle

ALTHOUGH ARISTOTLE SEEMS TO inveigh against Plato's teaching about Forms in certain of his writings, he seems not to have differed from him on the fundamental point of the superiority of the most divine things.[1] Theology, or the science of the things that do not change, is the highest science for Aristotle.[2] Yet surely Barnes is right in his summative remarks about Aristotle's attitude toward the sciences:

> Aristotle, like Plato, was impressed by the progress made in the most successful of Greek sciences, geometry; and in particular he was impressed by the way in which geometry could be presented as a unified area of knowledge. And he required, in effect, that the features to which geometry owed its unity should be transferred, so far as possible, to the other theoretical sciences. In short, knowledge is to be systematized in the form of axiomatized deductive sciences.[3]

More will be said about Aristotle and axiomatization; but for now we can admit that Aristotle himself seems to have been persuaded that—at least in theory—each science has its first principles from which its subject matter can properly be deduced. There are four main points I hope to make in this chapter: 1) Aristotle appears to say that each subject should proceed with as much rigor as possible. 2) Not every subject matter will be as rigorous as mathematics. 3) The geometry of the time was not as axiomatic as Aristotle required. 4) The rigor of Aristotelian axiomatics served anagogical ends and not epistemological.

1. See, for example, Chang, "Plato's Form." Questions such as: what description of the Forms does Aristotle take issue with? Did Aristotle's opinion of Plato develop over time? how relevant were Plato's teachings to Aristotle's own philosophical work? cannot be taken up here.

2. For this and the following points I am following Barnes, "Life and Work," 25–26.

3. "Life and Work," 25. Compare Ross, *Aristotle*, 43.

Let us begin by considering how Aristotle likely gleaned portions of his logical conception of demonstration from mathematics. I shall then present an instance where Aristotle's ideal was one that not even geometry pretended to live up to. To help the discussion along, I shall interact with ideas set forth by Barnes regarding what it is that Aristotle is trying to do in *APo*. Then I will attempt a reconstruction of a geometric example found in Aristotle's *On Sophistical Refutations* against which Aristotle has negative things to say in terms of its axiomatic efficacy.

The first topic to broach is Barnes' proposal that *APo*. "is concerned exclusively with the teaching of facts already won . . . it offers a formal model of how teachers should *present and impart* knowledge."[4] To sustain this thesis, Barnes argues that pedagogy is a primary concern for Aristotle, but others have rightly pointed out that pedagogical concerns are, at most, only incidentally in mind during the course of *APo*. (and elsewhere).[5] As a preliminary for his argument, Barnes argues that positions that posit a loose compatibility between *APo*. and some of the other writings are not easily sustained, but not a few scholars have managed to persuade themselves otherwise.[6] Yet we must not be unduly waylaid by ancillary discussions. Passing attention is called to Lloyd's survey of Aristotle's uses of "demonstration" in the *Rhetoric*, the ethical treatises, and the *Metaphysics* and Wians' assessment of Lloyd's survey that Aristotle indeed has more than one theory of demonstration in mind, each being partially articulated in the various writings according to the subject matter dealt with. Lloyd shows that Aristotle deliberately relaxes his axiomatic program at times.[7] This raises the question of how strict his axiomatic expectations really are.

Demonstrations in the strict sense—those from which it is required that the premises be "primary" and "immediate"—do not seem to be the only acceptable form of demonstration in *APo*. Rather, one might argue, they are the paradigms to which all other demonstrations should be ultimately compared.[8] Wians adduces at least three passages in *APo*. to

4. Barnes, "Aristotle's Theory," 77, italics in original.

5. See, for example, William Wians, "Aristotle"; M. F. Burnyeat, "Aristotle"; A R Perreiah, "Aristotle's Axiomatic."

6. See, for example, Gotthelf, "First Principles"; Lennox, "Divide"; Fraser, "Demonstrative Science"; McKirahan, "Aristotle's metaphysics."

7. See Lloyd, "Theories."

8. Compare Wians, "Commentary on Lloyd." Wians thinks that "the official theory

support this interpretation, but we have space here to refer only to one. The text in question merits an elaboration on Wians' brief remark that Aristotle is curiously not as explicit in this instance as he might have been in stating that his opponents "had failed."

When arguing against the extreme positions that nothing is demonstrable and, its reverse, that all truths are demonstrable, Aristotle makes the following points:

> Our own doctrine is that not all knowledge is demonstrative: on the contrary, knowledge of the immediate premises is independent of demonstration. (The necessity is obvious; for since we must know the prior premises from which the demonstration is drawn, and since the regress must end in immediate truths, those truths must be indemonstrable.) Such, then is our doctrine, and in addition we maintain that besides scientific understanding there is its originative source which enables us to recognize the definition.
>
> Now demonstration must be based on premises prior to and better known than the conclusion; and the same things cannot simultaneously be both prior and posterior to one another: so circular demonstration is clearly not possible in the unqualified sense of 'demonstration', but only possible if 'demonstration' be extended to include that other method of argument which rests on a distinction between truths prior to us and truths without qualification prior, i.e. the method by which induction produces knowledge. But if we accept this extension of its meaning, our definition of unqualified knowledge will prove faulty; for there seem to be two kinds of it. Perhaps, however, the second form of demonstration, that which proceeds from truths better known to us, is not demonstration in the unqualified sense of the term. (*APo.*, 72b18–32)

Considering the two extremes, Aristotle, in accord with his general practice, extracts the truths contained in each and then sets out to argue against their conclusions. The truth conceded in response to the first extreme—that nothing can be demonstrated—is that an infinite regress cannot be traversed.[9] Aristotle then proceeds to argue that although it is true that an infinite series cannot be traversed, it is not the case that there is an infinite regress here because the immediate premises do not require

---

[of demonstration] sounds a good deal less strict and more flexible than Lloyd's analysis implied." (407)

9. Just before our passage, Aristotle explicitly states: "wherein they are right, for one cannot traverse an infinite series" (72b9).

demonstration. Aristotle then turns to the truth to be gleaned from those who claim that everything is demonstrable: "Perhaps, however, the second form of demonstration, that which proceeds from truths better known to us, is not demonstration in the unqualified sense of the term." In other words, he affirms a distinction between demonstrations that rely upon immediate premises and those that rely upon premises that are prior by means of some other qualification. Aristotle, nonetheless, calls these types of arguments another form of "demonstration" (apodeixis). In other words, although demonstrations without qualification are "primary" (to use Wians' word), these are not the only type of demonstration to be permitted.

Hence mathematics is not the only science that Aristotle has in mind for comparison with the more strict form of demonstration. Other sciences should aspire, as appropriate, to more or less strict forms of demonstration. This interpretation seems to agree, for example, with what Aristotle says toward the beginning of *EN* (1094b11–14, 19–27):

> Our discussion will be adequate if it has as much clearness as the subject-matter admits of, for precision is not to be sought for alike in all discussions, any more than in all the products of the crafts . . .
>
> We must be content, then, in speaking of such subjects and with such premises to indicate the truth roughly and in outline, and in speaking about things which are only for the most part true and with premises of the same kind to reach conclusions that are no better. In the same spirit, therefore, should each type of statement be *received*; for it is the mark of an educated man to look for precision in each class of things just so far as the nature of the subject admits; it is evidently equally foolish to accept probable reasoning from a mathematician and to demand from a rhetorician scientific proofs.[10]

Yet it is interesting to note that in the *Rhetoric* (1355a7) Aristotle explains that there *is* a type of demonstration (apodeixis) appropriate to oratory.[11] Barring potentially disagreeable reconstructions of Aristotle's "philosophical development," it seems reasonable to conclude that "demonstration" for Aristotle is always science-dependent.[12]

Although the suggestion that *APo.* sets up mathematics as the paradigm for other sciences to follow as appropriate is not without its problems, it is a stronger candidate than Barnes lets on in his article. In response to

---

10. Translator's italics in Aristotle, *Basic Works*.

11. Compare Lloyd, "Theories and Practices," 381–84.

12. Compare D. K. W. Modrak, "Aristotle's Epistemology." Contra Furley, "Aristotle," 10.

his first objection—that the "interesting" examples are taken from natural science—one can hardly disagree with Wians' conclusion: "Aristotle in the *APo.* is preoccupied with mathematics."[13] In response to his second objection—that Aristotle's technical vocabulary did not originate in mathematics—attention can be drawn to an article by Gomez-Lobo that draws some very interesting parallels between *APo.* and Euclid's *Elements*.[14]

Gomez-Lobo observes that certain expressions in *APo.* 72a18–20 and 72a23–24 "are elliptical, i.e., that they have been reached by dropping certain terms from hypotheses actually in use."[15] He conjectures that demonstratives are implied to the effect that the putatively false hypotheses in *APo.* 76a40–42 should be understood as "let there be a one foot long line" and "let there be a straight line," mirroring "certain aspects of the practice of Greek mathematics as it is known to us in Euclid."[16]

Gomez-Lobo goes on to show that Aristotle's examples of primitive mathematical terms whose definitions need to be assumed are presented as assumptions in Euclid's *Elements*. Not only that, but further parallels can be seen in each writer's approach "towards primitive and derived terms and towards principles and conclusions":[17]

Pattern suggested by *APo.*   **Example taken from mathematics**

A1: What primitive terms mean is assumed → What is a unit in 76a34

A2: What derivative terms mean is assumed → What is a triangle in 76a35

A3: That the starting points are true is assumed → That this is a unit in 76a35

A4: That the derived propositions are true → That this is a triangle (?)
    is demonstrated

Actual practice of *Elements*

E1: What straight line means is assumed. (Definition 1.4)

E2: What triangle means is assumed. (Definition 1.20)

E3: That AB is a straight line. (ekthesis)

E4: That triangle ABC is an equilateral triangle is demonstrated. (sumperasma)[18]

---

13. Wians, "Scientific Examples," 140.

14. See Gomez-Lobo, "Aristotle's Hypothesis."

15. Ibid., 435.

16. Ibid., 436.

17. He offers a theoretical account for this parallel in Gomez-Lobo, "Aristotle's First Philosophy."

18. As Gomez-Lobo points out, this is precisely the format described by Proclus. Compare Proclus, *Commentary*, 159–60.

Gomez-Lobo has found a remarkable match between some of the parameters set by *APo.* and the pattern followed by Euclid. Yet he cautions, "All appearances to the contrary, I do not wish to suggest that Euclid knew and followed Aristotelian doctrine. On the contrary, I think I have been able to show that none of the items in Aristotle's classification of principles corresponds to the Euclidean postulates."[19] The correspondence may not be exact with actual geometric practice, but there still seems some intention to set forth in the *Analytics* a form of reasoning that mathematicians might methodically follow.[20]

Let us move on to Barnes' third objection: that there is no evidence for a "pre-Euclidean axiomatic presentation of mathematics." It is common knowledge that the definitions, common notions and great majority of theorems were already incorporated into works before Euclid's time.[21] Perhaps Aristotle had his eye on *somebody's* pre-Euclidean axiomatic work. But even if the case can be argued just as easily in the opposite direction, one can at least disagree with Barnes' skepticism with regard to Proclus' testimony: "[W]e may well wonder what authority he had for supposing that these men [Hippocrates, Leon, and Theudius] had anticipated Euclid in their presentation."[22] Barnes likewise extends his suspicions to Eudemus.[23] Not all writers, though, share his distrust for sources.

19. Gomez-Lobo, "Aristotle's Hypothesis," 439.

20. Surely there is some middle position to take up between Gomez-Lobo's "no correspondence" view and the traditional view. (The traditional view sees Euclid as consciously conforming his work to Aristotle's.) Germane to the broader argument of this book, however, is the observation that mathematicians and logicians of the modern period believed "Aristotle probably intended his *Prior Analytics* to set forth the form of geometric reasoning which Euclid intended in his *Elements* to follow." Anellis writes: "It appears to have been unanimously accepted, however, by eighteenth-century logicians, who regarded Euclid's *Elements,* especially the first book, as the epitome of logical reasoning and who, following Wolff, sought to apply the Euclidean method to every field of study." See Anellis, "Kant," 94. Something similar can be said for the seventeenth century.

21. See, for example, Artmann, "Euclid's *Elements.*"

22. Barnes, "Aristotle's Theory," 72.

23. Although it does not appear that any pre-Euclidean *Elements* are extant in Greek, in 1884 the editors of the Armenian journal *Pazmaveb* published a geometry fragment entitled, "A newly found Fragment of the Elements of Geometry by Euclid of Alexandria, translated into old Armenian by the ancients." About fifty years later A. A. Shaw happened upon it, translated it into English and compared the fragment with the standard editions of Euclid's *Elements.* It contains definitions numbered 20–35; common notions numbered 1–10; postulates numbered 1–5; and the first three propositions of Book 1. Shaw

In a lengthy essay that inquires into the proper historiographical methods for researches into Euclid's *Elements*, Knorr concludes:

> Euclid had access to a variety of exemplars from the preceding generation of technical writers, and he was surely more likely to take his expository model from them than embark on a conscious effort to create a formalism satisfying the prescriptions of one or another philosopher. To the extent that Euclid is consistent with philosophical precursors, this can be assigned to their shared acquaintance with that technical corpus.[24]

Far from eschewing mathematics on account of its Platonic uses in the Academy (Barnes' final objection), it is much more likely that "Eudoxus' tenure at the Academy coincided with that of the young Aristotle, so that the work of this geometer can hardly but have had its influence on the elaboration of the philosopher's views on logic and the formal structure of science."[25]

If *APo.* indeed had mathematics in view as its prime candidate as the ideal science,[26] some discrepancies still remain. Kullman, for example, shows how an examination of Aristotle's actual mathematical examples in *APo.* shows that they are "trivial" and even "feigned,"[27] but Wians probably has obtained better insight into the larger scheme of *APo.* when he posits that the motivation for incorporating mathematics into this discus-

---

found many variations that were "*not* improvements of the text of Euclid, on the contrary, they make the text definitely *primitive*, lacking in rigor." For example, in Proposition 2 the diorismos, the sumperasma, and common notion 1 are not given, common notion 1 being replaced with common notion 5 (i.e., 5 in the MS = 3 in Heath.). In fact the differences between the two were so pronounced in Shaw's judgment that he concluded "(a) the Armenian MS is a fragment of pre-Euclidean Elements written by Leon or Theudius of Magnesia whose works on the *Elements* are lost. (b) The Armenian MS is the *first* specimen of pre-Euclidean *Elements*, preserved through the medium of Armenian translation." See Shaw, "Pre-Euclidean Fragment," 81, 82. Whether Shaw's judgment still stands, Knorr's conclusion is still convincing.

24. Wilbur R. Knorr, "What Euclid Meant," 163. See also Knorr, "Infinity and Continuity.".

25. Knorr, *Traditions*, 50. Compare McKirahan, *Principles*, 19—although his "intermediate view" (135–43) involving Euclid's conscious decision to adhere to Aristotle's proposal is more difficult. See Barnes, "Aristotle's Philosophy of the Sciences," 237–41. Gould, too, finds a major role for Eudoxus in this story. See Gould, "Origins." Gould's interesting presentation of incommensurability as crisis, however, is no longer the consensual view.

26. For more on this interpretation of *APo.*, see Walter Leszl, "Mathematics."

27. See Kullman, "Funktion." Compare Wians, "Scientific Examples."

sion was Aristotle's perceived obligation to tackle the problem of mathematical truths in light of its overwhelming significance at the Academy.[28]
Hence it is not unreasonable to assume that the overlapping methods of
dialectic and mathematics in the *Republic* and elsewhere examined in the
previous chapter provide the ultimate context from within which Aristotle
ponders the roles and structures of demonstrations.[29] Perhaps, indeed,
it is Aristotle's philosophy of mathematics itself that inordinately drives
him to make some of his obscure methodological choices.[30] Burnyeat
contrasts *APo.* to Stoic conceptions of demonstration and persuasively
argues that the former is concerned with furthering *understanding* (and
not knowing) by way of *explanation* (as opposed to justification). Cleary
makes an insightful contribution as he completely Platonizes the problem, explicitly postulating that Aristotelian demonstration reasons *from*
principles whereas Aristotelian dialectic is a way for reasoning *to* principles.[31] Cleary's suggestion may actually go a long way toward reconcil-
ing *APo.* with *Met.*, for example.[32] The fundamental inquiry in each of
these considerations seems to be: What is "the nature of the faculty which
apprehends the first principles of the sciences"?[33] Let us now furnish at
least a preliminary answer to why the plethora of mathematical examples
in *APo.* seem so central *and* incidental *at the same time*: because Aristotle
is only formally interested in mathematics for its contextual metaphysical
peculiarity and possibility. After all, Aristotle may not have approached
his mathematical examples with sufficient competence in mathematics to
have an appreciable, material interest in them. Either way, redirecting the
discussion toward Aristotle's search for the metaphysical necessity of first
principles and the intellectual faculty that enables humans to apprehend
them can help explain why Aristotle has so many paradoxically ubiqui-
tous *and* perfunctory engagements with the discipline that allegedly touts
his methodological paradigm.

28. Compare Wians, "Scientific Examples."

29. See, for example, Robin Smith, "Dialectic."

30. Various accounts of Aristotle's philosophy of mathematics have been given. See,
for example, Cleary, *Aristotle and Mathematics*; Mueller, "Aristotle on Geometrical";
Modrak, "Aristotle"; and Halper, "Problems."

31. Cleary, *Aristotle and Mathematics*, 200–1, perhaps based on *Topics* 101a5–b4.

32. See, for example, Politis, "Aristotle"; Gomez-Lobo, "Aristotle's First Philosophy";
Fraser, "Demonstrative Science"; and Evans, *Aristotle's Concept*.

33. Evans, *Aristotle's Concept*, 33. Compare Smith, "Dialectic and Method"; Smith,
"What Use?"; Harari, *Knowledge*; Burnyeat, "Aristotle"; and Byrne, *Analysis*.

For example, consider how contemporary authors widely acknowledge that to produce a syllogism in the way that Aristotle describes—a syllogism that results in an unqualified demonstration—is a fairly daunting exercise. For Aristotle contends that in order for a demonstration to be a demonstration in an unqualified sense both its premises and its conclusion must be "eternal." Moreover, the conclusions drawn must be in the same genera as the premises *and* the premises used must be appropriate to the subject matter.[34] Thus, Aristotle writes: "Consequently a proof even from true, indemonstrable, and immediate premises does not constitute knowledge [unless the conclusion is demonstrated from its appropriate basic truths]." (*APo.* 176a13–14) For example, an ancient geometer, named Bryson, was taken to task by Aristotle and others for the way that he attempted to square a circle. Let us consider Aristotle's remarks in *SE* 172a10ff:[35]

> The contentious arguer bears much the same relation to the dialectician as the drawer of false geometrical figures to the geometrician . . . But the latter is not a contentious reasoner, because he constructs his false figure on the principles and conclusions which come under the art of geometry . . . For example, the squaring of the circle by means of lanules is not contentious, whereas Bryson's method *is* contentious. It is impossible to transfer the former outside the sphere of geometry because it is based on the principles which are peculiar to geometry, whereas the latter can be used against many disputants . . .

It is interesting to note that Aristotle's focus is not upon whether the conclusion drawn is true or false. His interest lies in the reasoning involved. To square a circle (also called a quadrature) is one of the three famous construction problems of antiquity.[36] In fact, it was not until some time in the nineteenth century that it was proven that such a construction is impossible. Aristotle's complaint seems to be that Bryson proceeded in a way that did not restrict itself to principles that were peculiar to ge-

---

34. Corcoran, "Aristotle's Natural," and Mendell, "Making Sense" argue that not all syllogisms must be confined to two premises.

35. Aristotle, *On Sophistical Refutations*, 65.

36. The other two were: doubling a cube and trisecting an angle. The task was to construct these with a straightedge and a compass. Pappas provides a concise overview of these three problems as well as Hippocrates' lunes (discussed below). O'Connor and Robertson suggest that the popular perception of ancient geometry as straightedge and compass construction is not entirely accurate.

ometry. An attempt to square a circle by means of lanules (or lunes, i.e., crescents) might conceivably involve constructing circles that overlap in such a way that they form lunes. The constructed lunes would then be used to measure the area of an inscribed triangle or square (or any polygon). If a specific relation could be established among the area of the lunes, the area of a circle, and the area of the square (or polygon), then, perhaps, all three could be shown equal. To give an idea of how one might go about squaring a circle by lunes, let us consider a way one might go about squaring a lune.[37] The key often lies in what relationship one is able to establish between the circles drawn. For example, the lune of the smaller circle shown above will be equal to the area of the inscribed triangle. The reasoning is as follows: Using the Pythagorean theorem and other results it can be shown that a quarter of the large circle is equal in area to the small semicircle. Clearly, a quarter of the large circle is also equal in area to the combined area of the triangle and the area of the lens that remains. The lens that remains when added to the area of the lune of the smaller circle is equal to the area of half of the smaller circle. It then follows that the area of half of the smaller circle minus the area of the lens of the large circle is equal to the area of the inscribed triangle.[38]

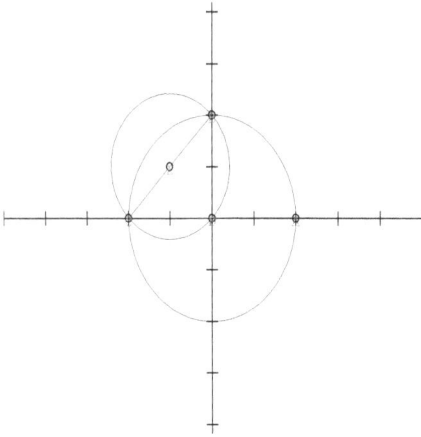

37. This example is adapted from Weisstein, "Lune." The tick marks on my graph indicate particular measures for easier frame of reference. See the website for the full proof. Many thanks to Russ Howell for helping me improve my explanation of the example that follows.

38. According to Simplicius, Hippocrates made use of a widely accepted result: "the squares on the diameters have the same ratios as their circles." See Thomas, *Thales to Euclid*, 239. Hippocrates (fifth century B.C.E.) famously attempted to solve the squaring of a circle using lunes in a similar way. Although I selected a different example to present, the reader can compare Hippocrates' diagram (below) with the one above. In Hippocrates' diagram, the lunes of the smaller circle turn out to be equal to the lune of the larger (the one delineated by the horizontal axis). The three together equal the triangle. For the proof, see Aaboe, *Episodes*,

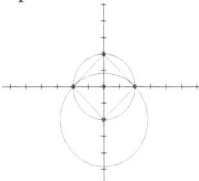

Aristotle writes that one who proceeds "by means of lanules is not contentious," presumably because the principles involved are peculiar to geometry.[39] The lunes are constructed geometrically, as are the other polygons. (However, the idea that a whole is equal to the sum of its parts does not seem to me peculiar to geometry, but, perhaps, the idea that areas can be equal to corresponding areas of other overlapping figures can only be said in geometry.[40]) By contrast, Aristotle rejected Bryson's alternate strategy as "sophistical." Bryson apparently suggested that one might square a circle by circumscribing and inscribing two squares, for example, using the same circle (see right). The circumscribed square would have an area greater than that of the circle and the inscribed square would have an area smaller than that of the circle. Bryson's argument has not been preserved but Heath surmises that it went as follows: "*[I]f a polygon intermediate in between the inscribed and circumscribed polygons could be drawn, the area of a circle would be equal to that of the intermediate polygon.*"[41] This approximation would seem to become more accurate as more sides are added to the initial polygon (which is in our case, a square).

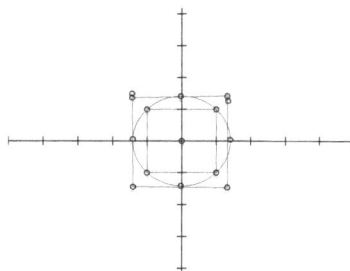

Many historians perceive Bryson's general approach to be noteworthy—a precursor of an approach (termed "exhaustion") that was applied more systematically and successfully by Eudoxus and Archimedes. Aristotle, by contrast, chides Bryson for importing intuitions that are common to all fields and not restricting himself to those that are specific to geometry. He explains: "[Proofs such as Bryson's] operate by taking as their middle a common character—a character, therefore, which the subject may share with another—and consequently they apply equally to subjects different in kind." (*APo.* 75b41–42) The nature of Aristotle's

---

39–40. (Hippocrates lunes: My larger circle may not provide the requisite 90° arc.)

39. Aristotle seems to reject extant attempts at quadratures, yet he does explicitly state that "the squaring of the circle by means of lanules is not contentious."

40. I.e., area by magnitudes. The fact that Aristotle approves the use of axioms such as 'take equals from equals and equals remain' seem to allow for a number of variations that do not restrict demonstrations as much as he seems to think.

41. Heath, *Manual*, 142, italics his. For other proposals, see Mueller, "Aristotle and the Quadrature"; and Knorr, *Traditions*.

critique is not clear,[42] especially since Bryson's own argument has not survived. Perhaps, we would not be wrong to infer that the conclusion drawn by Bryson could not count, according to Aristotle, as scientific knowledge:[43] "If, then, in controversy with a geometer qua geometer the disputant confines himself to geometry and proves anything from geometrical premises, he is clearly to be applauded; if he goes outside these he will be at fault, and obviously cannot even refute the geometer except accidentally." (*APo.* 77a10–15)

So in what way does Bryson's quadrature differ from the first proof presented above? How did Bryson "go outside" of geometry in a way that the first example did not? The methods on the whole seem comparable enough: using other geometric figures than those given to find the squares of the given figures. This general approach would not be used in any other discipline than geometry. The main difference between the two examples lies in the fact that whereas our first example yielded an explicit equality (area of lune = area of triangle, etc.): Bryson's strategy only *points* to inequalities that will *eventually* yield an equality. By using inequalities that grow presumably less and less as the sides of the inscribed and circumscribed polygons increase, one can make the claim that there must be some square that is equal in area to any given circle. But precisely what "middle" is taken from another discipline to render Bryson's argument "contentious"? If we are not to focus upon Bryson's conclusion (which seems correct), but rather his means of arriving at the conclusion (which also seems correct), where in the argument does Bryson depend upon principles that are dialectic and not specific to the discipline in question?

Given the subject matter of the work under consideration (*APo.*) and the immediate context of the present passage (75b37ff.), the mention of "middle" likely refers to the middle part of a categorical syllogism. Aristotle's forbidden middle is probably the reliance upon the combined inferential punch of limits and inequalities.[44] For the argument seems to

42. Heath refers to the question of Bryson's attempt to square the circle as "the most baffling in the history of Greek geometry." No satisfactory explanation has yet been found. See Heath, *Mathematics in Aristotle*, 48.

43. Compare Heath, *Mathematics in Aristotle*, 50. This is a very charitable reading: we may be giving Aristotle credit for a proficiency in geometry that he did not actually have. On the other hand, we might be giving Bryson credit where credit is not due. See, for example, the pertinent remarks in Alexander's *Commentary on Aristotle's Sophistical Refutations*. The relevant section is cited in Fauvel and Gray, *History*, 89.

44. And, perhaps, upon its crucial dependence upon a diagram? Although the use

depend upon two concurrently running strands of syllogistic reasoning, one that begins with the premise that any circumscribed polygon must have an area greater than that of the pertinent circle and one that begins with the premise that any inscribed polygon will have an area less than that of the pertinent circle. The running syllogisms might be formulated thus:

Inscribed

P1: $\text{Area}_{\text{inscribed}} < \text{Area}_{\text{circle}}$

P2: $\text{Area}_{n+1\text{polygon}} > \text{Area}_{n\text{-polygon}}$

C: $\text{Area}_{n\text{-polygon}} < \text{Area}_{n+1\text{polygon}} < \text{Area}_{\text{circle}}$

P1.1: $\dots \text{Area}_{n+1\text{polygon}} < \text{Area}_{\text{circle}}$

P2.1: $\text{Area}_{n+2\text{polygon}} > \text{Area}_{n+1\text{polygon}}$

CC: $\text{Area}_{n+1\text{polygon}} < \text{Area}_{n+2\text{polygon}} < \text{Area}_{\text{circle}}$

etc.

Circumscribed

P1': $\text{Area}_{\text{circumscribed}} > \text{Area}_{\text{circle}}$

P2': $\text{Area}_{n+1\text{polygon}} < \text{Area}_{n\text{-polygon}}$

C': $\text{Area}_{\text{circle}} < \text{Area}_{n+1\text{polygon}} < \text{Area}_{n\text{-polygon}}$

P1.1': $\text{Area}_{\text{circle}} < \text{Area}_{n+1\text{polygon}} \dots$

P2.1': $\text{Area}_{n+2\text{polygon}} > \text{Area}_{n+1\text{polygon}}$

CC': $\text{Area}_{\text{circle}} < \text{Area}_{n+2\text{polygon}} < \text{Area}_{n\text{-polygon}}$

etc.

These two lines of reasoning must overlap at some point such that the $\text{Area}_{n+m\text{polygon}}$ for each column above will become the identical polygon to the effect that *its* area must equal that of the circle.

Whether the conclusion is true or not (although one would not be faulted for being convinced that it is) is immaterial for our purposes. Our interest is in whether there exists a "middle" such that it can be said that it does not pertain to geometry alone. Aristotle does permit that if one "takes equals from equals then equals remain": this common axiom is permitted in any demonstration whatever. Heath's opinion is that Aristotle's concession regarding equals can easily be extended to apply to the "greater than" and "less than" relations that are employed by Bryson.[45] One might not agree with Aristotle's remarks if they were directed at our particular reconstruction of Bryson's reasoning—this is perfectly good geometry—yet, all the same, Bryson's method may have been too arithmetic for Aristotle's liking: the middle terms "greater than" and "less than" being geometrically unacceptable possibly because it was expected that

---

of diagrams seems perfectly acceptable to the geometers of the time; they would never count as proof in themselves. Compare Barnes: "Euclid's use of *diagrams* does not stop him from being an Aristotelian demonstrator." See Barnes, "Aristotle's Philosophy," 238.

45. For other suggestions, see Mueller, "Aristotle and the Quadrature."

measurement should have no place in rigorously conducted geometric practice.[46]

In any event, Aristotle's primary axiomatic strictures are so rigorous that Greek geometers seem to have little interest in upholding them.[47] How did geometers proceed if not strictly axiomatically according to the Aristotelian ideal?[48] If Aristotle's program is not practical for mathematics, does it prove useful for any science? Although these questions cannot be taken up here, we might say that Aristotle did indeed construe his most strict model of demonstration after his conception of what he thought mathematical reasoning should look like. Yet it does not take much to show that accepted mathematical practice consistently fell short of Aristotle's axiomatic expectation.[49] Yet if *APo.* is read within the larger context of "an exercise in Socratic *elenchus*," in continuity with what was taught at Plato's Academy,[50] we might have reason to expand upon the traditional interpretation of *APo.*, the interpretation that says that Aristotle is submitting a theoretical proposal for the criteria of an ideal science.[51] For within Aristotle's axiomatic proposal there seems sufficient conceptual leeway to accommodate less stringent methods that are more appropriate for non-mathematical disciplines. These less stringent methods can be regarded as analogous demonstrations in their own right within those disciplines.

Epistemology is clearly not in view here with regard to the human intellect in terms of its ability to apprehend first principles. For if the ability to apprehend first principles is intertwined with the means by which first principles are presented to the mind for understanding (and not to the mind for scientific knowledge), then the dialectical activity undertaken while searching out first principles will not serve an epistemological

---

46. Heath thinks that Aristotle evinces his limited exposure to mathematics when he criticizes Bryson. After all, the evidence suggests that Greek geometers were very much about the business of establishing equalities between areas and volumes. Compare Mueller, "Remarks," 287. See also Fowler, *Mathematics*; and Reed, *Figures*.

47. Compare with observations made in Suppes, "Limitations."

48. For an outline, see Mueller, *Philosophy*.

49. Robin Smith writes: "Greek mathematical demonstrations steadfastly resist any translation into categorical syllogisms." See Smith, "What Use?" 261.

50. Hintikka's phrase in "Commentary on Smith."

51. Lezl also sees a duality of purpose in *APo.* See Lezl, "Aristotle's Logical Works."

purpose.[52] Burnyeat is surely right: *APo.* occupies itself with furthering understanding by way of explanation and not by way of establishing epistemic justification. Even if Aristotle is concerned with justification, surely we must agree with Smith and say that *APo.* is decidedly not interested in the type of epistemic justification "that since the seventeenth century . . . has been seen as a remedy against the possibility of undetected error."[53] In other words, the emphasis is not on whether such and such first principles are veritable and indubitable or whether those principles' veracity guarantees their consequences as veritable and indubitable. Much rather the emphasis is on the process of anagogical maturation from epistemic activity to epistemic virtue, a process that requires one to have already worked through various series of deductions and to finally be in a position where one can appreciate this or that foundation can be authentically foundational "for me."[54] The next chapter considers how this translates to Euclidean geometry.

52. See, for example, Smith, "Dialectic and Method."
53. Smith, "What Use?" 265.
54. Compare Smith, "What Use?"

6

Euclid's Deductive Procedure

A COMPARISON OF ARISTOTLE'S axiomatic program with a roughly contemporary geometric example has proven illuminating, but perhaps we can learn even more by taking time to indulge in a mini-tour of the ancient geometric sense of axiomatic presentation firsthand. Although the parameters set for the current project will not allow for a comprehensive treatment, an inquiry into what Euclid intended to accomplish by the stipulation of one of his five postulates might help contribute to our larger panoramic theological investigation.

This chapter is a constructive inquiry into how the Euclidean tradition may have understood the argumentative strategy behind the *Elements'* stipulation of five geometric postulates toward the beginning of the first book.[1] The suggestion is that the postulates are hypotheses which direct the subsequent inquiry toward the "discovery" of the Pythagorean theorem. The strategy assumes that by arriving at the Pythagorean theorem, an already well-established proposition, the framers of the discussion help confirm the correctness of the hypotheses listed at the beginning of Book 1.

In the late modern period, scholars began asking whether the five postulates associated with Euclid were initially regarded as self-evident truths. The conclusion was that the Euclidean *Elements* is not as axiomatically rigorous as previously supposed. Nevertheless, modern textbooks still hold Euclid's *Elements* in high regard: "The great contribution of Euclid, for which he is justly renowned, is that he organized the geometrical knowledge of his time into a coherent logical framework, whereby

---

1. The documentary history of the *Elements* is not straightforward, especially regarding the postulates, but that has not prevented discussions surrounding the rationale for "Euclid's" five postulates from taking place. I use "Euclid" and "Euclidean tradition" to refer to the hypothetical authorial construct that facilitates such discussions.

each result could be deduced from those preceding it, starting with only a small number of 'postulates' regarded as self-evident."[2] And again: "The axiomatic method of sequential logical deduction, starting from a small number of initial definitions and assumptions, has become the basic structure of all subsequent mathematics. Euclid's *Elements* is the first great example of this method."[3] Virtually everyone who reads mathematics knows that Euclid did not succeed in deriving geometric theorems solely from given axioms.[4] We shall revisit these claims through the eyes of an ancient reader.

Losee explains that there are three general characteristics that comprise the ideal deductive system. First, the axioms and theorems are deductively related; second, the axioms are self-evident; and third, the theorems agree with observations.[5] Marchi and others, however, have mounted a very convincing case that the Euclidean postulates are not absolutely certain starting points, but rather hypotheses.[6] The idea has encountered some opposition but a recasting of the postulates may pay some methodologically valuable dividends.[7] In what follows, we shall take up Seidenberg's suggestion[8] and inquire into whether Euclid's fourth postulate is a theorem. Along the way, we shall attempt to ascertain the fourth postulate's particular meaning and, more importantly, its larger role in the *Elements* generally. Oftentimes, sustained inquiries into the role that the postulates play in Euclid succeed in presenting Greek geometry in a whole new light. A brief examination of the fourth postulate of Book 1 of the *Elements* can help show why.[9]

Seidenberg refreshingly raises the question of whether Euclid's postulates qualify as actual postulates; i.e., whether Euclid enumerated them

2. Hartshorne, *Geometry*, 9.

3. Ibid., 13.

4. At least according to modern standards. Euclid assumed the concept of betweenness, for example, a relation not justified by any of his starting points. But see Guggenheimer, "Axioms."

5. Losee, *Introduction*, 24.

6. See Marchi, "Method." See also Szabó, *Beginnings*, 282–304; compare Szabó, "Working"; and Szabó, "Greek Dialectic."

7. See, for example, Knorr, "Early History." Polarization is certainly an issue. See Kutrovátz, "Origins." Mueller concentrates on other factors in "Euclid's Elements."

8. See Seidenberg, "Euclid's Elements."

9. As a search of the literature will quickly show, "Postulate 4 has attracted the least attention from commentators . . ." See Reed, *Figures*, 18.

with the intention of providing self-evident grounds upon which to base his entire geometry. Seidenberg mentions in an article that "[i]t is strange to find [Postulate 4 of Book 1] postulated as it is very easy to prove."[10] In fact, "[t]he proof is so simple that I am sure that Euclid, Proclus, or any other ancient could have easily found it, if only someone told them to look."[11] Let us take Seidenberg's query more seriously than one might normally when met with such a counter-cultural claim and inquire more deeply into the meaning of Postulate 4 and what it is that it accomplishes for the *Elements*.

Postulate 4 of Book 1 of the *Elements* reads: "That all right angles are equal to one another."[12] Intuitively, one might agree with Seidenberg to the effect that Euclid's fourth postulate should be provable by way of Proposition 4. (In fact, Seidenberg claims more: that the postulate can be proven *without recourse to superposition* using Proposition 4.) Proclus had already offered a proof of Postulate 4 that was in circulation at least since the time of his commentary. Hilbert, far more recently, confidently claims that Euclid "unjustifiedly" places the "theorem" that all right angles are equal to each other among the postulates. Hilbert fits the right angle postulate into his schema at Theorem 21 and proves it by placing one right angle upon another in order to show that if the two are not congruent then they must be both greater than and less than each other at the same time. It would seem that on the evidence of Proclus' and Hilbert's proofs, at least, Seidenberg is right to raise the question of whether the fourth postulate is really a postulate at all. In fact, Albert Magnus, Gerard of Cremona, and Al-Nayrizi all present proofs for the postulate in their commentaries, just to name a few.[13] So what does the fourth postulate mean and why posit it in the first place?

Definition 8 reads: "A *plane angle* is the inclination to one another of two lines in a plane which meet one another and do not lie in a straight line."[14] Heath is surely right to understand that "Euclid really intended to define *rectilineal* angle,"[15] which emphasizes how each of these lines

10. Seidenberg, "Euclid's Elements," 269.

11. Ibid., 269–70.

12. Euclid, *Elements*, 1.200.

13. Lo Bello has published recent translations of these.

14. Euclid, *Elements*, 1.176. Seidenberg refers to it as Definition 7.

15. Ibid., 1.176.

is straight. Perhaps then it is understandable how Proclus sees the use of the fourth postulate in Euclid's Proposition 13 ("If a straight line set up on a straight line make angles, it will make either two right angles or angles equal to two right angles") even though it is never "really" required axiomatically.[16] Heath goes on, though, to interpret Postulate 4 "as equivalent to the principle of *invariability of figures* or its equivalent, the *homogeneity of space.*"[17] Seidenberg, by contrast, interprets Postulate 4 as being nearly equivalent to saying "that supplements of equal angles are equal."[18] In Heath's view, Euclid is assuming that everywhere on every plane space will behave in precisely the same way. Seidenberg seems to understand Euclid somewhat differently and in a more restricted sense for he compares Postulate 4 and Proposition 4 with Hilbert's Theorem 12 and Theorem 14 respectively. This is a very interesting train of thought in Seidenberg's article on whether Book 1 was intended as an axiomatic presentation of geometry because Hilbert himself remarks that "[a]n immediate corollary of Theorem 14 is the congruence theorem for vertical angles" and furthermore that "[t]he existence of right angles also follows from this theorem [Theorem 14]."[19] All this may hang on Hilbert's own definition of a right angle: "An angle that is congruent to one of its supplementary angles is called a *right angle.*"[20]

Comparing Hilbert's definition with Euclid's may prove instructive. Euclid, for his part, wrote: "When a straight line set up on a straight line makes the adjacent angles equal to one another, each of the equal angles is right, and the straight line standing on the other is called a perpendicular to that on which it stands."[21] The question of what Euclid means by Postulate 4, then, seems to turn, at least in part, on what a right angle is and on whether the fourth postulate should be closely associated with the fifth or whether it should be considered independently, as it were. Seidenberg raises a good question when he asks: If Euclid indeed intended to relate the fourth so closely to the fifth, why not then write the fourth and fifth postulates as one postulate? Although Heath's interpretation might be

16. Ibid., 1.275.

17. Ibid., 1.200.

18. Seidenberg, "Euclid's Elements," 269.

19. Hilbert, *Foundations*, 15.

20. Ibid., 13.

21. Definition 10 in Euclid, *Elements*, 1.181.

interpreted as the "necessary condition" for the possibility of Seidenberg's interpretation, these do not appear to be equivalent assumptions. The former rather seems an assumption about space as a whole, whereas the latter seems merely a feature of the specific rectilineal angles in question.[22]

In any event, Seidenberg does well to remind in this context (*contra* Heath) that superpositioning was an acceptable geometric practice for Euclid. It should not embarrass that Proclus offers a proof of Postulate 4 using the method of superposition. In fact, Euclid himself employs the method of superposition on noteworthy occasions, beginning with the fundamental triangle congruence of Proposition 4. Heath's translation of Proposition 4 reads as follows:

> If two triangles have the two sides equal to two sides respectively, and have the angles contained by the equal straight lines equal, they will also have the base equal to the base, the triangle will be equal to the triangle, and the remaining angles will be equal to the remaining angles, respectively, namely those which the equal sides subtend.[23]

This is commonly taught in modern-day geometry classes as *side-angle-side*.[24] The proposition that follows this one (and many others besides) literally employs superposition any time it relies upon Proposition 4's triangle congruence. Artmann does not exaggerate when he remarks: "Practically nothing can be done in elementary geometry without the congruence theorems."[25]

Let us then focus our attention on Postulate 4 specifically by considering why Proclus believes that the postulate is used in Proposition 13.[26] Both Mueller and Seidenberg, among others, claim that Proclus is mistaken here. Yet the case may not be so clear cut. His correct application of the postulate may very well depend on what is meant by "all right angles are equal to one

22. Compare Guggenheimer, "Axioms," 190.

23. Euclid, *Elements*, 1.247.

24. Incidentally, not a few high school text books follow Hilbert and present side-angle-side as a postulate (axiom) which goes to show our contemporary distaste for the ancient method of superposition. The same might be said for *side-side-side* (Euclid's Proposition 8). Euclid's reluctance to use superpositioning in 1.26 is often cited as evidence that Euclid himself was no fan of superpositioning. See Mueller, *Philosophy of Mathematics*, 22. Compare Heath in Euclid, *Elements*, 1.225, 1.249, etc. Seidenberg, of course, does not agree.

25. Artmann *Euclid*, 22.

26. Proclus, *Commentary*, 228 (293).

another." We can illustrate the case by proffering the following scenario for consideration:

Suppose someone was trying to prove Postulate 4 and proceeded as follows:

That all right angles are equal to one another.

Let AC be set upon BD so that angle ACB is a right angle. Since angle ACB is a right angle and since angle ACD is adjacent to angle ACB on the same straight line, angles ACD, ACB are equal (def. 10).

Thus it is required to show any constructed right angle is equal to right angle ACB.[27]

Let angle EGF be the given right angle with EGH adjacent to it on the same straight line.

I say that all right angles are equal to one another.

Apply FH on BD so that G is on C and GE is not on the same side of BD as CA. Since BCE, DCE are right angles, BCE, DCE are equal. Thus angles BCE, DCE are equal to two right angles and angles BCE, BCA are equal to two right angles.

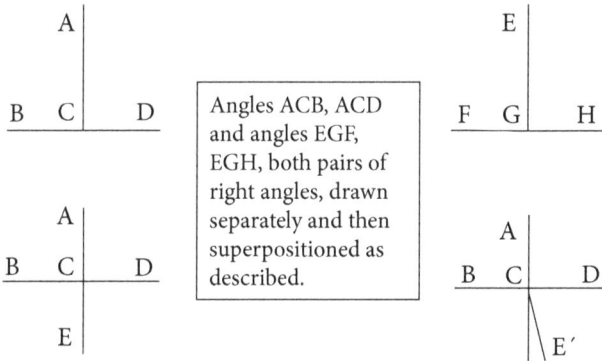

Angles ACB, ACD and angles EGF, EGH, both pairs of right angles, drawn separately and then superpositioned as described.

Here Proposition 13 comes immediately to my mind: "If a straight line set up on a straight line makes angles, it will make either two right angles or angles equal to two right angles."[28] In the situation just contrived we certainly have a number of adjacent angles that are equal to two

27. Mueller touches upon how Greek geometers considered one example sufficient for demonstration in *Philosophy of Mathematics*, 13–14.

28. Euclid, *Elements*, 1.275.

right angles. Might Proposition 13 be used, then, to help prove the fourth postulate? If Mueller, Seidenberg, and others are right and the fourth postulate is not required for Proposition 13, then it might imply that when Proclus reads the fourth postulate, he had in mind what must be true of all right angles (understood in at least two logically different senses) that are adjacent to each other, not least, *at a particular intersection*. This may help explain why he fails to mention it when discussing Propositions 14 and 15. Proclus writes of Proposition 13: "For when it makes two right angles, it makes angles equal to two right angles, since all right angles are equal to one another." In other words, according to his logical delineations that follow in the passage, *being* two right angles and *being equal to* two right angles must, at least in some sense, be the same thing and this sameness is provided for by the fourth postulate. He does not find occasion to expound these same logical distinctions in Propositions 14 and 15 even though Proposition 13 is used in both. Perhaps Proclus does not cite Postulate 4 since the distinction between simplicity and equality does not, as far as he can see—and as far as the text of Euclid's proposition is concerned—explicitly arise.

To continue with the attempted proof of the fourth postulate, we come across a situation closely related to that presented in Proposition 14 (in fact, its converse). Do adjacent right angles necessarily imply a straight line? Angles BCE, DCE are equal to two right angles and angles BCE, BCA are equal to two right angles. BD is a straight line by construction, but is AE? Here I think Seidenberg (and Seidenberg's Hilbert) are on the right track with their understanding of what the fourth postulate is asserting: supplements of equal supplements will turn out to be equal. Proclus helps us make an important distinction when he writes: "Vertical angles are different from adjacent angles, we say, in that they arise from the intersection of two straight lines, whereas adjacent angles are produced when one only of the two straight lines is divided by the other."[29] So right angles are explicitly described as being equal adjacent angles, leaving the possibility of vertical angles open. But when superimposed in the way done above, will they technically form vertical angles?

The angles vertical to each other, whether strictly vertical or not, are equal to two right angles. In fact they will be equal to the same two right angles as that of the two adjacent angles in question and this happens in

---

29. Proclus, *Commentary*, 233 (298).

both directions. It is easy to see here that the phrase "two right angles" is beginning to lose at least some of its initial meaning. Hence, Proclus may be justified after all in including his excursus on logical distinctions when discussing Proposition 13. Perhaps he would remark at this point that one's focus must remain upon adjacent angles being themselves two right angles, or at least that the transition to such a focus must be made logically possible. Are ACB and BCE adjacent in the relevant way? In other words, are they supplements? Are ACB and BCE still right angles? A rather unusual hypothetical phenomenon occurs here. ACB is a right angle when compared with ACD but not a right angle when compared with BCE even though BCE and ACD lie on the same line. In a similar way BCE is a right angle when compared with DCE but no longer when compared with ACB even though ACB and DCE are on the same line as it. Presumably, the fourth postulate minimally asserts that this cannot be. This is probably why Proclus thinks that without the fourth postulate, Proposition 13 makes little sense: Either these two angles are two right angles or they are equal to two right angles, and either way—*with the aid of the fourth postulate*—one can conclude that all senses of "two right angles" will in every instance locally amount to the same thing for geometric purposes.[30]

But what would hypothetically result if it were possible to take right angles ACB, ACD and "copy" them as adjacent angles in their respective positions and apply them to BD in such a way that the copied AC would be not on the same side as the original AC? It could be arranged that the copied C falls on the original C, but would the copied A fall on E? Suppose further (by Proposition 11) that a perpendicular were drawn to BD from E. What would be the case now? Would there be three sets of equal adjacent angles, all right, but all non-equal on the same line?

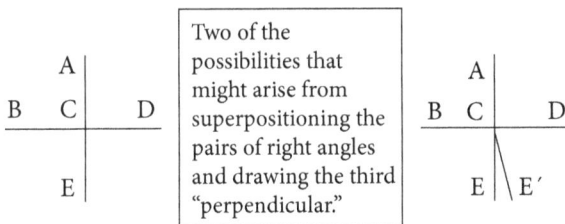

Two of the possibilities that might arise from superpositioning the pairs of right angles and drawing the third "perpendicular."

---

30. Compare Guggenheimer, "Axioms," 190.

At this point we have our choice of Proclus' or Hilbert's proofs to show that all right angles in question must be equal. This raises an interesting question: How is Hilbert able to assert that the congruence theorem of vertical angles is an immediate corollary of his Theorem 14 when in Euclid, according to Heath, Mueller and others, it follows immediately from Proposition 13 and Postulate 4? Part of an answer is given in the surmise that what Euclid is trying to describe with the fourth postulate is the standard nature of constructible right angles for the remainder of his treatise—especially the construction of right angles during the course of his proof of the Pythagorean theorem—and not primarily some fundamental feature of space.[31]

"Neutral geometry" famously proves that the right angle is the angle of parallelism.[32] Yet it is curious that parallelism does not apparently surface for Euclid until at least Proposition 29. It seems to me then, when all is said and done, that parallel postulates are what guarantee what Heath calls "the invariability of figures" and not right angles. One might even press a little further and suggest that Euclid's assumption of the homogeneity of space, to which Heath makes reference, is provided not so much by the fourth postulate as by the fourth proposition. Heath himself remarks that if indeed the fourth postulate is to be proved, "it can only be proved by the method of applying one pair of angles to another and so arguing their equality."[33] But there is no reference to the right angle postulate in Proposition 4 to substantiate the necessary assumption of the homogeneity of space. Perhaps this is why Seidenberg thinks it important to emphasize that he sees a proof for Postulate 4 without resorting to superposition. In any event, the fourth postulate might illuminatingly be restated in something like the following way: Being equal to two right angles is the same as being two right angles for geometric purposes. And the way one is to be convinced of this is to follow this hypothesis' trajectory as it "discovers" the Pythagorean theorem, a widely accepted theorem in ancient times.

In our proof attempt above, that was precisely the matter that came up: we wound up with a number of *combinations* of right angles that were equal to two right angles but were not all self-evidently right angles them-

31. Compare Mueller, *Philosophy of Mathematics*, 29–30.

32. See, for example, Bell, *Men of Mathematics*, 299–306, and Wallace and West, *Roads*, 255–57.

33. See Euclid, *Elements*, 1.200.

selves in the sense described by the Euclidean definition, and that made for a very unusual intersection. If our train of thought so far is not too far off the right track then it seems that if one can indeed prove that supplements of equal angles are equal (as Euclid partially does in Proposition 5) then one might be well on her way to proving our hypothesis itself, as Seidenberg's reading of Hilbert seems to suggest.

Whatever the proof Seidenberg has in mind, Postulate 4 seems not to be strictly a postulate in the sense that it stipulates something that is self-evident. Even so we must reiterate that there really is no problem with recourses to superpositioning.[34] Irrespective of whether the proof attempted above would satisfy a Tarski or a Hilbert (i.e., whether there lurk implicit axioms that a modern geometer would decry), a reason why a geometer in Euclid's time would reject it is not immediately apparent.[35] In response to Heath's interpretation of Postulate 4, one can justifiably point to Proposition 4 for the establishment of the homogeneity of space.[36]

In any event—aside from Seidenberg's article—Postulate 4 has not recently come under fire for being provable, but several of the postulates, common notions, and definitions have been subject to doubts on documentary grounds. Russo, for example, argues that Euclid's definitions are, in fact, taken from Heron's *Definitions* and that they were incorporated into Euclid's text at a much later date.[37] (However, Knorr had argued previously that Heron's work was not Heron's but that of Diophantus.[38]) Mueller considers only three of the five common notions to be Euclid's, the others being later interpolations.[39] Seidenberg himself reduces to three, which is what many scholars have done. Among those who accept Postulate 4, Heath and many others suppose that Postulate 4 was that crucial foundation upon which Euclid constructed his fifth. We have suggested here that Postulate 4 is more properly thought of as a hypothetical license to construct those figures with which Euclidean geometers were already familiar (along with other figures they might construct in the future) and were useful for formulating a series of demonstrations that culminated in the

34. Compare Mueller, *Philosophy of Mathematics*, 23–24.

35. Knorr argues (*contra* Szabó) that superpositioning was widely accepted among geometers even if philosophers saw problems with it. See Knorr, "Early History."

36. Compare Wagner, "Euclid's."

37. See Russo, "Definitions."

38. See Knorr, "'Arithmêtikê.'"

39. This is a common position. See Mueller, "Starting Point."

"discovery" of the Pythagorean theorem. This suggestion does not mean that Euclid doubted the "truth" behind each of the hypothetical licenses that he posits but rather that such licenses were set forth as "true" with the main objective of being given the practical space for trying to set forth in an orderly fashion consequences that might be said to "finally" arrive at the Pythagorean theorem, a theorem already everywhere known.

It is indeed stimulating to raise the question of whether the fourth postulate is really a postulate in terms of being a self-evident truth about the homogeneity of space. We, for our part, engaged in an exercise in-volving a hypothetical proof-attempt to illustrate what ambiguities might lurk therein; Proclus and Hilbert, among others, have proffered reasons why Postulate 4 is no self-evident assumption. Accordingly, perhaps not only Euclid, but several of his predecessors and successors, conceived of postulates quite differently than commonly supposed. If anything else, Seidenberg is certainly making a helpful gesture when he suggests that a definitive interpretation of Postulate 4, for example, should not be taken for granted.

The main question that we have broached here is: what were pos-tulates really supposed to accomplish? And what relationship, if any, can be observed among them once they are proposed? Perhaps one can get away with arguing that Aristotle was primarily interested in axioms in a very similar manner as contemporary logicians: starting points for entire disciplines that are so obvious that they are necessarily taken to be true simply by considering them—the ideal Aristotelian scientific thinker sup-posing to proceed strictly by syllogism.[40] Yet more in line with the con-ceptual equipment available to the ancients is the suggestion that ancient geometers sought more of a temporary, as it were, hypothetical license to construct whatever it was that they were already *doing* and wanted to *do*—in this case with the specific aim of deductively linking them to the Pythagorean theorem. According to Mueller, the postulates were math-ematical *hypotheses* and the ensuing arguments in the *Elements* should be thought of as geometric and arithmetical *thought experiments* that aimed to construct some proposed figure or prove that a figure possessed a cer-tain property.[41] Even if ancient geometers were duly challenged by Plato

40. Syllogisms were not always restricted to two premises. Conceptual differences are apparent between ancients and moderns. Compare the main argument of the first sec-tion of Ian Mueller, "Euclid's Elements."

41. See Mueller, "Euclid's Elements." Nikulin emphasizes that the figure constructed

or some other thinker(s) to provide theoretical grounds for their varied constructions (as some historians hold), the mathematicians themselves seemed infinitely more concerned with constructing whatever figures they thought would be useful in solving further seen and unforeseen problems. Epistemic justification was never at issue.[42]

In the next two chapters, we shall investigate the curious uses to which the hypothetical method was put by Proclus and Boethius in two of their metaphysical works. In both Proclus' *Elements of Theology* and Boethius' *De Hebdomadibus* we shall see that an ancient concern for validation of hypothesis and inquiring into hypothesis' connections to widely accepted theses has given way to pedagogical strategies that seek to better position students and other readers for a more mature appreciation of respective metaphysical positions.

---

was always conceived in its "intermediateness." See Nikulin, *Matter,* 223–27.

42. Knorr has argued that ancient mathematics was primarily concerned with the problems of their trade and not so much with philosophy.

7

Proclus' Deductive Metaphysics

IN THIS CHAPTER, I examine Proclus' *Elements of Theology* as a pedagogical use of the hypothetical method presented above. Proclus' decision to present the elements of platonic theology as if these comprised a
quasi-axiomatic system is an ordering device that gives his treatise the
appearance of a system where each successive platonic proposition follows deductively from a previous one. Although it was partly influenced
by his own neoplatonic heritage, Proclus' decision on behalf of a presentation *more geometrico* in both of his *Elements* represents a methodological
discontinuity from the regular expository and dialogical genres of the
classical metaphysical treatises. I suggest that the geometric presentation
of the *Elements* was attempted for the anagogical effect it might have on
his students.

On the way to making this suggestion, I set out here to contextual-
ize Proclus within the milieu of ancient Greek mathematical and logical
thought. Aristotle's treatises regarding first philosophy sought to establish
for metaphysics as well as for other disciplines certain logical and scientific principles. We have already proffered that Aristotle's works were profoundly informed by his considerations of mathematical procedure and
that the Euclidean *Elements* was an extension of the hypothetical method
to a textbook presentation of geometrical lemmas and theorems. In this
chapter, I consider how the presentation of an array of ordered propositions in Proclus' *Elements of Theology* was suggested to him, at least in
part, by Euclid's geometric and arithmetic *Elements* and that, inasmuch as
he could, Proclus was striving to try a new form of philosophical writing
toward the end that he might further dispose his readers to an anagogical
appropriation of the various tenets of neoplatonism in a way that prevailing pedagogical conventions could not. In other words, Proclus' imaginative appropriation of a quasi-axiomatic method in the *Elements* is a

spiritual exercise expressly designed to enhance the metaphysical progress and enlightenment of his already converted reader by further persuading them of the cogency of neoplatonism by positioning them to receive the intuition of the One as the origin of all that is. Without denying that neo-platonic influences lend themselves to the propositional structure of the *Elements of Theology*, the suggestion is that Euclid's classic geometric ar-rangement of propositions in his *Elements* formatively contributed to the structure of Proclus' *Elements*.[1] Proclus performs a persuasive act of great ingenuity when he allusively invokes the demonstrative flair of geometric deduction in his expository account of neoplatonic metaphysics.

I shall begin by reminding the reader of a founding assumption of this treatise, namely that the introduction of a deductive method for mathematics and its application in geometry is an innovation of Greek philosophy and mathematics. Tait explains:

> Cut-and-paste proofs of the kind found in Books I and II of Euclid existed long before fourth century B.C. and in cultures besides Greek . . .
>
> [However,] there is no reason to think that the idea of geometry as a deductive science based on *primary truths* . . . preceded the *Republic*.[2]

Tait interprets Plato's remarks against geometers in Books VI and VII of the *Republic* to indicate that "geometry had not yet been sufficiently founded on primary truths." The response to Plato's criticism, according to Tait, was Euclid's *Elements*.[3] This reconstruction is a popular one but it remains controversial.

With respect to the beginnings of a properly deductive geometry, a more nuanced understanding is Mueller's, according to whom:

> it seems likely that by Aristotle's time some mathematicians were being explicit about this sort of general quantitative assumption [referring to equals being taken from equals]. But it also seems to me and, I think, most scholars likely that these assumptions [com-

1. Compare Nikulin, "Physica."

2. Tait, *Provenance*, 191–92, italics his.

3. However, the Platonic method of which Tait boasts may have had Pythagorean roots. See Huffman, "Philolaic Method." Knorr states that one of the main purposes be-hind his magisterial *The Evolution of the Euclidean Elements* was precisely to "counterbal-ance a prevalent thesis that the impulse toward mathematical rigor was purely a response to the dialecticians' critique of foundations." See Knorr, *Evolution*, 1.

mon notions such as Euclid's] were not made explicit much before Aristotle's time.[4]

In another place, Mueller suggests that there is evidence that Plato played "some kind of role as general mathematical director" and that although he was not "a mathematician of real significance," he was, at the very least, "a source of challenge and inspiration to mathematicians."[5] Either way, one can reasonably conclude that it was the mathematicians who initially informed Plato's methods of analysis;[6] Plato, in turn, modified them for his purposes of disciplining dialectical philosophical procedure. Plato's methodological considerations, thus gleaned from the mathematicians, were then refined and further developed by Aristotle, who also had an eye on what at least some of the mathematicians of the time were doing.[7] The early interest in the idea of an axiomatic, deductive science was very familiar to Proclus.[8] Amongst Proclus' works is his well-known *A Commentary on the First Book of Euclid's Elements*. In it, he appeals to the same strictures found in Aristotle's work: "Let the geometer state that if four magnitudes are proportional they will also be proportional alternately and prove it by his own principles, which the arithmetician would not use; and again let the arithmetician lay it down that if four numbers are proportional they will also be proportional alternately and establish this from the starting-points of his own science."[9] This description seems uncannily modern for such an ancient discussion of scientific discourse.

4. Mueller, "Remarks," 290. Evans curiously traces the "equals from equals intuition to Euclid," but Aristotle, who antedates Euclid, invokes it time and again. Perhaps by "Euclid" she means "the pre-Euclidean tradition that stands behind him." See Evans, "'Sub-Euclidean.'"

5. Mueller, "Mathematical Method," 175.

6. Agashe, for example, speculates that an axiomatic method had already been developed by pre-Euclidean mathematicians during the course of trying to square a circle. See Agashe, "Axiomatic Method."

7. See also Einarson, "Mathematical Terms"; Mueller, "Starting Point"; Szabo, "Transformation"; and Stenius, "Foundations."

8. Corcoran helpfully distinguishes between axiomatic and deductive systems. Aristotle attempted to delineate a "natural deductive system" that formulates a science's "underlying logic." Euclid delineated an axiomatic system of geometry that isolated its starting points but paid little attention to underlying logic. See Corcoran, "Aristotle's."

9. Proclus, *Commentary*, 8 (Prologue 1.4). Interestingly enough, Jones observes how Euclid employs a less general definition of proportion in book seven than the one already enunciated in book five. He surmises that Euclid does this because of his understanding of geometry and arithmetic as two distinct disciplines. See Jones, "La influencia," 377–78.

To appreciate this, one might compare the Proclus quote above with a standard twentieth-century work on mathematical logic. Tarski, for example, includes a section that reiterates a concern for proceeding in the science in question in a way that only involves "the disciplines preceding the given discipline." His example reads as follows:

> Thus logic itself does not presuppose any preceding discipline; in the construction of arithmetic as a special mathematical discipline logic is presupposed as the only preceding discipline; on the other hand, in the case of geometry it is expedient—though not unavoidable—to presuppose not only logic but also arithmetic.[10]

To be properly deductive, in both ancient and modern times—or at least so it would seem—one must restrict oneself to the use of principles that are specific to the discipline in question.[11] However, it is important to note that Tarski's understanding stresses the unavoidable and primary use of logic in a way that is not typical of Euclid or Proclus. Mueller's observation made on a related matter is very perceptive in this regard: "It is a commonplace that people use logical principles unconsciously and correctly. However, logically correct reasoning must be distinguished from reasoning based on logic."[12]

The above comparison between Tarski and Euclid is comparable, I think, to a comparison between Aristotle and Euclid. For example, Robin Smith proposes that Aristotle's syllogistic was developed in the context of a "mathematized epistemology."[13] He posits that Aristotle began with a meta-mathematical theory of epistemology that eventually became a logical one. Irrespective of whether he is right about this, he is surely on to something when he observes that Aristotle was not trying "to codify the actual argumentative practice of actual mathematicians" but rather that he was aiming to formulate a meta-mathematical theory that could definitively establish the acceptable structures of mathematical proofs.[14]

---

10. Tarski, *Introduction*, 119.

11. Ibid.: "[A]ll requirements concerning the defining of expressions and the proving of statements which are specific for the discipline under construction, that is, those which do not belong to the preceding disciplines."

12. Mueller, "Euclid's Elements," 297–98.

13. See Smith, "Mathematical Origins."

14. Smith, "Axiomatic Method," 57.

The Aristotelian schema of demonstration ideally provides the disciplinary inquirer with a universal proposition that cannot be otherwise.[15] Euclidean demonstration can potentially supply such knowledge, but it just as often furnishes a particular construction that can at best be only a specific case solution to a very generally stated problem.[16] The Platonists (including Proclus) would never have admitted that constructions are universal and eternal. Constructions are, by their very nature, instantiations—the epitome of becoming. It is between these two proof-theoretic standards of the eternal and universal on the one hand and the "constructive-genetic" and particular on the other that Proclus finds himself caught. Of the tension that arises here, Parvu and Parvu comment:

> These two essential aspects of geometry will represent the starting point of a long-drawn polemic on the nature of the rationality and unity of geometry and of geometrical demonstration. They underlie also the vast *analytic-synthetic* dichotomy of the modern theory of knowledge.[17]

Of course, modern mathematicians have the option of eradicating the constructive aspects of geometry entirely when theorizing about it; there has been a revolutionary change in the perspective from which mathematics is studied and created:

> The deductive disciplines constitute the subject-matter of the methodology of the deductive sciences, which today, following Hilbert, is usually called metamathematics, in much the same

---

15. Or so it was supposed: "Aristotle himself, however, misconceived the importance of the categorical syllogism, supposing that the theory of it gave him the key to the nature of 'scientific' knowledge . . . This led him to characterize as 'sophistic,' and not 'scientific,' proof, the geometrical method of taking cases and shewing what holds in each one . . . Aristotle call this sort of inference, *though it leads to truth because it proceeds correctly from true premises*, 'sophistic' . . . " See Anscombe and Geach, *Three Philosophers*, 6, italics mine. Corcoran ("Aristotle's") thinks overly critical views of Aristotle's logic are unwarranted.

16. This is not a reference to diagrams employed in geometric proofs, but rather an attempt to take seriously the observation that a significant number of important proofs are in and of themselves proofs of *construction*—proofs that such-and-such thing *can be constructed.*

17. Parvu and Parvu, "Postulate Problem," 337, italics theirs. The authors go on to draw connections between these problems of ancient geometry with the development of the epistemological distinction between *a priori* and *a posteriori* knowledge. The phrase "constructive genesis" was taken from this article.

sense in which spatial entities constitute the subject-matter of geometry and animals that of zoology.[18]

In other words, with Hilbert, "[t]he subject of geometry has changed from
a study of space to the study of the logical interdependence of certain
statements about otherwise undefined objects."[19] But we should recall
that Proclus experiences no such shift in theoretical perspective. Rather,
he makes a heroic effort to preserve the best of both the metamathematical and the mathematical modes of presentation at the same time. The
dilemma, of course, is that the metatheoretical and the theoretical are not
so easily reconciled in the case of ancient Greek geometry.[20]

Nevertheless, Proclus strives to uphold both. He sought a "middle
path for geometry between tautological rigour and a fecundity liable to
free it from intelligible constraints."[21] Proclus' key to striking the right
balance between the metamathematical and mathematical aspects of geometric demonstration is

> the grouping within the same 'axiomatic system' of *hypotheses*—as
> the starting point of the demonstration of a particular science—
> and of *postulates*—as the starting point of its constructions. The
> axioms preserve—as in the case of Aristotle and Euclid—the hier-
> archical stage of some inter- or supra-disciplinary principles.[22]

In other words, Proclus stresses the Euclidean aspects of geometric postulates, i.e., that they give geometers the license to construct without having
to abandon Aristotelian logical strictures. At any time a new geometric
entity can be introduced for the purpose of establishing a further *theorem*,
without, at least in Proclus' eyes, apparently undermining the deductive
force of the science. These very considerations are creatively carried over
into his theological treatise, *Elements of Theology*. Such an imaginative

18. Tarski, *Logic, Semantics, Metamathematics*, 60.

19. Artmann, *Euclid*, 50. It has been said that "[a]bstract mathematics is introduced
in order to obtain finitary results in an easier and more elegant manner." See Shoenfield,
Mathematical Logic, 3.

20. Parvu and Parvu, "Postulate Problem," 333. Compare Lakatos, *Mathematics*, 61–69.
Also of interest here might be Luzzatto, "Philosophy?" On the other hand, Stenius seems
to challenge the distinction between mathematics and metamathematics. See Stenius,
"Foundations."

21. Parvu and Parvu, "Postulate Problem," 340.

22. Ibid.

integration marks an unprecedented development followed only sporadi-
cally in the course of the history of Western medieval philosophy.[23]

Proclus begins his *Elements of Theology* by articulating propositions
followed by their proofs:

Prop. 1. Every manifold in some way participates unity.

Prop. 2. All that participates unity is both one and not-one.

Prop. 3. All that becomes one does so by participation of unity.

Compare these with Euclid's first three propositions in Book 1 of his
Elements:

Proposition 1. On a given finite straight line to construct an equilateral
triangle.

Proposition 2. To place at a given point (as an extremity) a straight line equal
to a given straight line.

Proposition 3. Given two unequal straight lines, to cut off from the greater a
straight line equal to the less.

Here Euclid's first proposition allows him to construct the second and the
second permits the third. These three are constructions, licenses to create
additional geometrical entities as needed in subsequent demonstrations.

Consider now the role of Proclus' first three propositions. Proclus
does not begin his *Elements* with a list of definitions, postulates and common notions as Euclid does; however, it appears that he expects his first
three propositions to ground his entire scheme. By no means am I suggesting that Proclus' *Elements* is primarily a mathematical work or that it
adheres to the same rigor as Greek mathematics is said to do, but Proclus
does seem to be utilizing a quasi-mathematical style for the presentation
of his philosophical system.

Proclus' first three propositions act functionally as his so-called postulates in geometry, as his licenses to deductively create a system about
the One. The fact that he offers proofs for them does not in itself discount
the possibility that they play the same functional role as Euclid's first
three postulates did for his work. Above, I suggested that postulates for
the Greeks are not to be conceived primarily in terms of self-evident truth
and un-provability. They are rather theoretic and practical permission to

---

23. See, for example, Sweeney, "Literary Forms."

take a specific direction in thought, an expository tour of the discipline in question.

Proclus' common notions restrict themselves to the mundane logical laws that make all discourse possible (such as the laws of non-contradiction, modus ponens, etc.), as fundamental as these are to all thought, one should not expect him to enumerate them. Euclid, by comparison, remains silent regarding them even though he defers to them regularly.[24] Nevertheless Proclus' functional postulates are so crucial to his enterprise that they cannot be set forth without at least some minimal discussion. An overview of these discussions can help illuminate the kind of anagogical exercise Proclus expects his readers to undertake in their reading of his *Elements of Theology*.

Many of Proclus' proofs are indirect, and just as many are proven by cases. Both types of proof accord with acceptable geometric practices and may evince an added Aristotelian flair in the work, since Proclus often employs both proof methods in the selfsame proof.[25] Passing mention was made above that in Greek geometry a single generic example could legitimately prove a property for every conceivable case. One does not need to read Proclus' commentary on Euclid for long before she notices that Proclus goes much further than Euclid in introducing multiple cases. Such cases are only rarely entertained by the Euclidean demonstrations. Here we can detect Proclus' concern to exhaust all possibilities in the event that possible objections to a given proof are levied, calling the integrity of the Euclidean materials into question.

The proof by cases is an extension of the indirect proof, which considers the negative case only. Similarly, the method of exhaustion used by Bryson, Archimedes and others might be construed as an extension of proof by cases. Presumably, the rationale behind the multiplication of cases is to eliminate all contrary possibilities; such a task further establishes the soundness of the given proposition. Yet Proclus introduces cases almost *ad nauseum*, as it were, as he attempts to supplement several of Euclid's single example (and even cased) demonstrations, but in his own *Elements of Theology* Proclus' cases come across at times as somewhat contrived, to the effect that "[t]he dilemmata he sets up are ranked alternatives that are 'contrary' in the peculiar sense . . . in which *P* and *~P*

24. On Proclus as an Aristotelian logician trapped in a Platonic world, see Martin, "Proclus."

25. See Martin, "Proclus," 221.

are called 'contrary' yet $P \leq {\sim}P$."[26] I understand this as an indication that Proclus is conducting a pedagogical exercise wherein his methodological inspiration draws palpably from articulation *more geometrico* yet in a way that is careful not inadvertently to belie his neoplatonic teaching that all things find their source in the One.[27]

Consider, for example, Proclus' Proposition 1: Every manifold in some way participates unity. His proof begins: "For suppose a manifold in no way participates unity." An opening negation of the proposition prepares the reader for subsequent contradiction. By loosely patterning his proof on geometric indirect argument and then advancing to a subsequent proposition as if it follows in some deductive manner, Proclus breaks with the conventions of metaphysical treatises and thereby stretches his readers' perception and reception of the cosmological force of neoplatonic philosophy. This break constitutes, if not a new conception of first philosophy, at least a new way of doing first philosophy. So let us return to Proclus' proof by cases and offer a brief remark on the proof of Proposition 1, which, I think, is typical enough of what Proclus does in his *Elements* to serve as an exemplar for many of the proofs offered in the *Elements*. This, I propose, will allow the reader to see more clearly the possible motivation behind the pedagogical genre introduced by the *Elements of Theology*.

Proclus' *Elements* works in a way that recalls its Euclidean prototype. Students are expected to grow in their theological understanding via exposure to a deductive presentation of the teachings already taught to them. The understanding that Proclus' *Elements* aims for reaches beyond rational discourse toward the neoplatonic cosmological principle, the extra-rational, as it were, ground of all things that are. As Lowry remarks, "[Elements of Theology] can be considered as a kind of cosmological geometry. But unlike geometry the content of the [Elements of Theology] cannot allow there to be any ungrounded premise."[28]

Proclus takes up his proof of the first proposition by cases in the following way. Supposing that a manifold in no way participates unity, Proclus reasons that it has no part in oneness either as a whole or in any of its parts. The parts themselves then must be manifolds and the

26. Martin, "Proclus," 221.

27. Compare Lowry, *Logical Principles*.

28. Lowry, *Logical Principles*, 37.

manifolds' parts must each be manifolds as well and so forth. Similarly, for each of these parts it must either be one or not-one. Now, if it is not-one, it must either be many or nothing. My paraphrase seeks to highlight the contraries proffered by Proclus: one/not-one and many/nothing (i.e., not many and not-one). They, as noted above, satisfy a $P/ \sim P$ relation but Proclus implicitly expects that $P \leq \sim P$ at the same time according to each condition's proximity to the One. Contrast how this is not implied in, say, Euclid's Proposition 13 which states that every two lines that cut each other either form two right angles or two angles that are equal to two right angles. There is no indication whatever of a $P \leq \sim P$ value. In other words, there is no apparent ordering of states that can be readily discerned in Euclid's propositions or his proofs, whereas Proclus keenly has his eye on the One at all times and such a focus is evident throughout the *Elements*, not least by the way he elects to ground the treatise in his first three propositions.[29]

Proclus intends that his three cases in the proof of Proposition 1 of his *Elements* exhaust the possibilities: one, many, nothing. In his commentary on Euclid's Proposition 2, Proclus explains:

> A 'case' announces that there are different ways of making the construction, by changing the position of the points, lines, planes, or solids involved. Variations in case are generally made evident by changes in the diagram, wherefore it is called 'case,' because it is a transposition in the construction.[30]

On Proclus' treatment of Proposition 2, Heath writes:

> To distinguish a number of cases in this way was foreign to the really classical manner. Thus, as we shall see, Euclid's method is to give one case only, for choice the most difficult, leaving the reader to supply the rest for himself. Where there was a real distinction between cases, sufficient to necessitate a substantial difference in the proof, the practice was to give separate *enunciations* and proofs altogether . . . [31]

---

29. Compare Lowry, *Logical Principles*, 37: "There is the One and the descending procession of its productivity. There is the theorem and then the inherent working out of all its possibilities." Lowry considers the first six propositions as the foundation for all that follows.

30. Proclus, *Commentary*, 212.

31. Heath's remarks in Euclid, *Elements*, 246.

Proclus' cases for Proposition 2 are as follows: [32] A point's position may be "(1) outside the line or (2) on the line, and, if (1), it may be either (a) on the line produced or (situated) obliquely with regard to it; if (2), it may be either (a) one of the extremities of the line or (b) an intermediate point on it."[33] Heath makes mention of "Proclus' anxiety to subdivide," which a reader can also discern in Proposition 1 of *Elements of Theology*. Proclus explains that one might consider a manifold in terms of (1) a whole or (2) its parts, and if (2), each part again as either (a) a whole or (b) its parts; if (a), it may be either (i) one or (ii) not-one; if (ii), either (aa) many or (bb) nothing. Heath's complaint regarding Proclus' cases with respect to Euclid's Proposition 2 stems from the fact that at least one of Proclus' cases is trivial (2a) and that the others are implicit in the original Euclidean proof. For the cases presented in the proof of Proposition 1 of Proclus' *Elements*, the subdivisions strike one more as a dialectical analysis than a geometric demonstration, an analytical process metaphysically driven by the momentum gained from Proclus' directed movement from the composite to the fundamental—described as $P \leq \sim P$ above.[34]

That Proclus' *Elements* is a dialectical work is not to be disputed. Clearly the tension between the metatheoretical and theoretical aspects of Proclus' *Elements*, as it were, is resolved in favor of the metatheoretical.[35] That said, one might still discern by comparison what Proclus is trying to accomplish here. Knorr and others argue that Euclid intended his *Elements* to be an elementary textbook that touted a deductive presentation of geometric material without the giving of examples or explicit opportunities to practice.[36] Proclus reveals his understanding of what "Elements," or "elementary treatises," are supposed to accomplish:

> It is a difficult task in any science to select and arrange properly the elements out of which all other matter are produced and into which they can be resolved . . . Such a treatise ought to be free

32. The proposition reads: "To place at a given point (as an extremity) a straight line equal to a given straight line."

33. Heath's summary in Euclid, *Elements*, 245. Proclus' cases are in his *Commentary*, 223–28.

34. I am trying here to appropriate observations made in Martin, "Proclus." Lowry, for his part, suspects the influence of Iamblichus' doctrine of mean terms between extremes.

35. As Cleary has expertly shown. See Cleary, "El Papel."

36. See Knorr, "What Euclid Meant."

of everything superfluous, for that is a hindrance to learning; the selections chosen must all be coherent and conducive to the end proposed, in order to be of the greatest usefulness for knowledge; it must devote great attention both to clarity and to conciseness, for what lacks these qualities confuses our understanding; it ought to aim at the comprehension of its theorems in a general form, for dividing one's subject too minutely and teaching it by bits make knowledge of it difficult to attain. Judged by all these criteria you will find Euclid's introduction superior to others.[37]

Proclus' understanding of an "elementary treatise" is in line with the general ancient views on "Elements."[38] Proclus' *Elements of Theology*, then, is in all likelihood intended as an introductory textbook. Yet the innovative development that concerns us here is the *Elements'* evidently deductive manner of presentation of neoplatonic theology. Knorr writes of Euclid's *Elements*:

Euclid appears to assume a practical grounding in the discipline, for which he aims to provide the appropriate formal demonstrations. In effect, the *Elements* is a treatise on the causes relevant to the geometric field; it offers the learner models of how to secure the results of geometry as deductive consequences ultimately rooted in certain notions (namely, the postulates and axioms) of figure and quantity. The learner is expected to gain expertise in geometric theory through the study of finished models of formal exposition.[39]

In like manner, I propose that Proclus assumes a certain degree of technical know-how in the study of first philosophy (via dialectics) and expects the reader to gain in metaphysical knowledge and ability, even if on an introductory level, by way of working through a comprehensive account of the elements of platonic theology as if they all flowed naturally (read "deductively") from the One. The deductive arrangement encourages the reader to participate (and by this means, emphasize) in the more difficult of the two directions of dialectical inquiry in order that she might gain a greater understanding of the complexities of existence and the cosmological relation of these to the One, an anagogical exercise of immense proportions. Such a pedagogical endeavor seems to have a decidedly re-

---

37. Proclus, *Commentary*, 61 (Prologue 2, 73.17–74.14).
38. See Knorr, "What Euclid Meant," 162.
39. Knorr, "What Euclid Meant," 162.

ligious dimension insofar as the reader is led beyond discursive theology toward an intuition of the One as the origin of all that exists.

In a mathematical philosophy treatise, Lucas remarks that "[w]hereas Euclid's presentation is intelligible and has immense intellectual appeal, Hilbert's is unintelligible, except to those who already know their geometry backwards, and has no appeal for the wider public."[40] Similar remarks were probably said by non-mathematicians of Euclid's work in his time. Perhaps Euclid's *Elements* does not assume that its reader knows geometry backwards, but it does assume at least some technical exposure. The *Elements*, as an introductory textbook, sets out to increase one's knowledge of the science by reintroducing theorems already known—perhaps by other means—in a deductive fashion as theorems that are procedurally grounded by a body of earlier material.

Proclus' spiritual exercise, I propose, consists in the creative decision deductively to present to his students the fruits of a full-fledged, dialectically-earned platonic theology and to invite them to conceive it as such. Proclus, having studied in depth at least the first book of Euclid's *Elements* and having been steeped and trained in the neoplatonic philosophy of his tutors,[41] attempted to utilize the revolutionary pedagogical style of the former with hopes of further elucidating the profound tenets of the latter. The tension that persisted between the ideals of Aristotelian science and the actualities of geometric practice was a serious concern for Proclus, but his optimistic expectation that such a tension was worth overcoming in the realm of metaphysics for the sake of the philosophical edification of his students made the prospect of producing his *Elements of Theology* an eminently worthwhile pedagogical pursuit. For an initial, hypothetical acceptance of the axiomatic propositions regarding the One is to eventually give way to an intuitive and extra-discursive grasp of the reality that the propositions purport to describe. The aim is entirely anagogical and is one that the neo-platonist, Boethius, later decides to take up in one of his theological tractates.

---

40. Lucas, *Conceptual Roots*, 34.

41. For an outline of the neo-platonic curriculum, see Siorvanes, *Proclus*, 114–21.

8

Boethius' Recourse to Axiomatics

IN THIS CHAPTER, I posit that Boethius attempts a similar pedagogical use of the hypothetical method in his *How Substances are Good
in Virtue of Their Existence without Being Substantial Goods* (*Quomodo
Substantiae*, or *De Hebdomadibus* as it came to be called).[1] The work has
come up in contemporary discussions in the context of what impetus it
may or may not give to the story of Western philosophy told by Gilson.[2]
My own interest in *De Hebdomadibus* stems from the fact that it is one of
the only metaphysical treatises to explicitly assume a presentation *more
geometrico*. Accordingly, this chapter examines the axiomatic appearances
of Boethius' third tractate, specifically its purported use of seven axioms in
the course of arguing for a particular metaphysical conclusion. I claim that
Boethius was likely engaging in a pedagogical act similar to Proclus in his
Elements, a performative act, as it were, that disposes the reader to accept
a matter of faith that discursive activities can only vaguely comprehend.

Boethius' arguments in *De Hebdomadibus* regard how the things
which are are good. We shall set out to play the role of Boethius' "intelligent interpreter" and "supply the arguments appropriate to each point"
that he presents in his formulation of the dilemma. The emphasis will not
be upon Boethius' problematic *per se* nor on his particular solution to
that problem,[3] but upon his presentation *more geometrico* of a dilemma
and his proofs that purport to show that neither horn of the dilemma can
offer a viable solution to his question: how is it that the things that are are

---

1. Text citations are from Boethius, *Tractates*; axiom citations are from Aquinas,
Exposition. For the import of Boethius' *De Hebdomadibus*, see Scott Macdonald,
"Relation."

2. For a summary, see McInerny, *Boethius*, ix–xiv, 161–98, and McInerny., "Saint
Thomas." For an interesting account of the "story," see Etienne Gilson, *Being*.

3. For reflections upon these, see MacDonald, "Boethius's Claim."

good? We shall then go on to emphasize the same for Thomas Aquinas' reiteration of the dilemma in his commentary on Boethius and compare his remarks to Boethius' "proof."

In *De Hebdomadibus* Boethius jumped at the opportunity to follow "the example of the mathematical and cognate sciences and laid down bounds and rules according to which [he said] I shall develop all that follows." Boethius lists nine (or seven) premises from which his discussion proceeds axiomatically.[4] For simplicity's sake, we shall follow Schultz and Synan and posit a Boethian seven-axiom foundational schema for our elucidation of the dilemma that he poses.[5] The approach taken is influenced in part by a particular understanding of Boethius' use of "*hebdomad*."

There have been many conjectural explanations of the term *hebdomad*, especially given the fact that Boethius uses the phrase *Hebdomadibus nostris* (partially transliterated in translations as "my (or our) *Hebdomads*"). Aquinas himself (as do many other medieval writers) suggests that Boethius is referring to "editions," based upon the Greek verb "to edit." MacDonald promotes the older suggestion that Boethius here refers to a previous work of his that has not survived. Marenbon speculates that it was a term that John the Deacon had used to tease Boethius about having "philosophical pretensions."[6] On the other hand, Shultz and Synan consider the *hebdomads* to refer to the list of the seven axioms with which Boethius begins his treatise proper.[7] If one does not follow Aquinas' treatment of the requests made of him (Boethius), Boethius, in his own words, understands that he is about to write about the problem of how things are good "because the method of writings of this sort is not

---

4. A very interesting proposal for reading only seven axioms is proposed by Schultz and Synan in Aquinas, *Exposition*, xxiv–xxxii. That there are nine axioms is not believable. McInerny registers his complaint along these lines: "The nine Roman numerals in the Stewart-Rand-Tester edition are of scant help. By making the meta-axiom I, the editors get off to a bad start." See McInerny, "Saint Thomas," 76 n. 6. What follows is not at all affected by the fact that some writers delineate only four main axioms and their corollaries among Boethius' opening list of axioms.

5. Compare Chadwick, *Boethius*, 204. The axioms are taken from Aquinas, *Exposition*, xxxi–xxxii and for convenience are appended to the end of this chapter.

6. Aquinas, *Exposition*, 7; MacDonald, "Boethius' Claim," 247, n. 7; Marenbon, *Boethius*, 87–88.

7. Aquinas, *Exposition*, 7; Compare Boethius, *Tractates*, 38 n. a., where we might understand their suggested translation of "groups of seven" as my "group of seven [axioms]."

known to all."[8] Boethius, then, in addition to responding to a request for an explanation of a particular problem, is providing a clarification with respect to method. The reference to *hebdomads* in the opening section involves, at least minimally, the axiomatic task of arriving at the desired conclusion from the seven accepted premises.

This is certainly a plausible scenario.[9] Boethius writes how he was not willing to "share [his speculations] with any of those pert and frivolous persons who will not tolerate an argument unless it is made amusing." Augustine, Boethius, Anselm, Aquinas—virtually every church leader has had at one time or another to defend his or her practice of intellectually plumbing the tenets of the catholic faith. Augustine and Aquinas thought it fit to answer charges of impertinency by justifying the propriety of the philosophical exploration of the faith. Boethius, for his part, took much solace in philosophy and, at times, took pleasure in the "obscurities consequent on brevity, which are the sure treasure-house of secret doctrine and have the advantage that they speak only with those who are worthy." Accordingly, instead of explicitly drawing out the connections between his seven axioms and the arguments that follow, he leaves it to the "intelligent interpreter" to "supply the arguments appropriate to each point." This I maintain cannot be done based upon the axioms listed.

Our interest will be restricted to the dilemma that Boethius poses for the problem at hand. He claims that the "things which are, are good." He inquires, though, how it is that they are good: "We must, however, inquire how they are good—by participation or by substance." The dilemma is such that if things are good by participation a contradiction ensues. If things are good "in virtue of their own existence," another contradiction ensues. The preliminary conclusion drawn must be, says Boethius provisionally, that things are, in fact, not good after all since neither horn of the dilemma is superable.

Let us examine Boethius' treatment of both horns of the dilemma.

---

8. See Aquinas, *Exposition*, 59 n. 2. See also the translation provided by MacDonald in the appendix of "Boethius' Claim." Compare Boethius, *Tractates*, 39: "You urge that this demonstration is necessary because the method of this kind of treatise is not clear to all."

9. Another interesting scenario emphasizes how Boethius was influenced by Nicomachus' numerology. See Pessin, "Hebdomads." Pessin is undoubtedly right that Boethius felt socially and culturally pressured to cloak his over-indebtedness to certain philosophical ways of thinking. However, Boethius' talk of "flow" should probably not be understood in terms of a strict Neopythagorean genealogy for it also has a very Plotinian (i.e., Neoplatonic) ring to it.

FIRST HORN OF THE DILEMMA.[10]

No thing can be good by participation. (To be proven)[11]

1. Any thing that is is good. (lemma).[12]

2. Any thing will tend toward good. (lemma)

3. Any thing that is good is good by participation. (Supposed)

4. Any thing that is good by participation is not good by substance. (lemma)[13]

5. Only good things by substance tend toward good. (Axiom 7)

6. No thing can tend toward good. (4 and 5 above)

→← (Contradiction)

Conclusion: No thing can be good by participation.

Indirect proofs, though necessary, were not as satisfactory as direct deductive proofs among mathematicians in antiquity. A *reductio ad absurdum* proof, when successful, always involves a contradiction, but as is the case with *Sorites* paradoxes, the cause may not always be that an initial premise is false. In the first (and the second) horn, the proof offered seems to turn on a presumed lemma that is not brought to the fore by Boethius. A first lemma (1) has to do with the fact that every thing will tend toward good.[14] A second (4) posits that if a thing is good, it is either good by participation or by substance. Even if the former lemma is to be accepted for argument's sake; the latter still deserves brief comment.

That a thing must be good either extrinsically or intrinsically seems reasonable enough (although it might theoretically be disputed that both

10. For alternate schematizations and analysis, see MacDonald, "Boethius' Claim," 252 and Aertsen, "Good," 60–61.

11. For simplicity's sake, I have, following Boethius, not distinguished between axioms and their corollaries.

12. Boethius does not seem to list this as an axiom. Aertsen rightly describes this claim that all things are good as Boethius' "permanent presupposition" and goes on to say that Boethius should have fleshed it out more in order that his solution to his ultimate problem might be more compelling. See Aertsen, "Good," 64.

13. "A thing is good either by participation or by its substance." No justification is given for this.

14. Boethius claims that this is a "common opinion of the learned." Aquinas traces it to *Eth. Nic.*

or neither is the case[15]). A question still arises whether extrinsically and intrinsically are suitable synonyms for "by participation" and "by substance" respectively. A thing could conceivably be good extrinsically by some means other than by participation. Conversely, a thing could conceivably be good intrinsically but by some means other than by substance. Perhaps, these two options (by participation and by substance) loosely correspond to J. P. Moreland's "non-identity assumption" and "self-predication assumption" respectively. Moreland defines the former as follows: "F things are F in virtue of some other thing, F-ness, which makes them F"; and the latter as follows: "F-ness is itself F."[16] For "F" one might substitute "good" and adapt Moreland's definitions to the effect: "Either good things are good in virtue of some other thing, goodness, which makes them good" or "Goodness is itself good [and not in virtue of some other thing]."[17] But should one go on to say with McInerny that "[i]n short, the distinction is equivalent to that between *per se* and *per accidens* predication?"[18]

This problem can only briefly be touched upon here.[19] Two responses must suffice. First, according to Marenbon, Boethius in his *On Division* explores what types of divisions are commonly made by philosophers. Of these there were basically two types: *per se* and *per accidens*.[20] Boethius insists that these types should not be confused and goes on to distinguish division sub-types for each basic type of division (though he focuses primarily on *per se* division sub-types involving genera and species). Hence it seems fair to conclude that the first horn of the *De Hebdomadibus* dilemma misapplies an excluded middle insofar as "good by participation" can be further divided into types of participation. This could render Boethius' proffered proof irrelevant if it can be shown that an unrelated type of participation is involved. The same could be said of "good by substance."[21]

---

15. Which seems the way in which the problem was actually resolved by Boethius and many others in the tradition (e.g., Aquinas claims in *Summa Th.,* 1.6.4: "And so of all things there is one goodness and yet many goodnesses.").

16. Moreland, *Universals*, 9.

17. Moreland is treating another topic and has no disjunction in mind.

18. McInerny, *Boethius*, 220.

19. See chapter nine below.

20. Marenbon, *Boethius*, 44.

21. Compare McInerny, *Boethius*, 220 n. 32: "Actually both 'participation' and '*per se* predication' have several senses."

Second and more importantly, Vallicella's recent onto-theological project purports "to answer the question as to what it is for an individual to exist, and in so doing answer the question as to why contingent individuals exist."[22] He has cogently argued that the basic problem of the relation between things and their properties, accidents, etc. can be recast in a different mold once a "paradigm existent" is introduced. Whether this is a special case of the first response or not, Boethius' dilemma is a false one inasmuch as he fails to justify a very important assumption (the lemma). By so doing, he opens his proof to invalidity (or at the very least inconclusiveness) by virtue of his use of illegitimate postulates as reasons for his statements.[23] Boethius seems here to compromise his axiomatic methodology.

SECOND HORN OF THE DILEMMA.[24]

No thing is good by substance. (To be proven)
[Any thing that is is good.] (lemma)[25]

1. Any thing that is good is good by substance. (Supposed)

2. Any thing that is good is good insofar as it is. (Def. "good by substance")

3. That which any thing is it possesses from that which is <being>. (Axiom 5)[26]

4. Any thing's <being> is good. (2 and 3 above)

5. The very <being> of any thing is good. (lemma)

6. Any thing is good as far as it is. (4 and 5 above)

7. For any thing to be is the same as for it to be good. (6 above)

---

22. Vallicella, *Paradigm*, 29.

23. *APo.*, 76b28–30.

24. For an alternate schematization, see MacDonald, "Boethius' Claim," 252. The present schema for the argument is admittedly longer than others that appear in the literature; however, it may help to be as explicit as possible. Note how they are rarely used as reasons. "Def." = "definition." The definitions of "First Good" and "God" seem to be those inherited from Plato and Augustine, for example.

25. Although it did not play a visible role in the first proof, it is more aggressively presupposed in this one.

26. Though disagreement persists over the meaning of Boethius' *esse* ("essence," "being," "existence"?), the form of the argument would not necessarily be affected by one meaning in the stead of another.

8. Any thing that is good is a substantial good. (7 and Def. "substantial goods")

9. The First Good is a substantial Good. (Def. "First Good")

10. There is nothing outside the Good Itself which is like it. (lemma)

11. The First Good is God. (Def. "God")

12. Any thing that is a substantial good is God. (8, 9, 10, 11)[27]

→← (Contradiction, i.e., an "impious assertion")

Conclusion: No thing is good by substance.

Again, there are lemmata that creep into the proof. Ignore for now the lemma about all things being good since we touched upon that above. Focus rather upon the other two (5 and 10). Rather, the second (10) will be investigated first and the first (5) second.

The second lemma (10) claims that there is nothing outside the First Good that is like unto it. This seems to require proof, but Boethius gives none. This may have been an oversight or perhaps Boethius assumes familiarity with a proof that is extant in the traditional authorities. Although many discussions arise involving the Good throughout *Met.* and *Eth. Nic.*, there does not appear to be a proof for this particular lemma in Aristotle. It may be the case that a proof lurks somewhere in his writings or the writings of Plato (*Rep.* 4?). Perhaps, Boethius merely makes a Plotinian assumption as in *Enn.* 5.4.1 and many parts of 6. It could even be that Boethius was satisfied with Augustine's line of reasoning:

> This thing is good and that good, but take away this and that, and regard good itself if thou canst; so wilt thou see God, not good by a good that is other than Himself, but the good of all good. For in all these good things, whether those that I have mentioned, or any else that are to be discerned or thought, we could not say that one was better than another, when we judge truly, unless a conception of the good itself had been impressed upon us, such that according to it we might approve some things as good, and prefer one good to another. So God is to be loved, not this or that good, but the good itself.[28]

---

27. It may seem unusual to provide the conjunction of four statements as a reason. A 9a might read, "Both anything that is good and the First Good are substantial goods" (8 and 9). If 11 is handled otherwise, that might reduce it to two; but I prefer the present arrangement.

28. *De Trin.*, 8.3. In the same section he picks up this line of thought again: "Wherefore

Very few would be satisfied with Augustine's argument as a proof *qua* proof. As an argument for the said position, Augustine's remarks are acceptable enough,[29] but there is a difference between argument and proof, and of that Boethius was surely aware.[30] If the difference between argument and proof is unclear to the reader, it is probably because the reader has a different sense of proof in mind. And since this is precisely what we are comparing with respect to Boethius and Aquinas—that they each have different senses of proof in mind when it comes to what is appropriate for this section of *De Hebdomadibus*—it behooves us to pause for a remark on the different senses of proof.

Simon Blackburn has the following to say about the different senses of proof:

> Informally, [it is] a procedure that brings conviction. More formally, [it is] a deductively valid argument starting from true premises, that yields the conclusion. Most formally, in proof theory, a proof is a sequence of formulae of which each member is either an axiom or is derived from a set of preceding members by application of a rule of inference, and which terminates with the proposition proved.[31]

Although "argument" is sometimes used as a synonym for the informal and formal senses of proof, clearly the most formal sense (what we are calling "mathematical proof") is what is presently in mind. It should be clearer now how the Augustinian citation does not qualify as a proof *qua* (most formal) proof.

---

there would be no changeable goods, unless there were the unchangeable good. Whenever then thou art told of this good thing and that good thing, which things can also in other respects be called not good, if thou canst put aside those things which are good by the participation of the good, and discern that good itself by the participation of which they are good (for when this or that good thing is spoken of, thou understandest together with them the good itself also): if, then, I say thou canst remove these things, and canst discern the good in itself, then thou wilt have discerned God."

29. Augustine has written much on the topic of goodness. For a defense of his concept of the good, see Asiedu, "Augustine's."

30. In addition, Augustine never approaches the problem that Boethius is wrestling with nor does he approach problems generally in a manner similar to Boethius. Compare Asiedu, "Augustine's" 340: "As far as I know, Augustine almost never speaks of 'substantial being' or 'accidental being.' This is language one can find in Aristotle's *Categories* and *Metaphysics*. . .and certainly in Boethius's *De hebdomadibus*, but not in Augustine." For Aquinas' approach to the present problem, see *Summa Th.*, 1.6.2.

31. Blackburn, *Dictionary*, 306.

In defense of Boethius and in order to move the present discussion along (since a search of the traditional authorities did not turn up the pertinent proof), let us offer the following (almost most formal[32]) proof on his behalf: The Good Itself is the most final end.[33] Let x and y be ends that are both said to be the most final end. x is therefore a more final end than y since x is the most final end. y is therefore a more final end than x since y is the most final end. The only way that both of these last two statements can be true is if x and y are the same final end.[34] Hence, there is nothing "outside" the most final end that is a most final end.

Now that the second lemma (10) has been established as veritable let us briefly consider the first lemma (5) above. The first lemma (5) claims that the very <being> of any thing is good. Irrespective of the debate over Boethius' use of *esse*, it seems reasonable to understand that reference is being made in this particular case to existence *qua* existence. It should be noted that to say that the very existence of any thing is good is different from saying that any thing's existence is good. It is not simply that it is good *that* a thing exists. In fact, it is conceivable that it could be very bad that a thing that is good exists.[35] Rather, it is the case that to the extent that existence comprises the fundamental being of a thing, goodness becomes fundamental to the existence of the thing. In short, wherever there is existence, there is goodness and in this not separately, but coherently.

Thus stated, the lemma is very close to what MacDonald calls the "Interchangeability Thesis for Being and Goodness."[36] Whereas MacDonald explores the role of this thesis in the writings of Albert the Great, we shall note that Thomas Aquinas in *Summa Th.* writes, "Goodness and Being are really the same and differ only in idea . . . Now it is clear that a thing is desirable only in so far as it is perfect . . . But everything is perfect so far as it is actual. Therefore it is clear that a thing is perfect so far as it exists . . . Hence it is clear that goodness and being are the same really."[37] The con-

32. To explore the reasons behind each statement would take us too far afield. In my opinion, the proof is straightforward; the reasons for each statement are evident enough. The claim is simply that two (or more) final ends that both claim to be most final ends have to be the same final end else neither is a most final end.

33. Aristotle, *Eth. Nic.*, 1.7.

34. Compare the tact taken in Boethius' argument in *Cons. Phil.*, 3pr11.

35. See, for example, Stump and Kretzmann, "Being and Goodness."

36. See MacDonald, "Metaphysics."

37. *Summa Th.*, 1.5.1. MacDonald's Interchangeability Thesis is a special case of a

vertibility of transcendentals[38] is certainly not new with Albert the Great or Thomas Aquinas.[39] The idea is that in some profound way goodness is related to being to the extent that where one is the other will necessarily be also (and precisely to the degree that a being is ontologically actualized it is said to be ontologically good).[40] Being and goodness are distinguishable in our minds in a way that they do not seem to be in reality.

The reasoning seems to be that if a thing ceases to be good then it will cease to be period (exist, it becomes another thing). And vice versa: if a thing ceases to be (exist) then it can no longer be good since it no longer exists. The lemma that states that the very <being> of a thing is good assumes a massive philosophical discussion that has actually taken several different directions. This certainly needs to be fleshed out in a proof. In addition, Boethius should give attention to the lemma's relation with the foundational lemma that posits that all things are good. The proof, for its completeness, at the very least, is in need of a more exacting explication of these two foundational lemmata and especially how they relate to each other.

That said, it seems that this horn of the dilemma is more sound than the first.[41] But recall that the supposition that things are good by substance did not technically lead to a contradiction; rather it led to an absurdity, or in Boethius' mind, an impious remark—these are not necessarily the

---

general thesis regarding the interchangeability of transcendentals.

38. Wolter explains: "For the schoolmen understood by 'transcendentals' those abstract yet very real concepts which escape classification in the Aristotelian categories by reason of their greater extension and universality of application." See Wolter, *Transcendentals*, 1.

39. See Aristotle, *Met.*, 1003b23ff. for the interchangeability of being and unity and *Met.* 1091a29ff. for the suggestion that the first principle is also good; also Plotinus, *Enn.* 6.15–42 and Augustine, *Conf.*, 7.10–15. See Boethius, *Cons. Phil.*, 3pr11 and Aquinas, *Summa Th.* 1.6.4 for the "convertibility" of all three. McInerny insists that Boethius was indeed familiar with "a doctrine of transcendentals." See McInerny, "Saint Thomas," 76–82.

40. See Wolter, *Transcendentals*, 120–21. Some contemporary philosophers have cautioned that more care should be taken with phraseology so as not to imply that things may exist in greater or lesser degrees.

41. Gilbert of Poitier was of the opinion that this horn of the dilemma was fraught with ambiguities. He claimed that Boethius concealed two senses of "good" in his use of the term. See MacDonald, "Gilbert Poitier's." MacDonald points out in his essay that the ambiguity that was detected by Gilbert did not actually involve the word "good" but rather the phrase "by substance." We have already drawn attention to this ambiguity above. MacDonald claims that Augustine does not equivocate in his use of "good." See MacDonald, "Augustine's." Asiedu does not agree.

same thing. Although the name given to this type of proof is *reductio ad absurdum*, absurdity and contradiction are not identical. One might reasonably hold that all contradictions are absurdities, but the converse is certainly not true. Therefore, it may or may not be significant that the second horn of the dilemma led Boethius to "an impious remark" and not an outright contradiction.[42] Notwithstanding, we have said enough to show that the proposed dilemma is a false one. Considering the stated problem in this particular way (as a dilemma) does not necessarily lead to the impasse that Boethius suggests.

42. It should be pointed out that the assertion would only be impious to those who shared Boethius' view of God.

9

Aquinas' Commentary on Boethius

AQUINAS' COMMENTARY ON THIS section of Boethius' tractate revisits some of the same issues raised in the previous section. He provides supporting arguments for those lemmata that are not supported in Boethius' presentation of the dilemma. Let us look briefly at certain of these supplements—though, the reader should be reminded that as far as possible we wish to circumvent the Thomist storm over whether Aquinas was a faithful interpreter of Boethius.[1] Because Aquinas closely follows Boethius when he comments upon the dilemma at hand, it will suffice to highlight those points wherein Aquinas introduces (or fails to introduce) the implicit lemmata of Boethius' proof.

FIRST HORN OF THE DILEMMA

When Aquinas comes to the first horn of the dilemma, he immediately recognizes the lemma that is presupposed by Boethius: Any thing that is good by participation is not good by substance. Aquinas comments, "And this indeed is true if 'through themselves' be taken for the inherence that

---

1. The dispute arises over whether Boethius meant that "essence" and "the thing that is" are different or that "Existence" and "the thing that is" are different. Many argue that though Boethius meant the former, Aquinas wrongly imputes to him the latter. For example, Maurer writes that "St. Thomas offers a radically new interpretation of being by emphasizing the existential side. This was a decisive moment in the history of Western metaphysics . . ." See Aquinas, *Being*, 10. In *Boethius*, McInerny argues against this interpretation, claiming that Boethius and Aquinas both meant the latter (which is not to say that Boethius and Aquinas agreed with respect to goodness). See also McInerny, "Saint Thomas," 94. On another front, Nijenhuis argues that Aquinas did not even have "existence" in mind—at least in the way that it is commonly conceived of today. See the intra-Thomist discussion between Pannier and Sullivan and Nijenhuis as recorded in the pages of *American Catholic Philosophical Quarterly*. See Panier and Sullivan, "Aquinas"; Nijenhuis, "'Ens'"; Panier and Sullivan, "Being"; Nijenhuis, "Existence." Suffice it to say that we shall attempt to steer clear of the dispute.

is posited in the definition of what is defined, as a human being 'through itself' is an animal."[2] Aquinas identifies the lemma at the outset and immediately qualifies: "[The lemma] is indeed true *if...*"

There are at least two different senses of "by substance" as there are at least two different senses of "by participation," says Aquinas.

> By participation 1: as a subject participates in an accident.
>
> By participation 2: as a species participates in a genus.
>
> By substance 1: as a definition pertains to an essence.[3]
>
> By substance 2: as a definition pertains to a predicate.

"By participation" 1 has to do with subjects and attributes while "by participation" 2 has to do with species and genera. Similarly, "by substance" 1 has to do with the way an essence "inherits" its definition while "by substance" 2 has to do with a different way in which a definition of a predicate pertains to a subject. Aquinas recognizes that neither of these should be restricted to one type of participation or substance. That is because, as McInerny observes, "[O]n the Aristotelian view, according to which man truly is animal and there is no animal existing independently of the differences constitutive of species, something predicated by way of participation is also predicated substantially."[4] Therefore, Aquinas is careful to point out that Boethius' lemma is really "Any thing that is good by Participation 1 is not good by Substance 1."

Aquinas succeeds in uncovering a tacit lemma, partially vindicating Boethius' first horn of the dilemma. However, in so doing, he also undermines it precisely by drawing attention to the ambiguity inherent in Boethius' terms of argument. That goodness cannot be present either by Participation 1 or by Substance 1 looses much of its punch once it is realized that these do not exhaust the possibilities. To the extent the possibilities are left unexplored in a proof, the proof becomes less a most formal proof and more an informal proof, or in other words, less a mathematical

2. Aquinas, *Exposition*, 35.

3. In *On Being and Essence*, 6.1, Aquinas explains that "essence is what the definition signifies." See Aquinas, *Being*, 66.

4. McInerny, *Boethius*, 220. McInerny mentions three modes of participation that Aquinas delineates at different points in his commentary. McInerny's taxonomy seems to me to align nicely with those of the Aristotelian, the Platonic and the Neoplatonic understandings of participation respectively. See McInerny, *Boethius*, 204–5.

proof and more an argumentative nudge in the right direction. But this does not appear to trouble Aquinas.

SECOND HORN OF THE DILEMMA

Once again Aquinas follows Boethius very closely and agrees with much of what is said. As was admitted above, this horn of the dilemma is by far the more sound. Even so, it should be pointed out that as Aquinas follows Boethius' proof of the second horn, when he comes to (our) line 5, "The very <being> of any thing is good," he adds these words: "And since the premises from which he has proceeded in his argument are convertibles, he reasons from their converse."[5] Aquinas, once again, explicitly mentions the lemma that Boethius omits from his proof.

A theory of the convertibility of transcendentals or, more specifically, of the interchangeability of goodness and being is supposed here. Aquinas explains, "For it follows from the converse *that if the being* of all things be *good*, then those things that are inasmuch as they are, are good, namely, in such a way that "*to be*" and "*to be* good" are the same for each thing."[6] That is, *if* we grant the controvertibility of transcendentals, then we are able to go on to the next line of the proof. But that's a big if!

It does not seem to me that a theory of the controvertibility of transcendentals was uncontroversial during Boethius' or Aquinas' time. Or at the very least the issue had not been clearly settled.[7] For example, is Being a transcendental, an accident, a category, an Idea/Form, etc.? Perhaps the answer to this question will in great measure match the answer given to the question of whether one was a Platonist or an Aristotelian. Gilson confidently writes of Boethius in the following way:

> Acquainted as we are with history, we cannot fail to see the fundamental Platonism of Boethius, but some of his mediaeval readers have hesitated over the true meaning of his thought. They have imagined him hesitating between Plato and Aristotle, listening first to the one and then to the other, without ever reaching a decision . . . In fact the real Boethius of history did not waver.[8]

5. Aquinas, *Exposition*, 37.

6. Ibid., italics in the original.

7. For an attempt to characterize the whole of medieval philosophy as primarily a philosophy of transcendentals, see Aertsen, *Medieval Philosophy*.

8. Gilson, *History*, 100–1.

He did not waver, according to Gilson, because Boethius always envisioned God as "the Sovereign Good," as absolutely, perfectly One. He was most interested in the Idea, says Gilson. But we must keep in mind that

> [t]he inquiry that is both the hardest of all and the most necessary for knowledge is whether being and unity are the substances of things, and whether each of them, without being anything else, is being or unity respectively, or we must inquire what being and unity are, with the implication that they have some other underlying nature.[9]

Gilson is suggesting, *inter alia*, that Boethius had definitely made up his mind regarding the "hardest" and "most necessary" question. But it may even be the case that Plato himself had not definitely made up his mind. Steel comments upon the ambiguity that can be found in Plato when contrasted with the main Neoplatonic tenet that Good transcends Being and cannot be identified with it.

> Modern scholars have argued that this Neoplatonic interpretation does not conform to the intention of Plato. Of course, the scholars do not deny that Plato himself, in the conclusion of his argument, strongly emphasizes the transcendence of the good . . . But, the scholars argue, in many other passages the good is enumerated among the other principal ideas (such as beauty or justice) and is not set apart or above them.[10]

He observes how "[i]n many other texts the idea of the good functions like other ideas."[11] Without involving ourselves in discussions over what characteristics constitute Neoplatonism over against Platonism,[12] we should remind ourselves that simply because "'good' is necessarily coextensive with 'being', it does not follow that good is transcendental in the way being is."[13] One might further suggest as Pseudo-Dionysius did (in the words of Gilson) that "[t]o say that God is the 'Hyper-Good' is to

9. Aristotle, *Met.* 1001a 2–7.

10. Steel, "Greatest Thing," 17.

11. Ibid., 18.

12. See Reale, "Fundamentos." Reale concedes that much of what had been traditionally thought to be genuinely Neoplatonic can legitimately be said to be genuinely Platonic. He then outlines three main features that distinguish Neoplatonism from Platonism. Compare Sweeney, "Plotinus?"

13. MacDonald's comments directed at Albert the Great in Macdonald, "Goodness and the Transcendentals," 38.

name him with regard to creation, of which his goodness is the cause; with regard to himself, the best name which we can borrow from creatures in order to designate him is 'Being.'[14] This would explain an apparent wavering in Boethius that he does not bring to the fore in *De Hebdomadibus*. Boethius was trying to be both Platonic and Artistotelian while at the same time proceeding by means of an axiomatic methodology.

Alexander of Hales (d. 1245) attributes the following saying to Boethius: *bonum et ens convertuntur*, but that is precisely the lemma that he never states![15] One important question is whether this implies that the good is the "appetibility" itself or the reason why things are "appetible" in the first place.[16] McInerny surmises that "[i]f one searched the Boethian tractate for a *ratio boni*, some expression or account that could be substituted for "good," he would come back empty."[17] But if one had to guess, "The Aristotelian account is implicit in the argument developed in the course of stating the problem." This seems contrary to Gilson's judgment issued above. Perhaps MacDonald's insight illuminates a cause for confusion: "Philosophers such as Boethius who believed in the reconcilability of the Aristotelian and Platonic systems tended to use Aristotelian logical notions together with Platonist metaphysical views."[18] But the situation may be messier still for, in addition to sifting for Neoplatonist influences, one might further inquire into whether Aristotelian "logic" is metaphysically neutral—an interesting question that cannot be taken up here.

Thomas Aquinas, for his part, "does not succeed in proving the identity of the good with being in an intrinsic manner."[19] Again, this does not seem to trouble Aquinas. It seems rather to suggest that this failure has not only to do with the immensity of the problem but also bears upon the fact that Aquinas has a different sense of proof in mind and thus a different conception of what it is he is to set out to do in his philosophical writings.

---

14. Gilson, *History*, 84. For more on Pseudo-Dionysius, see Perl, "Hierarchy."

15. At least it does not appear in the extant versions.

16. Wolter, *Transcendentals*, 121.

17. McInerny, *Boethius*, 232.

18. MacDonald, "Boethius' Claim," 249 n. 14. This conciliatory approach seems to have started with Porphyry. See Evangeliou, *Aristotle's*.

19. Te Velde, "Good," 101, speaking of *De Veritate*. The same can certainly be said of the commentary under consideration. Anderson helpfully gathers a number of relevant Aquinas texts in *Introduction*. For more on Aquinas and the problem of the transcendentals, see Aertsen, *Medieval Philosophy*.

Argumentation in both Boethius and Aquinas is seen as a means to persuade an interlocutor of a specific point. Above, the point feigned to be proven by recourse to axiomatics was that no thing is good. The argument was "feigned" in at least two ways. First, Boethius did not make much use of his axioms in the argument. Second, Boethius ignores crucial lemmata that he relies upon for his arguments. Insofar as Boethius perceives himself to be proceeding in a way comparable to the geometers and other mathematicians, he seems only to be going through the motions of doing so. Yet his display is convincing enough that Chadwick can write of Boethius' approach in *De Hebdomadibus* that "the West learnt from him demonstrative method."[20] In fact, "[Boethius' method] turns out to have been very different," Marenbon remarks, "from that of the philosophically educated theologians, such as Augustine and Marius Victorinus, who certainly influenced Boethius in his terminology and positions."[21] In other words, Boethius understands Aristotelian logic to be "the way" to explain Christian philosophy "insofar as [it] can be explained."[22] Marenbon's remarks here allude to, among other things, the axiomatic project of Aristotle's *APo*. Chadwick encapsulates the pedagogical act affected by Boethius' choice in genre when he writes: "Boethius' third tractate taught the Latin West, above all else, the method of axiomatization" and its propriety for Christian philosophy.[23]

But in what way could Boethius' axiomatic venture be appropriate to Christian philosophy? I propose that the said propriety does not lie in the actual deductive progression of an axiomatic system. For Boethius was clearly not very interested in deductive schemas *qua* rigorous, inferential system—as our comparison of Boethius and Aquinas has shown. It would appear rather that Boethius is far more interested in what types of conclusions might be drawn from a given set of hypotheses. A good example of Boethius' occupation with determining what conclusions might follow from a set of premises is given in *Cons. Phil.*, when Boethius responds to Lady Philosophy's appeal to geometric methods and interprets them as a search for corollaries.[24] A corollary typically refers to a related conclusion

20. Chadwick, *Boethius*, 108, 210.

21. Ibid., 76.

22. Ibid., 94–95.

23. Ibid., 210. Compare Hall, *Trinity*, 26; and Evans, "More Geometrico."

24. "That is both a beautiful and precious thing, whether you prefer it to be called a *porisma* or a corollary." (3pr10).

that is already implied in a previous conclusion, or in Lady Philosophy's words: a conclusion "which reason persuades us should be added to what we have said." Attention can be drawn here to one of Boethius' responses to a relevant strand of Lady Philosophy's hypothetical argument. Boethius' primary interest is in where the hypotheses lead: "No conclusion could be drawn more genuinely true, more firmly based on argument, or more worthy of God." What is the philosophical context within which Boethius' interest in corollaries arises, i.e., his interest in what conclusions follow from a given prior conclusion, in *Cons. Phil.*? Precisely the matter of how God can be good and whether he is good in another way than how all that is is good.

The prose section of III 10, 22 of *Cons. Phil.* begins with Boethius' satisfaction with Lady Philosophy's line of argument thus far: "I agree, for all is bound together by most firm reasoning." Lady Philosophy chimes in after Boethius admits how excited he is about the prospect of learning what the good itself is: "I shall indeed make that clear too, with most valid reasoning, provided those conclusions stand which have just now been reached." The force of the argument here is brought about hypothetically as propositions are demonstrated to Boethius' satisfaction. The arguments are based upon preliminaries and at each stage certain corollaries are carefully tweaked out of the propositions. The effect on the reader of this argument *more geometrico* is summarized by Boethius in the following reply to Lady Philosophy: "I both am unable to refute your previous propositions and see that this inference follows from them." (3pr10)

The hypothetical search in Christian philosophy is—as Boethius admits in the first quote above—a search for metaphysical conclusions that satisfy three general criteria: the conclusions are to be "genuinely true, firmly based on argument, [and] worthy of God." Given Boethius' strong Aristotelian commitments, he readily supposes that a conclusion that meets any one of the criteria will consequently meet all three. For Boethius any proposition firmly based on inferential argument will by its very nature be worthy of God and genuinely true. Yet one should bear in mind that the stated purpose for writing *De Hebdomadibus* was not that certain *conclusions* had proven unacceptable but that *the method employed* proved obscure to certain readers.

Still, we noted above that Thomas Aquinas took care to make explicit certain lemmata that Boethius had neglected in his presentation of the dilemma. From at least one perspective, then, we can duly regard Aquinas as a more keen axiomatizer than Boethius. If the axiomatic method involves "analysing argument and making explicit the fundamental presuppositions and definitions on which its cogency rests" and trying "to state truths in terms of first principles and then to trace how particular conclusions follow therefrom", as Chadwick says, then Aquinas is clearly more of a master of the axiomatic method than Boethius. The supplementary material provided in Aquinas' *Commentary* provides the unstated lemmata and reasons that Boethius fails to mention.

We have examined the dilemma that follows Boethius' list of axioms and suggested that the dilemma is a false one, not least because Boethius disregards pertinent lemmata. Comments were then made on Boethius' neglect for these lemmata to the effect that he was not as thoroughgoing in method as he purported to be: his actual procedure was shown to be disparate with his initial methodological stance. We also noted that Aquinas, for his part, proceeds with much more care in his recounting of Boethius' dilemma. The axiomatic approach is used for anagogical reasons.

AXIOMS GIVEN IN *DE HEBDOMADIBUS*[25]

1. Being (*esse*) and that which is (*id quod est*) are diverse. For being itself (*ipsum esse*) as yet is not. That-which-is however, once the form of being (*essendi*) has been taken on, is and stands together.

2. What-is (*quod est*) can participate in something, but being itself (*ipsum esse*) in no way participates in anything. For participation occurs when something already is. Something is, however, when it has received being (*esse*).

3. That-which-is (*id quod est*) can possess something other than what it itself is (*quod ipsum est*). Being itself, however (*ipsum uero esse*), has nothing else outside itself as an admixture.

4. However, to be something (*tamen esse aliquid*), and to be something in this, that <a thing> is (*esse aliquid in eo quod est*), are diverse. For by the former (*illic*), accident is signified; by the latter (*hic*), substance.

5. Everything that is participates in that which is being (*eo quod est esse*) with the result that it be. It participates in something else with the result that it be something. And through this, that-which-is (*id quod est*) participates in that which is being (*eo quod est esse*) with the result that it be. It is, however, with the result that it can participate in anything else you like.

6. In every composite, being (*esse*) is other than the item itself. Every simple item possesses its being (*esse*) and that-which-is (*id quod est*) as one.

7. All diversity is discordant, whereas similitude must be sought. And what seeks something else is shown to be itself by nature such as that which it seeks.

---

25. Boethius' seven axioms as translated and delineated in Aquinas, *Exposition*, xxxi–xxxiii.

10

By Good and Necessary Consequence

THE OBJECTIVE IN THE foregoing chapters has been to trace the historic use of deductive and axiomatic method. After rehearsing what skeptical pressures characterized the intellectual milieu within which the good-and-necessary-consequence approach was first introduced into Reformed confessions, I discussed the token methods and aims of deductive procedure in the work of the Pythagoreans, Plato, Aristotle, Euclid, Proclus and Boethius. In chapter three, I began with the Pythagoreans and argued that during the course of conducting number-generating investigations some early Pythagoreans stumbled upon a proof for the fact that adding even numbers to even numbers always yields an even number. This general theorem was likely discovered deductively, once it was realized that the pebbles used for addition could abstractly represent any number of even addends and that the sum of those addends—whatever they may be—would always be even. It is quite plausible that several closely related theorems were also discovered in similar ways. The example selected is a very early example of deductive mathematical proof. The proof is compelling and succinct.

In chapter four, I took a look at three of Plato's works that make explicit mention of a mathematical procedure that can and should be used in philosophical dialogue. *The Republic, Meno* and *Phaedo* were brought to bear upon two methods of inquiry proposed by Socrates during the course of the dialogues: hypothetical and dialectical. Although the former was said to be that carried out by mathematicians, Plato understood the latter to be more capable insofar as it could reverse in direction and cross-examine initial hypotheses. Strict deductive reasoning may have met with success for the Pythagoreans but it turned out to be a dead end for Plato. One of the reasons why Plato's foray into deductivism proved a failure is that the argument that ensued from the initial hypothesis proved not to be convertible. The reverse examination of the initial hypothesis showed problems with its assumption. This meant that the interlocutors had to go beyond arguing from hypotheses and enlist a dialectical method if they wanted to critically reflect upon the procedure itself.

The Pythagoreans and Plato can be read as two early theorists who were interested in axiomatic method in the areas of mathematics and philosophy respectively. An axiomatic approach proved eminently successful for the Pythagoreans' work in mathematics but not as helpful for Plato's philosophy. Each proceeded without a general theory of axiomatics to guide them. Such a theory awaited Aristotle and his foray into the uses of mathematics for philosophy. Aristotle introduced a theoretical ideal for demonstrative science in *APo.* and, interestingly enough, presented his work as an argumentative procedure where a Pythagoras and a Plato might meet, (i.e., where mathematical and philosophical methods might intersect). The axiomatic ideal adumbrated by Aristotle was gleaned—or so it was suggested—from his exposure to mathematics in the Academy. Why did Aristotle employ so many mathematical examples during the course of *APo.*? At the very least, we can say that Aristotle was interested in giving an account of the demonstrative prowess of his ideal science and the most suitable subject for comparison was mathematics. Yet *APo.* makes a very telling concession when it allows for various kinds of demonstrations, demonstrations that are not nearly as strict as the immediate premise kind. In fact, the conclusion reached in this chapter was that even for Aristotle, the notion of demonstration has to be science-dependent.

To help us appreciate just how demanding Aristotle's proposal was—a proposal whose method, we should recall, was to be extended as far as possible: to all the other sciences in accord with the rigor appropriate to each—a comparison was made between the requirements stipulated in *APo.* and the actual practice of the geometer Bryson. Interestingly enough, the geometric example fell short of Aristotle's demonstrative strictures. Although *APo.* reads as an axiomatic proposal to be followed by every science insofar as possible, there is another purpose accomplished by the work: the presentation of fundamental principles for the mind to *understand* (not know) during the course of habitual dialectical exercises as performed in the several disciplines. Aristotle's axiomatics is useful for increasing the understanding of the fundamental truths that underlie a discipline but axiomatics had not been called upon to gain an epistemological advantage. For one thing, the skeptic challenge had yet to be raised.

This means that the use to which early modern scientists and philosophers put axiomatic method necessarily differed from that which Aristotle had in mind. The seventeenth century had set for itself the task of employing strict deductive procedures in an attempt to stem off skepticism. Wallace has shown, for example, how instrumental *APo.* was for Galileo and his construction of a logic of discovery.[1] In a certain sense, the same might be said for Descartes, and perhaps also for Newton. In each case, while reflecting upon what method might help them progress in metaphysics (Descartes) or physics (Newton), each thinker plundered mathematical deductivism for methodological direction.[2] The issues Descartes raises about deduction are similar to those already discussed, but still there is an appreciable difference: a newfound emphasis on epistemology.[3]

Consider, for example, a little remark Descartes makes in his *Geometry*. The remark reads as follows:

> This is one thing which I believe the ancient mathematicians did not observe, for otherwise they would not have put so much labor into writing so many books in which the very sequence of the propositions shows that they did not have a sure method of finding all, but rather gathered together those propositions on which they had happened by accident.[4]

Among the many things that this passage refers to is the absence of "a sure method of finding all" amongst the Greeks. The context for this remark is the presentation of what Descartes understands to be four geometric diagrams to which *every* problem that has occupied the history of ordinary geometry up till Descartes' time can be reduced. Descartes announces that he has made a definite advance over his predecessors, having "[reduced] to a single construction all the problems of one class," enabling him to "[easily] find the rest" through variations derived from his initial constructions.[5]

---

1. See Wallace, *Galileo's Logic*.

2. See, for example, Grabiner, "Descartes"; and Gaukroger, *Descartes' System*. Newton improved upon Descartes by being less inclined to speculative hypotheses.

3. See, for example, Barbin, "Meanings."

4. Descartes, *Geometry*, 17.

5. Ibid., 240.

Descartes was well aware of how novel his reductive constructions were. He candidly admits as much in the *Discourse* and in *Geometry* (which was initially published as one of several appendices to the *Discourse*). For our purposes, it is important to note that it was his formative success in geometry that spurred Descartes on to extend the application of his reductive method to other fields as well. Although the tradition of the Euclidean *Elements* provided a working model for scientific demonstration, geometry was not the sole impetus for Descartes' methodological program.[6] Yet Euclidean geometry was central enough that it will be the only component to receive attention here.

Descartes evinces great dissatisfaction with the methodological prowess of geometry, at least insofar as it was supposed to be the exemplar science.[7] He complains that "the very sequence of the propositions shows that they did not have a sure method of finding all." In Descartes' view, all one needs to do is look at the order in which the geometric propositions were being presented and one will notice that the ancients "merely gathered together the propositions on which they had happened by accident." Descartes decries how not even geometry could help but learn "by accident." As a remedy, he enumerates five basic principles in his *Principles of Philosophy*:

1. Insofar as it is possible, everything should be doubted once in a lifetime by whoever is in search for the truth.

2. Things which are doubtful should be considered as if they were false.

3. It is not helpful to extend doubts to our daily lives.

4. We can doubt observable things.

5. We can even doubt mathematical things.[8]

Both in the *Principles* and the *Meditations* Descartes mentions how even mathematical demonstrations can be subject to doubt. There are two main reasons he gives for such pervasive skepticism. First, if they are honest, practitioners will admit that they themselves have at times been

6. Optics and mechanics also played important roles. For an overview, see Mahoney, "Mathematical Realm."

7. A view held throughout the medieval era. See, for example, Evans, "More Geometrico."

8. Descartes, *Mediations*, 112–13.

mistaken (either that or know someone who has been mistaken). Second, Descartes reminds that we have reason to doubt "especially because we have learned about God, who is omnipotent and by whom we were all created."[9] Perhaps God created us in such a way that we remain deceived, even regarding matters that appear certain to us.

In his *Discourse on Method*, Descartes writes, "Above all else, I was interested in mathematics because of the certainty and self-evidence of the way it reasons; but I had not yet noticed its real use and, since I thought it was useful only for mathematical applications, I was surprised that nothing more noteworthy had been built on such solid and firm foundations."[10] He picks up again on this train of thought:

> As regards the analysis of the ancients or the algebra of the moderns, apart from the fact that they apply only to very abstract questions which seem to have no use, the former is always so tied to the discussion of shapes that it cannot exercise the understanding without greatly tiring the imagination; and in the latter, one is so constrained by certain rules and symbols that it has become a confused and obscure art that hinders the mind, rather than a science that assists it.[11]

In the spirit of Aristotle, Descartes muses that the theoretical power of geometry was being wasted: he sees no reason why its deductive powers could not extend to other disciplines:

> The long chains of inferences, all of them simple and easy, that geometers normally use to construct their most difficult demonstrations had given me an opportunity to think that all the things that can fall within the scope of human knowledge follow from each other in a similar way, and that as long as one avoids accepting something as true which is not so, and as long as one always observes the order required to deduce them from each other, there cannot be anything so remote that it cannot eventually be reached nor anything so hidden that it cannot be uncovered.[12]

In short, Descartes calls upon deduction to prove everything that is doubtful. Careful inferential reasoning must be applied—in every sci-

9. Ibid., 113.
10. Descartes, *Discourse*, 9.
11. Ibid., 15.
12. Ibid., 16.

ence—so that no methodical room for error remains.[13] This is reminiscent of the ideal conception of demonstration encountered in Aristotle's *APo.*[14] Yet Descartes goes much further than Aristotle in setting out to achieve for *all* of human knowledge an epistemologically sure foundation: a foundation that geometry itself had not been able to achieve—a certain body of knowledge constructed axiomatically and to which knowledge can be continually added by means of strict deduction.[15] Descartes concludes that the same can be done in philosophy.

He explains that he waited until he was of sufficient age, i.e., until he possessed adequate life-experience (age twenty-three, he says), before inquiring after philosophy's first principles. Such an inquiry should be governed by four simple laws:

> The first was never to accept anything as true if I did not know clearly that it was so. . .The second was to subdivide each of the problems that I was about to examine into as many parts as possible and necessary to resolve them better. The third was to guide my thoughts in an orderly way by beginning with the objects that are the simplest and easiest to know and to rise gradually, as if by steps, to knowledge of the most complex, and even by assuming an order among objects in cases where there is no natural order among them. And the final rule was: in all cases, to make such comprehensive enumerations and such general reviews that I was certain not to omit anything.[16]

This is reminiscent of Pappus' discussion of analysis and synthesis in his *Collections*, the general discussion of which already had a long pedigree and was well known to geometers and philosophers alike.[17] Yet there is a very important and distinctly modern difference: Descartes is moving up through the series of consequences with a radically skeptical eye, deliberately refusing to suppose any preceding consequence true if it admits the least bit of doubt.[18] Proceeding in this way, Descartes purports to establish

---

13. For the seventeenth century appeal of such a proposal, see Jardine, "Epistemology"; and Mancosu, "Aristotelian Logic."

14. See chapter five above.

15. Contrast Aristotle's cautious remarks in *Eth. Nic.* 1094b13ff.

16. Descartes, *Discourse*, 16.

17. Mentioned in chapter four.

18. For Descartes' own remarks on synthesis as "a method not as satisfying as analysis" even though used by geometers, see Descartes' second set of replies (2.111) in Descartes, *Philosophical Writings*, 156. For discussion, see Curley, "Analysis."

the existence of the soul and of God, along with the immortality of the soul, to his own satisfaction. Through his foundationalist deductivism—a method that is said to be superior to that of geometry—Descartes believes he has imbued his metaphysics with a certainty unattainable since the beginning of geometry.[19] Only after securing indubitable metaphysical foundations does Descartes inferentially and methodically establish all the sciences.[20]

Yet history shows Cartesianism a failure. As early as Leibniz was Descartes' deductivist, geometric project being challenged: "I claim that there is yet another analysis in geometry which is completely different from the analysis of Viete and of Descartes, who did not advance sufficiently in this, since its most important problems do not depend on the equations to which all of Descartes's geometry reduces."[21] In fact, Leibniz claims that Florimond De Beaune (1601–1652) had already written to Descartes about a significant problem with his project, after which Descartes had to admit that "he did not yet see it clearly enough." Although the specter of Sextus Empiricus had not raised its ugly head during the time of Plato and Aristotle, it had successfully staged a coup in seventeenth century Europe.[22] And it was deductive procedure that came to the rescue.

In chapter six, we turned again to mathematics, hoping to glean some insight from the Euclidean approach, the paragon of argumentation *more geometrico*. We revisited the meaning of the fourth postulate and nodded toward Proclus' explanation of it. We pondered how various proofs could be offered in the commentary tradition if it purported to be a self-evident postulate. The moral of the chapter was that Euclid's postulates were not initially conceived as self-evident truths, but rather served as hypotheses as prescribed in our discussion of Plato's dialogues. The *Elements* was un-

19. See here Dear, "Mersennes' Suggestion."

20. Foremost among them (whether for political, religious, and/or philosophical reasons) was theology. From at least one perspective, it would seem that Descartes is the culmination of over three centuries of medieval deliberation on the nature of theology and the method that is proper to it. See Evans, *Old Arts*. It should be noted that some historians of science are insisting that it was not Descartes' method but his choice of metaphysical positions that led to his success. See, for example, Schuster, "Cartesian Method?"

21. Leibniz, "Letter to Countess Elizabeth (?), On God and Formal Logic (1678?)" (*Philosophical Essays*, 236).

22. See Burnyeat, "Platonism," who claims that this is one of the reasons *APo.* is so hard for moderns to read.

derstood to be a textbook for those already familiar with geometry so that they might gain more insight into the geometry they were doing.[23]

In chapter seven, Proclus was presented as conducting a "spiritual exercise" in which a dialectically earned theology was presented as a deductive sequence. (Proclus does the same in his *Elements of Physics*.) Nikulun recognizes a presentation *more geometrico* in Proclus' work and notes that "[s]uch a form of presenting physics is a novelty in antiquity, and before Proclus it was only used either in mathematics, which in antiquity is geometry *par excellence*, or in mathematics related sciences . . ."[24] Borrowing phraseology from Hadot, we observed that Proclus had the spiritual growth of his students in mind as he wrote. In his *Elements*, Proclus precipitated a profound anagogical exercise by way of a presentation *more geometrico*.

In chapters eight and nine we compared Boethius' third tractate with Aquinas' commentary on it. Boethius thought that the axiomatic method was serviceable for theological inquiry—at least for an inquiry into how good things can be good. Boethius enumerates his axioms explicitly and claims that he will base his arguments solely upon them. An examination of his arguments shows unacknowledged lemmas. Aquinas, for his part, mentions each of the lemmas that Boethius neglects, showing himself the better axiomatizer. Yet he evinced a greater reluctance toward axiomatics for Christian philosophy, preferring the procedure of question-and-answer dialectic.

What I suggest we take away from all this is that when it comes to epistemology, the axiomatic method does not serve well in philosophy or theology. For one thing, the first systematic discussion of axiomatics (Aristotle's) was formulated in a philosophical context where skepticism was not pressing. Second, in contemporary geometry, independent and consistent systems have been founded on the basis of different and contrary sets of axiomatic postulates. Third, there is an insidious sense of certainty associated with axiomatics that is not commensurate with how axiomatics gets done. Surely Reviel Netz is right to protest when pretenses of certainty conceal the open choices would-be axiomatizers have to make.[25] If Netz bases his observations on what he has seen mathematics, how much greater should we be wary of axiomatic certainty in theology!

23. Compare Burnyeat's pedagogical concession with respect to the *APo.* in "Platonism."

24. Nikulun, "Physica," 202, italics in original.

25. See Netz, "Why?"

Insofar as the Westminster Confession of Faith is influenced by the same skeptical culture as Descartes and the same epistemological concerns as he, it will suffer from the same failures and find itself less and less serviceable. A strictly deductive theology like that sanctioned by the Westminster Confession of Faith—where the good and necessary consequences are strictly deduced from other scriptural truths—is not recommended for contemporary use for at least two reasons: 1) It was adopted for a perceived epistemological advantage that it cannot deliver; and 2) It gives the appearance of doing away with the "problem" of open choice—choices that all believers make—under the rhetoric of God's divine authority. Gillespie's explications of the good-and-necessary-consequence clause illustrate both tendencies:

> This assertion must neither be so farre inlarged as to comprehend the erroneous reasonings and consequences from Scripture which this or that man or this or that Church, apprehend and believe to be strong and necessary consequences. I speak of what is, not of what is thought to be a necessary consequence, neither yet must it be so far [narrowed] and straitened, as the *Arminians* would have it, who admit of no proofes from Scripture, but either plaine explicit Texts, or such consequences as are *nulli non obvie*, as neither are nor can be controverted by any man who is *rationis compos* . . . By which principle, if imbraced, we must renounce many necessary truths which the reformed Churches hold against the *Arians*, *Antitrinitarians*, *Socinians*, *Papists*, because the consequences and arguments from Scripture brought to prove them, are not admitted as good by the adversaries . . .
>
> For although the consequence or argumentation be drawn foorth by mens reasons, yet the consequent it self or conclusion is not believed nor embraced by the strength of reason, but because it is the truth and will of God . . .[26]

Seventeenth century Protestants wanted to be sure of what doctrines to believe and which practices to follow—both thought to be commanded by God. They convinced themselves that by turning to scripture and the consequences that necessarily follow from scripture they could achieve certainty. Yet what is "so farre inlarged" and what is "so far [narrowed] and straitened" is an open question to say the least. Despite the human subjectivity inherent in the biblicist-foundationalist enterprise, conservatives, such as Gillespie, insist that the good and necessary consequences neces-

---

26. Gillespie, *Treatise*, 238.

sarily deduced from scripture must be accepted because they are "the truth and will of God." For almost all conservatives agree that if scripture is God's word and an interpretation gives the full sense of what is written in scripture then that interpretation should be binding. The problem is that the language of "good and necessary consequence" effectively obscures the hermeneutical uncertainties attending interpretive acts.[27] In fact, even today how far the good and necessary approach extends is a matter of intra-confessional dispute, and that among self-professed Westminster adherents![28]

C. J. Williams downplays the subjective element in deducing consequences from scripture by necessarily inferring it, as it were, from the subjective element involved even in understanding scripture's clearer statements:

> There is no way of raising doubts about deduction as a hermeneutical method without also raising doubts about the process of interpreting the more explicit statements of Scripture. Either way, the exegete must subject his mind to the guidance of the Spirit and the Word, but he must use his mind. We cannot escape the need to interpret the text, and deduction is one element of interpretation.[29]

Since deduction is understood to tie consequences necessarily to premises, doubts regarding deduction double as doubts about the axioms seems to be the reasoning here. If so, the concern may reveal a misunderstanding of what deduction can accomplish and of what uses to which it has

27. Muller, for example, tries to show how "the prelapsarian covenant [was] supplied as the necessary conclusion demanded by the collation of the texts." Yet it is certainly debatable whether the prelapsarian conclusion is necessary, for it might be "[a] good [consequence] to prove a sutablenesse or agreablenes of this or that to Scripture, though another thing may be also proved to be agreeable unto the same Scripture in the same or another place." To say the least, the question is open. See Muller, *Scripture and Worship*, 80–81; and Gillespie, *Treatise*, 240.

28. Compare Gordon's remarks: "the entire thing [WCF 1.6] would have been better expressed had the divines articulated a more manifestly covenantal statement, indicating that the scriptures are a sufficient guide to the various covenants God has made with his various covenant people through the centuries, and that the entire canon, taken in its entirety, is sufficient therefore to govern the members of the New Covenant made in Christ. . . . I would want to argue now that scripture is not a sufficient guide to many aspects of life, other than in the sense of providing religious direction and motivation to all of life." See T. David Gordon, "The Insufficiency of Scripture." Source: http://www.covopc.org/Papers/Insufficiency_of_Scripture.html.

29. Williams, "Good," 179–80.

historically been put. According to Peter Smith, the informal ideal of Euclidean deduction is still taught in schools in order to accomplish two main goals: the development of "a unified body of results that we can be confident must hold if the initial Euclidean axioms are true" and the appreciation of how hard it really is to make as explicit as possible *all* the fundamental assumptions involved in the system. He also mentions that the major objective of all formalization is to ensure that no one is cheating when they offer arguments for this or that conclusion.[30] None of these pedagogical objectives involve the binding of deduction to the axioms in such a way that if deduction should somehow prove impotent then the axioms are rendered useless.

In fact, Kurt Gödel's work has shown that when dealing with formal deductive systems several possibilities remain open:

> [T]here are an endless number of true arithmetical statements which cannot be formally deduced from any given set of axioms by a closed set of rules of inference. It follows that an axiomatic approach to number theory cannot fully characterize the nature of number-theoretical truth. It follows, also, that what we understand by the process of mathematical proof does not coincide with the exploitation of a formalized axiomatic method . . . no antecedent limits can be placed on the inventiveness of mathematicians in devising new methods of proof.[31]

In my view, an analogous application to the deduction of consequences scripture would suggest: 1) There are a number of scriptural teachings on doctrine, ritual, church practice and administration that cannot be reached by good and necessary deduction from scripture. 2) A deductive approach to scripture cannot fully characterize the nature of scriptural truth. 3) There are other ways to connect such truths to scripture without having to insist upon a good-and-necessary-consequence approach. 4) There is no limit to the inventiveness of ministers and scholars who regularly engage scripture in coming up with new ways to provide proofs for theological truths.[32]

---

30. Smith, *Introduction*, 18.

31. Nagel and Newman, *Gödel's Proof*, 109–10.

32. I see various critiques of biblical inerrancy, such as those lodged by Donald Dayton and Clark Pinnock, dovetailing some of the concerns outlined here. See Donald Dayton, "Pietist Critique"; and Pinnock, *Scripture Principle*. For more on incompleteness and the Westminster Confession, see Bovell, "Two Examples."

Compare Warfield's remarks on the subject:

> Men are required to believe and to obey not only what is "expressly set down in Scripture," but also what "by good and necessary consequence may be deduced from Scripture." This is the strenuous and universal contention of the Reformed theology against Socinians and Arminians, who desired to confine the authority of scripture to its literal asseverations; and it involves a characteristic honoring of reason as the instrument for the ascertainment of truth. We must depend upon our human faculties to ascertain what Scripture says; we cannot suddenly abnegate them and refuse their guidance in determining what Scripture *means* . . .
>
> The Confession is only zealous, as it declares that only Scripture is the authoritative rule of faith and practice, so to declare that the whole of Scripture is authoritative, in the whole stretch of its involved meaning. It is the Reformed contention, reflected here by the Confession, that the sense of Scripture is Scripture, and that men are bound by its whole sense in all its implications. The reëmergence in recent controversies of the plea that the authority of Scripture is to be confined to its expressed declarations, and that human logic is not to be trusted in divine things, is, therefore, a direct denial of a fundamental position of Reformed theology, explicitly affirmed in the Confession, as well as an abnegation of fundamental reason, which would not only render thinking in a system impossible, but would discredit at a stroke many of the fundamentals of the faith, such e.g. as the doctrine of the Trinity, and would logically involve the denial of the authority of all doctrine whatsoever, since no single doctrine of whatever simplicity can be ascertained from Scripture except by the use of the processes of the understanding. It is, therefore, an unimportant incident that the recent plea against the use of human logic in determining doctrine has been most sharply put forward in order to justify the rejection of a doctrine which is explicitly taught, and that repeatedly, in the very letter of Scripture; if the plea is valid at all, it destroys at once our confidence in all doctrines, no one of which is ascertained or formulated without the aid of human logic.[33]

Warfield acknowledges the need for the church to interpret the scriptures but is forced by the Confession to articulate his observation in terms of logic and in terms of good and necessary consequences. This is to be done against the concerns of other Protestant groups regarding the fallacious nature of human reasoning. Notwithstanding, various groups

33. Warfield, *Westminster*, 6.3.3.

continue to make conflicting claims with regard to what good and necessary consequences follow. And not only is there disagreement regarding consequences, but also about express statements too! This raises some honest questions about the nature of the "necessity" allegedly provided for by biblicist foundationalism. In my view, biblicist foundationalism cannot possibly deliver what it promises.

A more realistic expectation for a good-and-necessary-consequence theology is one that acknowledges deductivism as a fruitful way to help show up inherent contradictions. Or perhaps a version of biblicist foundationalism can help bring to light specific undesirable consequences that may follow from this or that theological hypothesis. Additionally, an adaptation of deductive procedure might be put to good spiritual use when it has as its goal the presentation to the mind of certain fundamental Christian principles for anagogical and meditative enrichment. None of this has to do with epistemological fortification.

What I am after is a more historically aware appreciation of what a biblicist deductivism can do. Our foray into ancient geometry concluded that the *Elements*, as a hypothetical venture, was eager to show that a deductive link could be made between its postulates and the Pythagorean theorem. This added to the plausibility of the initial hypotheses, but the same epistemological emphasis that preoccupies us today was not a concern then. Analogously, Proclus' adaptation of axiomatics was presented as having the anagogical effect of showing how all things flow out from the One. In fact, both Proclus and Boethius engaged in spiritual exercises by creatively presenting elements of neoplatonic and Christian theology as if they comprised a deductive system. Although steeped in neoplatonic heritage, their decisions on behalf of argumentation *more geometrico* represent profound, methodological departures from the regular expository and dialogical genres of classical and early medieval metaphysics. The axiomatic genre was adapted by Proclus and Boethius toward the end of persuading readers of an anagogical "necessity." Perhaps biblicist foundationalism might likewise illuminate what principles are operative within the theologies of particular Christian communities.

In this context, consider Pierre Hadot's observation: "[E]very school practices exercises designed to ensure spiritual progress toward the ideal state of wisdom, exercises of reason that will be, for the soul, analogous to the athlete's training or to the application of a medical care."[34] The recourse to axiomatics in each case studied above was made with an eye toward the mathematical, philosophical and religious edification of prospective readers. By parity of reasoning, good-and-necessary-consequence theology should be seen in the same light: as a spiritual exercise. But more often than not, believers abandon the context of spiritual exercise and easily succumb to illusions of certainty as a result of the rhetoric of deduction. These same believers will find themselves bound to a set of choices, under the pretenses of "necessity," decided upon centuries ago in response to a specific set of historical circumstances. Mistaking cultural contingency for necessity, these believers become blind to the variety of choices their tradition has made at several turns.

For one, there are choices to be made about scripture itself *without the help of scripture*. As Adrian Thatcher remarks, the Bible "has no consciousness of itself."[35]

I made this observation in the first "recognition" of *Inerrancy and the Spiritual Formation of Younger Evangelicals* when I observed how "believers have intuited at some basic level that the Christian faith does not have the resources with which to answer its own questions." In order to answer such questions, believers naturally adopt multiple worldviews as dictated by given situations. This fits with what we observed above: a system of deduced theological tenets must find a way to transcend itself in order to apprehend any theological and spiritual truths that are deductively beyond its reach. One way to do this is by "naturally shift[ing] into different worldviews depending upon for what a particular occasion calls . . . [T]he Christian faith may naturally lend itself to multiple worldviews in order that the faithful may responsibly and practically reckon with their mystery-filled beliefs and their relation to day-to-day living."[36] The Christian experience then forms what Hofstadter calls a "strange loop" and Bloesch a "theological circle."[37] Christian tradition has always been able to introduce innovative ways for enabling spiritual and doctrinal self-transcendence.

The ordering of geometric propositions in the geometry that Descartes knew did not sit well with him. For all their mathematical suc-

34. Hadot calls these practices "spiritual exercises." See Hadot, *Philosophy*, 59, 102–4, among other places.

35. Thatcher, *Savage Text*, 4.

36. Bovell, *Inerrancy*, 23.

37. See Hofstadter, *Strange Loop*; and Bloesch, *Ground*, 75.

cess, ancient deductive efforts had "merely gathered together the propositions on which they had happened by accident." According to Descartes, geometers never bothered to proceed by means of good and necessary consequence, as it were. This is a very important observation: one that I cannot stress enough. Descartes' philosophical reflections upon his mathematical work led him to search for a surer and more certain method for disciplined investigation, but in his experience, not even geometry could help but learn "by accident." His grievance against geometry (and philosophy and theology) was that its practitioners repeatedly learned by accident under the guise of proceeding deductively. In my mind, his grievance should also be raised against contemporary, conservative Reformed and evangelical theology.

That the church cannot help but do theology by accident (even if under the pretense of good and necessary consequence) is precisely my contention. There are a host of open choices to be made at all levels of theological reflection. This becomes an even more pressing issue when what one is proclaiming as "necessary" conclusion is presented to honestly seeking parishioners as God's final, authoritative word. In my view, the time has come *to let go* of the good-and-necessary-consequence pretense. For then we might begin speaking plainly to each other, in light of how people actually make their decisions. Granted, the lines of discussion I am opening are still preliminary, yet I hope they are enough to draw others into conversation.

11

A Consequence of Biblicist Foundationalism

THIS CHAPTER INQUIRES INTO the relationship between biblicist foundationalist propaganda and a conservative evangelical interpretation of Bart Ehrman's loss of faith. An examination of Ehrman's spiritual journey seems to suggest that when inerrancy is framed as the epistemological foundation for all beliefs that comprise the doctrinal system of "true" Christianity, believers will socially construct their faith in such a way that should inerrancy ever prove untenable, they will be in danger of losing their faith entirely. In the first half of the chapter, I outline the contours of my conservative evangelical interpretation of Ehrman's spiritual journey from faith to agnosticism.[1] In the second half, I draw out pedagogical implications regarding the negative role that inerrantist apologetics can play in a believer's loss of faith.

Nowhere does Ehrman give a detailed account of his spiritual journey but he does supply enough information, I think, to get a general idea of what seems to have happened. Ehrman's journey, at least insofar as I have been able to reconstruct it from syndicate interviews, newspaper articles, and Ehrman's own writings, might be recounted as follows:

Bart Ehrman became a fundamentalist in his teenage years upon undergoing an evangelically-styled religious conversion. Although his born

---

1. The reason I keep talking about "a conservative evangelical interpretation" of Bart Ehrman's spiritual journey is because when I talked to Ehrman about this chapter (both by email and in person) he denied that this explanation gets at the heart of what happened to him. Yet, interestingly enough, he refused to offer an alternate explanation. Rather, he encouraged me to read more of his books. At first, he directed me to *Misquoting Jesus*, then to *God's Problem*. Most recently he told me to wait for a book he intends to begin writing soon and assures me that this one will finally explain it all. However, in *God's Problem*, Ehrman writes, "But the problems of the Bible are not what led me to leave the faith. (3)" Accordingly, what I offer here is "a conservative evangelical interpretation" and not Ehrman's own account.

again experience was what originally grounded his newly found faith, his subsequent faith was quickly understood to be existentially and soteriologically tied up with a particular view of scripture. Accordingly, whenever that view of scripture came under attack, it was as if the entire faith was coming under attack—and that in a most elemental way. Over time, a sustained critical study of scripture eviscerated the inerrantist view of his teenage years. In the meantime the memory of the initial conversion experience began to fade, meaning that the initially intense existential component of the evangelical religion had been allowed to gradually erode over time. In fact, over the course of twenty years or so, Ehrman gradually traveled down a long and windy academic road that sadly ended with his ultimate renunciation of faith.

This conservative evangelical interpretation seems at least partially borne out by what Ehrman has publicly related on various occasions. On the Diane Rehm show, for example, Ehrman recounts the early phase of his journey as follows:

> In attending this group, [I] realized that the people who were most active in the group had a different religious experience from the one that I had had in my Episcopal church, that they were more fervently religious and were more certain about their faith and seemed to have a lot of answers to questions that I had. That seemed attractive to me and so I actually joined the group and had this born again experience . . . I threw myself completely into this experience and became very active in this Youth for Christ group. The leader of the group convinced me that if I wanted to be a really serious Christian I would commit my life to it and go off to study Bible in college . . . But as I started working through the Greek New Testament I realized that there are places where we don't know what the original words were because we don't have the originals in any of the books of the New Testament. We only have copies that are made many years later, centuries and centuries later. And these copies all have differences from one another so much so that there are places where we don't know what the original text said. That started me down a different path where I started realizing that the certainties that I had been holding onto, in fact, were uncertain even to the point of not knowing what the words of the Bible were.[2]

---

2. Interview with Diane Rehm on The Diane Rehm Show, WAMU 88.5, December 8, 2005. Online: http://wamu.org/programs/dr/05/12/08.php

In his bestseller, *Misquoting Jesus*, Ehrman describes his early interest in scripture: "Those of us who had these born-again experiences considered ourselves to be 'real' Christians . . . One of the ways we differentiated ourselves from these others was in our commitment to Bible study and prayer. Especially Bible study . . . I soon became envious of [Bruce's, the person who led Ehrman to faith] ability to quote scripture and got involved with Bible studies myself . . ."[3] So Ehrman went to Moody and became a "serious" Christian, "studying scripture full time." Every course there was taught from the perspective that "the Bible is the inerrant word of God. It contains no mistakes." And this was a "'step up,'" writes Ehrman, "from the milquetoast view of the Bible I had had as a socializing Episcopalian in my younger youth. This was hard-core Christianity, for the fully committed."[4] He explains, ". . . starting with my born-again experience in high school, through my fundamentalist days at Moody, and on through my evangelical days at Wheaton—my faith had been based completely on a certain view of the Bible."[5]

Likewise, in an article in the *Washington Post*, Ehrman recounts that after becoming born again, he was socially and spiritually encouraged to take the Bible more seriously: "I told my friends, family, everyone about Christ . . . The study of the Bible was a religious experience. The more you studied the Bible, the more spiritual you were. I memorized large parts of it. It was a spiritual exercise, like meditation." When recounting the later phases of his de-conversion, Ehrman makes explicit mention of what an overwhelming part the Bible played in the religious culture that had nurtured him: "I just began to lose it [. . .] It wasn't for lack of trying. But I just couldn't believe there was a God in charge of this mess . . . It was so emotionally charged. This whole business of 'the Bible is your life, and anyone who doesn't believe it is going to roast in hell.'"[6] In *Misquoting Jesus*, Ehrman retrospectively recounts that even while at Wheaton, "[t]hese doubts both plagued me and drove me to dig deeper and deeper,

---

3. Ehrman, *Misquoting Jesus*, 4.

4 Ibid..

5. Ibid., 11.

6. Interview with Neely Tucker in Tucker, "The Book of Bart: In the Bestseller 'Misquoting Jesus,' Agnostic Author Bart Ehrman Picks Apart the Gospels That Made a Disbeliever Out of Him," *Washington Post* Online: http://www.washingtonpost.com /wp-dyn/content/article/2006/03/04/AR2006030401369_pf.html. Ehrman's later doubts involved the problem of evil. See Ehrman, *God's Problem*..

to understand what the Bible really was."[7] "As I've indicated, already at Wheaton I had begun to question some of the foundational aspects of my commitment to the Bible as the inerrant word of God. That commitment came under serious assault in my detailed studies at Princeton."

> I resisted any temptation to change my views, and found a number of friends who, like me, came from conservative evangelical schools and were trying to 'keep the faith' (a funny way of putting it—looking back—since we were, after all, in a Christian divinity program). But my studies started catching up with me.[8]

A climax seems to have come when Ehrman conceded a professor's point to the effect that it is quite possible that the evangelist Mark had simply made a mistake in Mark 2.26, where he had Jesus say, "Abiathar," instead of "Ahimelech." "Once I made that admission," Ehrman writes, "the flood gates opened. For if there could be one little, picayune mistake in Mark 2, maybe there could be mistakes in other places as well."[9] "This kind of realization coincided with the problems I was encountering the more closely I studied the surviving Greek manuscripts of the New Testament."[10] Together, these two strands of doubt precipitated a gradual de-conversion process:

> This is a radical shift from reading the Bible as an inerrant blueprint for our faith, life, and future to seeing it as a very human book, with very human points of view, many of which differ from one another and none of which provides the inerrant guide to how we should live. This is the shift in my own thinking that I ended up making, and to which I am now fully committed.[11]

> What if the book you take as giving you God's words instead contains human words? What if the Bible doesn't give a foolproof answer to the questions of the modern age—abortion, women's rights, gay rights, religious supremacy, Western-style democracy, and the like? What if we have to figure out how to live and what to believe on our own, without setting up the Bible as a false idol—or an oracle that gives a direct line of communication with

7. Ehrman, *Misquoting Jesus*, 4.

8. Ibid., 8.

9. Ehrman, *Misquoting Jesus*, 9.

10. Ibid., 10.

11. Ibid., 13.

the Almighty? There are clear reasons for thinking that, in fact, the Bible is not this kind of inerrant guide to our lives: *among other things*, as I've been pointing out, in many places we (as scholars, or just regular readers) don't even know what the original words of the Bible actually were.[12]

The conservative evangelical interpretation that I am relating here, that Bart Ehrman became a Christian through a potent religious experience and then, for whatever reason, understood that his faith was inextricably tied to the veracity of the Bible, may or may not coincide with how Ehrman would recount his own story. Even so, there are countless former evangelicals who experienced *something* like this during the course of their de-conversion process. This conservative evangelical account of Ehrman's journey—even if it does not strictly fit what actually happened to him—is representative of what has happened to any number of former evangelicals who have defected from faith. For these, as apparently for Ehrman, inerrancy encapsulated "hard-core Christianity, for the fully committed," a frame of mind adopted by those who would not settle for taking half-measures with their faith.[13] In Ehrman's case, he became so committed to the scriptures that James Arlandson muses that his conception of scripture was "super high, too high in fact, and this lands him into false dilemmas."[14] When asked about Ehrman, Darrell Bock candidly remarks, "[S]ometimes I wonder if we are not all guilty of asking the Bible to do too much."[15] Robert Gundry observes: "Ehrman's evangelical faith died by way of a hardening of the categories [of human and divine with respect to the inspiration of the Bible]; and his self-reported post-mortem stands as a warning to evangelicals, from whom he inherited some of that hardening of categories."[16] And Dan Wallace speaks of "Bart's black and

---

12. Ehrman, *Misquoting Jesus*, 14, italics mine. Ehrman's critics have gone to great lengths to defend inerrancy from his "original words" argument (since that is what *Misquoting Jesus* is primarily about), but this argument could also be interpreted as a metonymy for a more expansive, cumulative case against inerrancy. In a more charitable reading, readers might bear in mind Ehrman's qualification, "among other things," in the quote cited above. I tease out what some of these "other things" were for me in *Inerrancy*.

13. Ehrman, *Misquoting Jesus*, 4.

14. Arlandson, "Review."

15. Tucker, "Book of Bart."

16. Gundry, "Post-Mortem."

white mentality" by which he was taught to "frontload [his] critical investigation of the text of the Bible with bibliological presuppositions."[17]

Any way you slice it, at least from a conservative evangelical point of
view, something happened to Ehrman's doctrine of scripture that caused
his faith to diminish in vibrancy and incrementally reduce as his understanding of the biblical texts gained in critical probity. If this is the case,
then it is most unfortunate that biblicist foundationalism has become the
mainstay of untold numbers of Christians within conservative Reformed
and evangelical Christianity. Conservatives are renown for using their
foundationalist view of the Bible to help identify themselves over against
the "liberals," yet the way that this biblicist foundationalism is culturally
promulgated in the States seems to place evangelical believers—especially
those pursuing higher levels of education—in a far more precarious position than they are wont to admit.[18] As was the case for Ehrman, biblicist
foundationalism can have the adverse effect of clouding evangelical awareness of the actual process of Christian conversion: religious experience first;
doctrinal considerations second. After all, it is God who first reaches out to
his people through the Christian lifeworld, which would include other believers, tradition, scripture, the Holy Spirit. Then, new believers begin, each
at their own pace, to reflect upon the faith as they set out to articulate what
it is that actually happened to them and gradually learn whether and how
the faith can help make sense of the their lives.[19] In other words, the foundation is not scripture and certainly not a biblicist view of them. Much rather,
as the Christian philosophical tradition has learned: faith comes first, and
understanding second. That is the patent Christian expectation and this is
what Ehrman appears to have experienced.

Yet inerrantist propaganda, in its apologetic fervor to justify, promote
and defend the faith, fails to recognize the spiritual trajectory set by con-
versions that progress from faith to understanding. Instead, inerrantists
set out to unnaturally integrate inerrancy into the existential equation. In
others words, the inerrantist message practically amounts to an inversion
of the experiential progression to the effect that faith comes first, *inerrancy
second*, and then seeking third, a seeking, we should point out, that must
never show itself to be in contradiction with the inerrantist foundation.

17. Wallace, "Gospel."

18. See Bovell, *Inerrancy*.

19. Compare Whitehouse, *Modes*. See also Fowler, *Stages*.

The foundational status of an inerrant scripture is inculcated tacitly, and sometimes explicitly, very early on in terms of a believer's developmental progress. Apologetic arguments for inerrancy at this stage—or at any stage of faith, for that matter—set out to establish not only the rationality of the doctrine but also its cruciality. That is where a number of the problems set in. Fundamentalist and evangelical faith is constructed in such a way that the consequences for disavowing inerrancy are deliberately made to be so costly that disaffirming inerrancy jeopardizes the entire faith construct. To illustrate this, one need look no further than the arguments proffered by inerrantists themselves in defense of their "high" view of scripture.

Let us consider, then, three of the main arguments used by conservative thinkers to help reassure themselves and others of the theoretical viability (viz., necessity) of an inerrant scripture. The three arguments I have in mind are conveniently discussed in one place in a work by Stephen T. Davis, published, incidentally, a year before Ehrman graduated from Wheaton. According to Davis, inerrantists marshal the following three arguments in support of their position: a biblical argument, an epistemological argument, and a slippery slope argument.[20] The biblical argument he describes as an attempt to trace the doctrine of inerrancy back to the biblical authors themselves. The conservative history of the doctrine takes on various forms, yet the tenor of the argument suggests that even a cursory perusal of scripture reveals how the prophets, the apostles, and especially Jesus Christ himself all thought the Bible inerrant. On the authority of the biblical authors, the argument runs, it behooves evangelicals to accept their conclusion. As Davis points out, this particular argument strategically avails itself of the fact that evangelical believers are "in a sense *obligated* to inquire after and accept the Bible's view of itself . . . If an evangelical rejects what he discovers to be the Bible's view of itself, he rejects the procedure by which any suggested doctrine is to be accepted or rejected."[21]

A second argument that Davis recounts is the epistemological argument. It takes a very similar strategy as Quine did when he argued for the indispensability of mathematics for scientific practice in his effort to legitimize mathematics in spite of its abstract nature. Davis explans: "The basic idea is quite clear: Unless the Bible is inerrant, Christians have no

20. Davis, *Debate*, 49–93.
21. Ibid., 51, italics his.

sound epistemological foundation on which to base their beliefs. Thus inerrancy is crucial for Christians."[22] If the Bible is not inerrant, Christianity has no way to achieve its own self-articulation.

A third argument Davis calls the slippery slope argument (SSA) and he delineates as follows:

> Belief in doctrine A is crucial for Christians because those who reject it are likely also to doubt doctrines B, C, and D, which places them on the slippery slide that leads to liberalism and ultimately to no faith at all. Theoretically, A, B, C, and D can be any doctrines of Christianity, but the SSA is perhaps most often presented as an argument in support of the claim that the Bible is inerrant.[23]

Once again, the consequences of disbelieving inerrancy are emphasized and leave the evangelical believer in dire straits.

The three arguments above pressure evangelicals to understand their faith in ways that seem to fly in the face of how evangelicals actually come to believe in an authoritative Bible. Mascord illuminates the matter considerably during the course of an extended argument against Reformed epistemology:

> Although it is true that the gospel frequently does just "seem right" to people, and has a "ring of truth" about it, a good part of the reason for that is that it lines up, often in profound and unexpected ways, with what people already believe or suspect. The Christian teaching on human sin *is* likely to touch a deep chord within people when they encounter it in Scripture . . . There is within Scripture a cuttingly accurate diagnosis of the human which contributes to the gospel's plausibility, giving it that "ring of truth" when it is preached or read . . . The Bible makes claims both about itself and us which are proven true in experience.[24]

The Bible proves itself authentic in a way that might very well be described as "true." Yet inerrantists imprudently capitalize upon this intuitive notion of "truthfulness" and aggrandize its significance beyond credulity to encompass virtually every manner of truth imaginable. For an interpretation of how this is actually done, I defer to Mark Wynn's account of the role of emotion in religious understanding.

22. Ibid., 66.

23. Davis, *Debate*, 83.

24. Mascord, *Alvin Plantinga*, 149–50.

Writing on religion, William James speculated that theological and philosophical conceptions should be "classed as over-beliefs, buildings-out performed by the intellect into directions of which feeling originally supplied the hint." Wynn expounds in precisely what respect James' analysis seems to have gotten things right:

> [P]rimitive, religiously informed affects . . . can help to guide our discursive enquiries, in so far as such enquiries seek to spell out the content of such experience . . . or again, feelings may render a certain religiously significant subject matter salient, and encourage the posing of certain questions in relation to that subject matter; and they may properly constitute a "paradigm" which shapes the reading of evidence pertaining to these questions. Feelings may also give shape to theological reflection by grounding value claims which invite completion in metaphysical terms.[25]

In our case, the observation to be made is that the "feeling"—for lack of a better word—that the gospel "accurately" describes the human condition and that the scriptures give an account of a gospel that "fits" the human condition is unwittingly theologically articulated by fundamentalists and evangelicals in such a way that the authority of scripture becomes *the* symbolic metaphor for this initial spiritual insight. The discovery that the gospel disclosed in scripture is "true" is discursively expressed in terms of comprehensive biblical authority. The initial "decision" or "belief" in the direction of faith is embraced so enthusiastically that perspective is lost with regard to a forced transition from "implicational" to "rational" modes of thought. So Wynn: "[f]eeling has a certain explanatory priority when we consider religion as a sociological phenomenon: the doctrines only get going because of the feelings. . .[I]f the doxastic commitments of religious believers are profoundly shaped by feeling, then the epistemic standing of those commitments may well depend upon the capacity of feeling to bear a positive cognitive significance."[26]

This, I propose, helps account for how someone like Ehrman (and any number of fundamentalists/evangelicals besides) can come to express his own conception of faith with the sentiment, "Those of us who had these born-again experiences considered ourselves to be 'real' Christians

---

25. Wynn, *Emotional Experience*, 146–47. The James quote from *The Varieties of Religious Experience* is cited by Wynn (123). "Paradigm" is a reference to Ronald de Souza's model for understanding emotions.

26. Wynn, *Emotional Experience*, 147.

. . . One of the ways we differentiated ourselves from these others was in our commitment to Bible study and prayer. Especially Bible study." In a perceived continuity with Reformation and post-Reformation tradition, the emotions of evangelical religious experience that initially ground one's faith cry out for foundational discursive articulation involving metaphors that evoke absolute biblical authority.

The prevailing metaphor at the time of Ehrman's schooling (and even today in conservative evangelicalism) is one of plenary inspiration, an inspiration reified in a text that cannot contain a mistake. Thus, Barr was very much in the right when he refused to define fundamentalism in terms of an insistence upon the literal interpretation of scripture. His proposal was rather that fundamentalism be identified with that family of interpretive traditions that exhibits the following three attitudes: (1) "'a very strong emphasis on the inerrancy of the Bible,' (2) 'a strong hostility to modern theology' and 'the modern critical study of the Bible,' and (3) a sharp distinction between 'nominal' and 'true' Christians (i.e., fundamentalists)."[27] For all his vitriol, Barr rightly saw the intrinsic connection made by fundamentalist communities, both academic and lay, between the doctrine of inerrancy and the nature of "true" Christianity *and* "true" Christianity's defensive stance against critical biblical studies.

In order to overcome the taboo against critical study, some fundamentalists and conservative evangelicals feel that in order to muster the courage to go against the cultural mindset, one must resolve oneself to a "quest for truth wherever it might take me, trusting that any truth I learned was no less true for being unexpected or difficult to fit into the pigeonholes provided by my evangelical background."[28] More often than not, inerrancy does not successfully sustain this kind of all-out critical examination, which has far-reaching ramifications for the believer who initiates the quest.

Max Heirich observes, "If experiences or encounters take place that cannot be encompassed within current explanatory schemes yet cannot be ignored, present understandings of root reality may come into question. Alternatively, when quite unacceptable outcomes appear imminent and inevitable, if current understandings of root reality are correct, many persons begin to reexamine their most basic assumptions." But in the fun-

---

27. Dayton, "Evangelicalism."
28. Ehrman, *Misquoting Jesus*, 8. Compare Avalos, *Se puede?* 280–81.

damentalist and conservative evangelical context, such a reexamination can be difficult to carry out. Heirich continues, "One need not abandon one's sense of basic order to avoid undesired outcomes; but one might be more likely to question it under such circumstances and to look seriously at alternative claims that provide more options."[29] However, the fundamentalist assumptions that 1) inerrancy is the watershed issue for "true" Christianity and 2) inerrancy is indispensable to the very possibility of any Christianity worthy of the name emotionally preclude consideration of bibliological alternatives.

Not only that, but the believer quickly discovers that without the doctrine of inerrancy one finds oneself without a place to lay his head. There is no place for such a "liberal" among the community of "true" believers and once *this* observation is made, the floodgates are truly opened. In fact, they are not only open to a new prospect of finding errors in scripture (as if that were not bad enough). The believer who discounts inerrancy soon finds himself spiritually homeless, an ecclesial exile, a persona non grata, existentially discounted, disconnected, disoriented. The fact that there may be errors in the Bible proves to be the least of his concerns.

The moral of the story seems to be that in the long run it is not ultimately helpful to Christ's kingdom to argue for inerrancy in such a way that it is understood to belong so intrinsically to faith that faith cannot do without it and spiritual understanding cannot be gained divorced from it. Many religious communities express a "willingness . . . to see their scriptures as sources of knowledge both of the world and of what is assumed to lie beyond it."[30] Even if one cedes to Biderman that scripture "both provides knowledge (in an entangled verbal form) and constitutes the evidence by means of which this knowledge is justified,"[31] Ehrman's journey seems to argue that (within Protestantism, at least) theological constructs of scripture should never be articulated in such exclusive ways that seekers and believers are left without alternatives for consideration. For if it turns out that belief in inerrancy yields to critical scrutiny, it is not merely one doctrine that is jettisoned, but the entire faith construct. When inerrancy is constructed *post facto* in such a way that it is said to belong *ipso facto* to the religious conversion experience, an existential and

29. "Change of Heart: A Test of Some Widely Held Theories About Religious Conversion," *The American Journal of Sociology* 83 (1977): 674–75.

30. Biderman, *Scripture*, 100.

31. Ibid., 105–6.

epistemological idol is made out of the Bible. When a believer comes to recognize this way of constructing the faith for what it is—an inversion of the faith seeking understanding process—the faith can easily fall, and how great will that fall be!

When Ehrman (or any conservative for that matter) asks, "What is my faith based on?" His answer should never have been, "The Bible," much less "completely on a certain view of the Bible [inerrancy]," but rather, "Religious experience." The Christian faith must be based on religious experience, understood within the framework of the historic Christian tradition. In other words, a sense of God or encounter with God culturally and relevantly interpreted through the meta-narrative of the Christian story—*that* is what ultimately gets one to buy into Christianity and *that* is what ultimately continues to sustain faith subsequent to initial conversion.[32] Bibliology is neither here nor there in this context (as, indeed, it should not be). Inerrancy, said to be the condition for the possibility of biblicist foundationalism, should no longer be inculcated to believers, whether new or veteran, as a central doctrine of faith. For an inability to maintain that doctrine's integrity should never count as a reason for the understanding that one is no longer a believer.

32. Compare, for example, Craig, "Classical Apologetics," 28–36; and van de Beek, "Being Convinced"; Mascord, *Alvin Plantinga*, 148–67. Of course, I am not talking about experience *alone*. Bloesch, *Ground of Certainty*, 68–77.

12

A Husserlian Alternative
to Biblicist Foundationalism

A FORMER PROFESSOR WOULD frequently tell his students that it is
always easier to tear something down than to construct an alternative. I shall accordingly end the book by making a brief and tentative
proposal for how the authority of scripture might be presented to conservative Christians. To help make this suggestion I appeal to insights made
by phenomenologist Edmund Husserl. Specifically, I set out to explore
what Husserl's insistence upon 'genesis,' his phenomenological quest
for original sources, and his concern for progressive transformations of
meaning indicate for how instrumental epistemological foci have become
in Western culture. In a suggestive, comparative analysis, I compare an
instance of the acquisition of mathematical knowledge with an example
of the acquisition of religious knowledge and attempt to subject both to
the rigor of Husserl's *epoche*. In my view, biblicist foundationalism encourages an instrumental attitude toward knowledge that is killing the
ethos of conservative Reformed and evangelical spiritual formation. This
final chapter offers a tentative suggestion for how leaders and teachers
can spiritually form those under their care by guiding them through a
firsthand existential and spiritual sifting of the canonical texts from non-
canonical hagiography. Perhaps in this way, they may come to experience
the Spirit's putative divine attestation of sacred scripture for themselves
and appreciate its authority firsthand without being seduced by the epistemological certainty exuded by biblicist foundationalists.

Early in his career, Edmund Husserl wrote an article entitled,
"Psychological Studies for Elementary Logic."[1] Although Husserl's later

---

1. Edmund Husserl, "Psychological Studies for Elementary Logic," in *Husserl: Shorter*

phenomenological turn in descriptive psychology disabused him of psy-
chologism's impulse to reduce logic to psychology, this early article contains material that he later incorporated into his *Logical Investigations*.
Let us consider some remarks he makes toward the end of this article regarding the import of continued psychological (and for Husserl, purely
logical) investigations into the relationship between intuition and representation. Husserl's explorations into epistemology were inspired by
his previous researches in mathematics and subsequent ponderings into
the possibility of mathematical knowledge. His explorations convinced
him that epistemology and psychology of knowledge are not the same
thing.

It is amazing, if not a bit troubling, remarks Husserl, that the disar-
ray present in the foundations of mathematics is virtually inversely pro-
portionate to the perceived soundness of its conclusions. Commenting on
how Cauchy "defended totally different theories of imaginary numbers"
during various periods of his life, Husserl astutely observes that

> one cannot object [to Husserl's skeptical epistemological rumina-
> tions by saying] that two different things are involved here, insight
> and reflecting on such insight reasonably. For in these theories
> it is not a matter at all of mere reflection but a matter of certain
> and actually very complicated chains of conclusions which must
> necessarily mediate scientific thought if such thought is to be rea-
> sonable. Theories change but the procedure remains the same. The
> evidence produced by such a procedure—there is no doubt about
> this at all—is mere illusion.[2]

Husserl explains that he does not want

> to deny in any way now that one can considerably advance the
> logical understanding of the soundness of symbolic thinking (first
> of all naturally of mathematical thinking) without a more deeply
> penetrating insight into the essence of those elementary processes
> of intuition and representation which mediate this understanding
> throughout.[3]

Works, ed. P. McCormick and F. Elliston (Notre Dame, IN: University of Notre Dame
Press, 1981), 120–42.

2. Husserl, "Psychological," 140.

3. Ibid., 141.

Nevertheless, Husserl is after a "full and really satisfactory under-standing" of how one comes to know mathematics. The end result of his early foray into philosophy of mathematics is described in his "Vienna Lecture" as the emergence of "a third form of universal attitude" which is "that of the universal critique of all life and all life-goals, all cultural products and systems that have already arisen out of the life of man; and thus it also becomes a critique of mankind itself and of the values which guide it explicitly and implicitly."[4] What interests us here is what Husserl has to say about mathematical knowledge—mathematics being for Husserl the ideal science.

It should be noted that Husserl's epistemological work is not af-ter what most analytic philosophical theories of knowledge are after. Traditional readers in epistemology typically consist of essays about what can be known, how people can know things, and how a person knows that she knows things. In other words, the authors would minimally provide a carefully worded definition of knowledge along with a comprehensive discussion about epistemic justification. Husserl decides rather to under-take a purely descriptive philosophical project, one he terms "pure logic." Whenever he touches upon things epistemological, he is primarily after a description of knowledge unencumbered by scientific and philosophical theories. For his epistemological efforts always work toward the discovery of the universal structures of consciousness.

In another early piece entitled, "On the Logic of Signs (Semiotic)," Husserl writes:

> Every conventional operation with signs serves, in a certain man-ner, the purposes of knowledge. But not every one of them actually leads to what counts as knowledge, in the true and pure sense of logical *insights*. It is only in cases where the procedure itself is a logical one, and where we have logical insight into the fact that, such as it is and because it is so, it must lead to truth, that its result becomes, not a mere *de facto* truth, but rather a knowledge of the truth . . . In this sense we distinguish: *pre-logical sign operations*, which are oriented toward truth, and which perhaps attain to it, but do so without the employment (certainly also the invention) of these modes of procedure being based upon logical understand-

---

4. Husserl, "Vienna Lecture," 283.

ing; and *logical sign operations*, which are followed on the basis of knowledge, and therefore do not merely provide us with truth, but rather with assured truth.[5]

Of course, Husserl intends this distinction to pertain to "all symbolic judgment processes whatsoever: even the natural ones resulting from the efficacy of idea-association alone and excluding all logical motives. These latter belong totally to the pre-logical level."[6] At precisely this point in the text, Husserl makes a marginal note. He pauses to comment on what he calls an "analogous investigation." He asks, "How does it happen that we can calculate for centuries without an understanding of the calculatory system?" The perennial Husserlian question, I submit, is how does the pre-logical ever become logical? Husserl's contemporaries argued that the logical is merely reasoned reflections upon insights that are intuitively gleaned. According to Husserl, all evidences presented by his contemporaries in support of their position are "illusions."

Imagine Edmund Husserl sitting in on a typical high school trigonometry lesson:

> Begin with triangle ABC, not a right triangle. Suppose that students already know that $\sin \theta = \frac{\text{opp.}}{\text{hyp}}$ and that this ratio holds only for right triangles (which ABC is not).

> From here, students are taken step by step by their teacher from what is already known about $\sin \theta$ to what is called the "law of sines." The teacher might proceed as follows:

> Begin with triangle ABC, not a right triangle (Fig. 1). So far we know that $\sin \theta = \frac{\text{opp.}}{\text{hyp}}$ So let's draw the perpendicular (altitude) from C to side c, and suppose this has length h. Then note that $\sin B = h/a$. You can rewrite this as $h = a \cdot \sin B$. Similarly, $\sin A = h/b$. This, too, can be rewritten as $h = b \cdot \sin A$. Therefore: $a \cdot \sin B = b \cdot \sin A$ or $\frac{\sin B}{b} = \frac{\sin A}{a}$, where a and $b \neq 0$. (Law of Sines)

---

5. Husserl, "Logic," 47.

6. Ibid.

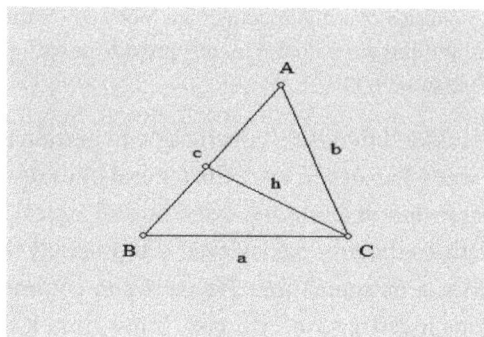

Fig. 1

In the language of Husserl's *Origins of Geometry*,[7] my "so far we know" fact about sin θ is a "sedimented tradition," a piece of knowledge established long before our high school class ever dreamed of the law of sines. Its mobility is illustrated in two ways, internally and externally. "Externally" describes the way that the sedimented tradition is being "passed on," in this case to the students from the math teacher. Whether the fact that $\sin θ = \frac{\text{opp.}}{\text{hyp}}$ is being heard for the first time or whether it was once heard before but has since been long forgotten (are these the same thing?), there is an inheritance being passed on—an external mobility. For anyone already familiar with sin θ, there is another type of mobility, i.e., the awareness of the possibility of the appropriation of the sedimented tradition regarding sin θ, not to mention all requisite mathematics necessary for knowing and saying that $\sin θ = \frac{\text{opp.}}{\text{hyp}}$. Thus, a new-found awareness opens up for the possibility of appropriation of the sedimented tradition to a *non*-right triangle, causing students to experience what Husserl calls a "progressive transformation of meaning."[8] This is an internal mobility.

Husserl's concern would be that "the sources of meaning have not been handed down" along with the "proposition" $\sin θ = \frac{\text{opp.}}{\text{hyp}}$. The law of sines and everything more that one can now do with it (not to mention how much more quickly one can do things) transform not only the meaning of sine for our hypothetical mathematics learners but also *the corresponding horizon of triangles under consideration* (in this case, the students are no longer restricted to right triangles).[9] Such transformations

7. Husserl, "Origins."

8. Ibid., 170.

9. I think it really does change the meaning. Students regularly use a calculator to

of meaning "work to the benefit of logical method," acknowledges Husserl in a marginal note, "but they remove one further and further from the origins and make one insensitive to the problem of origin and thus to the actual ontic and truth-meaning of all these sciences."[10] Of course Husserl was never one to stay the advancements of any logical method; however, he cautions that

> what we know—namely, that the presently vital cultural configura-
> tion "geometry" is a tradition and is still being handed down—is
> not knowledge concerning an external causality which effects the
> succession of historical configurations, as if it were knowledge
> based on induction, the presupposition of which would amount to
> an absurdity here; rather, to understand geometry or any given cul-
> tural fact is to be conscious of its historicity, albeit "implicitly."[11]

Or again: "The ruling dogma of the separation in principle between epis-temological elucidation and historical, even humanistic-psychological explanation, between epistemological and genetic origin is fundamentally mistaken . . ."[12] Here one can see with what aptness Jacques Derrida re-ferred to Husserl's phenomenon of "crisis" as "forgetfulness of origins."[13] Husserl's concern for the forgetfulness of origins signifies a contemporary crisis in Western culture's overly instrumental regard for epistemology, a crisis in which, I suggest, a biblicist foundationalism eagerly participates.

For our purposes, let us say that instrumental knowledge comprises an approach to knowledge that cherishes knowledge primarily as a means to some end. In other words, interest in epistemology is maintained pri-marily by what this or that piece of knowledge will ultimately help the knower accomplish. In the present age, one might term such knowledge, "technological knowledge" or "imperial knowledge," as some have. Yet neither I nor Husserl—at least as far as I can tell—would in any way

---

find sin θ (they used to consult tables) both before and after learning the law of sines But before learning the law of sines, sin θ may have been thought of as a ratio between sides of a right triangle. After learning it, it too easily becomes another *variable* and its geometric context conveniently forgotten. For example, textbooks never relate the law of sines to circles (its original context) as ancient geometers were in the habit of doing (e.g., Ptolemy).

10. Husserl, "Origins," 170.

11. Ibid., 173.

12. Ibid., 172.

13. Derrida, *Edmund*, 33.

imply that the instrumental dimension of knowledge is inherently and necessarily violent or injurious. In any event, we should applaud Husserl's rediscovery of the significance of historicity as a "'primally establishing' function" for the developmental advances of all "sciences," under which heading Husserl implicitly means every human cultural achievement.[14]

The law of sines, to take our present example, can be said to help further the remove of students from the primally establishing function of the "co-consciousness" of the original trigonometric ratio (of a triangle's sides in relation to the angle they form) by catapulting them toward a potentially meaningless sine button on a calculator with an emphasis on its numerical output. To help preserve the liveliness of mathematics and the authenticity of high school students' mathematical knowledge, educational communities should deliberately ensure that the original ontic meanings of mathematical premises are invariably included in the students' mathematical acquisitions, *even as they move and look forward* to new acquisitions in successive school years.[15]

The crisis of instrumental knowledge is both more foundational and far-reaching than often realized. Although Husserl's philosophical explorations began with an analysis and critique of his own mathematical practice, his phenomenological enterprise eventually encompassed all of humankind's activities and values. In time he even reserved an epistemological space for the religio-mythical attitude that characterizes and influences a great deal of ancient, and, whether to a lesser or greater extent, contemporary human thought and action.

In what remains, then, I propose to compare these patterns in mathematical learning to the religious analogue in question: the inculcation of the authority of Christian scripture to conservative Christian adherents. Christian conservatives learn at some point during the course of their religious education that God has provided the Church (however construed) with a written revelation, the Bible. It seems fair to say that its canonical form is no longer a major item of dispute amongst the churches even if there remains a diversity of canons and a variety of arguments for each. Let us consider then the acquisition of knowledge regarding one specific aspect of the authority of scripture in the context of Husserl's phenom-

14. Husserl, "Origins," 158.
15. Ibid., 159.

enology. To do this, we shall take a look at some of the earliest arguments made for the exclusive canonical use of four gospel books.

The earliest arguments made for an exclusive four-gospel canon appear to have been made by Irenaeus. Interestingly enough, it does not seem that the majority of Christians would accept these arguments today. Even so, the conclusions inferred from these early arguments have not (and will likely never be) officially overruled. Husserl's genius insight—his insight that the foundations of epistemology must probe beyond the standard distinction that is made between discovery and reasoned reflection upon discover—also bears fruit here. A contextualized Husserlian emphasis on genesis (which in the present example would be an emphasis on the origins of the belief that the Bible, as a product of special revelation, contains only four gospels) reveals how the crisis of instrumental knowledge has spread even to conservative Reformed and evangelical conceptions of scripture.

During the second century C. E., the bishop Irenaeus found himself in the unenviable position of having to defend the emerging clerical opinion that four primary religious documents should have special authority in the church: the Gospels according to Matthew, Mark, Luke and John. Over the course of his career, he defended the scriptural status of many other works that eventually found their way into the New Testament along with a few other works that never made it into the canon. In a major work entitled *Against Heresies*, Irenaeus penned the following words:

> It is not possible that the Gospels can be either more or fewer in number than they are, since there are four directions of the world in which we are, and four principal winds . . . The four living creatures [of Rev. iv. 9] symbolize the four Gospels . . . and there were four principal covenants made with humanity, through Noah, Abraham, Moses, and Christ.[16]

Here we have a very early argument for a fourfold gospel. The historical context seems to be that numerous gospels had been produced anonymously or pseudonymously and that different Christian sects had seized several of these gospels and developed diverse sets of theological views regarding the life and mission of Jesus Christ. In the opposite direction headed a reactionary argument that said that if a gospel were really going to be given by God—i.e., if it were really to be perfect and trustworthy in

---

16. *Adv. Haer.* 3.11.8, cited in Metzger, *Canon*, 155.

its redemptive message—then that gospel would be single, contained in one gospel only.

In contradistinction to these opinions, Irenaeus argued for the cosmological, if not redemptive, significance of the number four. Arguments from number symbolism were not uncommon in antiquity. They were used, for example, to originally legitimate the inclusion of seven Pauline epistles in the canon and to argue for the applicability of the book of Revelation to all churches everywhere, comprised, as it were, as a compilation of seven epistles.[17] When Hans Von Campenhausen considered Irenaean thinking to be crucial to the emergence of the Christian Bible, he had in mind the fundamentally proto-orthodox thrust of Irenaeus' theological arguments; however what of the arguments themselves?[18] What of the archaic arguments that purportedly lend support to the surmise that there are only four gospels? This is where I think we are met with an instance where the majority of Christians have conveniently and primarily interested themselves in the consensus that there are four gospels precisely for what it enables their students to do: get on with the business of reading and learning about the life and work of Jesus, and so on. It seems to me that one would not be wrong to cite this as a very real instance of Husserl's forgetfulness of origins.

It is not so much that Christians are by and large not interested in origins in the sense of philological and historical research into the emergence of the Christian Bible. As can be seen in chapters five and six of my *Inerrancy and the Spiritual Formation of Younger Evangelicals*, there has been somewhat of a scholarly renaissance in the field of canonics even if evangelicals themselves seem not to be as interested as non-evangelical believers are. Yet there seems little concern that "the sources of meaning have not been handed down" along with the "proposition," which in this case is the orthodox Christian proposition that there are only and properly four gospels in the New Testament. Perhaps David Dunbar comes closest when he observes that the fourfold canon is comprised of those gospels and only those gospels that the church *experienced* as foundational to its own existence.[19] He concedes:

17. See Metzger, *Canon*, 262ff.

18. See, for example, von Campenhausen, *Formation*.

19. Dunbar, "Canon," 358.

> The fact that the arguments used to defend the canonicity of certain books appear inadequate to some streams of modern scholarship does not necessarily disqualify the particular books in view since ... these arguments were generally *a posteriori*. The determining factor was usage, that is, the church's recognition of its own origins.[20]

Dunbar is emphatic that these origins were best discerned by the early church and points out that throughout the history of Christianity, ecclesiastical authorities have generally agreed with the original assessment. However, it seems to me that this is precisely where the crisis of instrumental knowledge shows what a powerful hold it has over contemporary conservative Christianity.

According to Dunbar, Ridderbos, and other Christian writers, it is precisely the sovereignty of God that assures Christians that there are exactly four gospels in the Bible. Yet I fear that these types of traditionally epistemological concerns tend to encourage an overly instrumental understanding of the Bible for the sake of theological construction, or for spiritual devotion, moral exhortation, or political recommendation. I should clarify that I do not see anything inherently wrong with pursuing any of these types of uses of Scripture. That said, Husserl's complicated chain of transformations of meaning seems to quickly and forcefully separate Christian biblicists from the ontic truth meaning of a very important aspect of their religion. The Husserlian phenomenological approach to attaining a faithfully Christian view of scriptures would be to inextricably intertwine the rigorous investigation and phenomenological appreciation of the Bible's epistemic origins with its genetic origins, which, to be fair, I think Dunbar tries to do. Yet it does not appear that someone like Dunbar would allow for contemporary Christian readers themselves to personally pursue the biblical geneses in a phenomenologically robust way—his fear presumably being that there is always the potential that the said phenenomenological investigation could lead one straight to heterodoxy or worse.

This is not to say that a concern for heterodoxy is something to be dismissed as a frivolous, fundamentalist preoccupation. Nor does the prospect of raising a specter of skepticism with regard to the biblical canon always have a desirable outcome. That said, is there not a very important way in which the original ontic meaning of the proposition "there are four gospels

---

20. Dunbar, "Canon," 359.

in the Christian Bible" fails to be passed on to Christian learners? This has the net effect of perpetuating a faith that is essentially and foundationally conceived as instrument. Surely, this raises serious concerns: a primary pedagogical moment in the spiritual formation of believers is couched in its very construal from the beginning as an instrument for epistemology. And if that were not bad enough in itself, a good and necessary consequence approach to Christianity exacerbates the problem immensely.

Younger conservatives, especially, as they investigate and explore what the scriptures are and how they are to be used do so with admirable enthusiasm and a potentially critical acumen. Yet they are severely handicapped by the fact that in the back of their minds they know that the verdict is already out on how to view the Bible and that it has only four Gospels. Not only that, but they already know in the back of their mind that the Bible contains no errors and that it is the Word of God from which we glean the whole counsel of God by good and necessary consequence. This pattern is not wholly positive, exhibiting many of the received patterns of what has been termed an "intratextual search for meaning."[21] As an alternative, I suggest that foundationalist-bibliological verdicts be suspended. This way, Christian learners can be given a real chance to return to origins, yet not in a biblicist-foundationalist way but in a searching Spirit-led epoche, and that to great avail. For now Christians might learn for themselves, as it were *for the first time*, how comparatively bereft of spiritual teaching and nourishment the uncanonical materials putatively are. Preferably, conservative leaders and teachers lead and personally escort those in their care through a phenomenological examination of the biblical and extant nonbiblical Gospels. This will allow them to discover for themselves the phenomenological genesis of the Gospels' selection process, a genesis to be experienced firsthand prior to the transformation of meaning. As the process progresses into the development of a sedimented tradition, believers can faithfully grow into a position where they are capable of passing tradition along without losing the originary sources of meaning. A delicate and arduous task to be sure—one that will raise profound questions for all involved (about the uniqueness of Scriptures, for example)—but the effort should also prove an early and very important step toward formatively impressing upon believers the actual nature of scriptural authority and inspiration. Pedagogical measures

---

21. See Hood, Hill, and Williamson, *Psychology*, 11–29.

such as these should not be left to themselves, much to the whims of a Cartesian biblicist foundationalism!

William Alston relates (although not as a "general recipe") how one can be "attached to Christianity for the wrong reasons, for radically wrong reasons, and that when that is the case, the best thing to do may be to get out and give yourself a chance to make a fresh a start under new circumstances at some later time."[22] I proffer that if conservative believers have been spiritually formed in such a way that they have been taught to crucially and irrevocably link inerrancy to a good and necessary consequence view of historic Christianity, perhaps it will prove existentially profitable for these believers to re-experience the originary process for a fresh bibliological start.

22. Alston, "Philosopher's Way," 25.

Bibliography

Aaboe, Asger. *Episodes from the Early History of Mathematics*. Washington, D.C.: The Mathematical Association of America, 1964.

Abraham, William J. *Canon and Criterion in Christian Theology: From the Fathers to Feminism*. New York: Oxford University Press, 1998.

———. "Canonical Theism: Thirty Theses." In *Canonical Theism: A Proposal for Theology and the Church*, edited by W. J. Abraham, J. E. Vickers, and N. B. van Kirk. Grand Rapids: Eerdmans, 2008.

Achinstein, P., editor. *Science Rules: A Historical Introduction to Scientific Methods*. Baltimore: The Johns Hopkins University Press, 2004.

ad-Andalusi, Said. *Science in the Medieval World: "Book of the Categories of Nations."* Translated and edited by S. I. Salem and A. Kumar. Austin: University of Texas Press, 1991.

Aertsen, Jan. "Good as Transcendental and the Transcendence of the Good." In *Being and Goodness: The Concept of the Good in Metaphysics and Philosophical Theology*, edited by Scott MacDonald, 56–73. Ithaca, NY: Cornell University Press, 1991.

——— . *Medieval Philosophy and the Transcendentals: The Case of Thomas Aquinas*. Leiden: Brill, 1996.

Agashe, D. "The Axiomatic Method: Its Origin and Purpose." *Journal of Indian Council of Philosophical Research* 7 (1989): 109–18.

Alston, William. "A Philosopher's Way Back to Faith." In *God and the Philosophers: The Reconciliation of Faith and Reason*, edited by T. V. Morris, 19–30. New York: Oxford University Press, 1994.

Annas, Julia. *An Introduction to Plato's Republic*. New York: Oxford University Press, 1981.

Anderson, James F. *An Introduction to the Metaphysics of St. Thomas Aquinas*. Washington, D.C: Regnery Publishing, 1977.

Anellis, Irving H. "Kant, Axiomatics, Logic and Geometry." *Modern Logic* 2 (1991): 77–103.

Anscombe, G. E. M. and P. T. Geach. *Three Philosophers: Aristotle, Aquinas, Frege*. Malden, MA: Basil Blackwell and Mott, Ltd., 1961.

Aquinas, Thomas. *An Exposition of the "On the Hebdomads" of Boethius*. Translated by J. L. Schultz and E. A. Synan. Washington, D.C.: The Catholic University of America Press, 2001.

——— . *On Being and Essence*. 2nd ed. Translated by A. Maurer. Toronto: Pontifical Institute of Mediaeval Studies, 1968.

Arena, Luis. "Matematicas, metodo y '*mathesis universalis*' en las 'Regulae' de Descartes." *Revista de Filosofia (Spain)* 8 (1996): 37–61.

Ariew, Roger. *Descartes and the Last Scholastics*. Ithaca, NY: Cornell University Press, 1999.

Ariew, Roger, John Cottingham, and Tom Sorell, editors, *Descartes' Meditations: Background Source Materials*. New York: Cambridge University Press, 1998.

Aristotle, *The Basic Works of Aristotle*. Edited by R. McKeon. New York: Random House, 2001.

———. *Nicomachean Ethics*. Loeb Classical Library. Translated by H. Rackham. Cambridge, MA: Harvard University Press, 1934.

———. *On Sophistical Refutations, On Coming-To-Be and Passing Away, On the Cosmos*. Loeb Classical Library. Translated by E. S. Forster and D. J. Furley; Cambridge, MA: Harvard University Press, 1955.

Arlandson, James. "Review of Bart D. Ehrman's Misquoting Jesus." *American Thinker* March 10, 2007. Source: http://www.americanthinker.com/2007/03/review_of _bart_d_ehrmans_misqu.html.

Artmann, Benno. *Euclid—The Creation of Mathematics*. New York: Springer-Verlag, 1999.

———. "Euclid's *Elements* and Its Prehistory." In *PERI TWN MAQHMATWN*, edited by Ian Mueller, 1–47. Edmonton: Academic Printing and Publishing, 1991.

Asiedu, F. B. A. 'Augustine's Christian-Platonist Account of Goodness: A Reconsideration.' *Heythrop Journal* 18 (2002): 328–43.

Avalos, Hector. *Se puede saber si Dios existe?* Amherst, NY: Prometheus Press, 2003.

Bambrough, R., editor. *New Essays on Plato and Aristotle*. London: Routledge and Kegan Paul, 1965.

Barbin, Evelyne. "The Meanings of Mathematical Proof: On Relations Between History and Mathematical Education." In *In Eves' Circles*, edited by J. M. Anthony, 41–52. Washington, D. C.: Mathematical Association of America, 1994.

Barnes, Jonathan. "Aristotle's Philosophy of the Sciences." In *Oxford Studies in Ancient Philosophy, Volume XI*, 225–41. New York: Oxford University Press, 1993.

———. "Aristotle's Theory of Demonstration." In *Articles on Aristotle: 1. Science*, edited by J. Barnes, M. Schofield, and R. Sorabji, 65–87. London: Gerald Duckworth & Company Limited, 1975.

———. "Life and Work." In *The Cambridge Companion to Aristotle*, edited by J. Barnes, 1–26. New York: Cambridge University Press, 1995.

Barnes, Jonathan, editor, *Early Greek Philosophy*. New York: Penguin Book, 1987.

Barnes, Jonathan, Malcolm Schofield, and Richard Sorabji, editors, *Articles on Aristotle: 1. Science*. London: Gerald Duckworth and Company Limited, 1975.

———. *Articles on Aristotle: 3. Science*. London: Gerald Duckworth and Company Limited, 1979.

Becker, O. "Die Lehre von Geraden und Ungeraden im neunten Buch der euklidischen Elemente." *Quellen und Studien zur Geschichte der Mathematik, Astronomie und Physik*, Abteilung B. 3 (1936): 533–53.

Bedu-Addo, J. T. "Recollection and the 'Argument from a Hypothesis' in Plato's Meno." *The Journal of Hellenic Studies* 104 (1984): 1–14.

Behboud, Ali. "Greek Geometrical Analysis" *Centaurus* 37 (1994): 52–86.

Bell, E. T. *Men of Mathematics: The Lives and Achievements of the Great Mathematicians from Zeno to Poincare*. New York: Simon and Schuster, 1965.

Bennett, Jonathan. "Infallibility and Modal Knowledge in Some Early Modern Philosophers." *Proceedings of the British Academy* 103 (2000): 139–66

Benson, Hugh. "Plato's Method of Dialectic." In *A Companion to Plato*, edited by H. Benson, 85–99. Malden, MA: Blackwell Publishing, 2006.

———. "Plato's Rationalistic Method." In *A Companion to Rationalism*, edited by A. Nelson, 85–99. Malden, MA: Blackwell Publishing, 2005.

———. "The Method of Hypothesis in the *Meno*." In *Proceedings of the Boston Area Colloquium in Ancient Philosophy Volume XVIII, 2002*, edited by J. J. Cleary and G. M Gurtler, 95–126. Boston: Brill, 2003.

Berka, Karel "Was There an Eleatic Background to Pre-Euclidean Mathematics?" In *Change, Ancient Axiomatics and Galileo's Methodology: Proceedings of the 1978 Pisa Conference on the History and Philosophy of Science Volume 1*, edited by Jaakko Hintikka, David Gruender, and Evandro Agazzi, 125–32. Boston: D. Reidel Publishing Company, 1981.

Berlinghoff William P. and Fernando Q. Goêvea, *Math through the Ages: A Gentle History for Teachers and Others*. Expanded Edition. Oxton House Publishers and The Mathematical Association of America, 2004.

Berti, Enrico. "Does Aristotle's Conception of Dialectic Develop?" In *Aristotle's Philosophical Development: Problems and Prospects*, edited by William Wians, 105 –30. Lanham, MD: Rowman and Littlefield Publishers, Inc., 1996.

Biderman, Shlomo. *Scripture and Knowledge: An Essay on Religious Epistemology*. Leiden: E. J. Brill, 1995.

Blackburn, Simon. *The Oxford Dictionary of Philosophy*. New York: Oxford University Press, 1994.

Bloesch, Donald. *The Ground of Certainty: Toward an Evangelical Theology of Revelation*. Grand Rapids: Eerdmans, 1971.

Bochner, Salomen. *The Role of Mathematics in the Rise of Science*. Princeton: Princeton University Press, 1966.

Boethius, *Tractates, De Consolatione Philosophiae*. Loeb Classical Library. Translated by H. F. Steweart, E. K. Rand and S. J. Tester. Cambridge, MA: Harvard, 1973.

Bold, Benjamin. *Famous Problems of Geometry and How to Solve Them*. Van Nostrand Reinhold Company, 1969; repr., New York: Dover Publications, Inc., 1982.

Bolton, Robert. "Plato's Discovery of Metaphysics: The New *Methodos* of the *Phaedo*" In *Method in Ancient Philosophy*, edited by J. Gentzler, 93–111. New York: Oxford University Press, 1998.

Bos, H. J. M. *Redefining Geometrical Exactness: Descartes' Transformation of the Early Modern Concept of Construction*. New York: Springer-Verlag, 2001.

Boucher, David. "Ambiguity and Originality in the Context of Discursive Relations." In *Objectivity, Method and Point of View: Essays in the Philosophy of History*, edited by W. J. Van der Dussen and L. Rubinoff, 22–46. New York: E. J. Brill, 1991.

Bovell, Carlos. *Inerrancy and the Spiritual Formation of Younger Evangelicals*. Eugene, OR: Wipf and Stock Publishers, 2007.

———. "Two Examples of How the History of Mathematics Can Inform Theology." *Theology and Science* (forthcoming).

Boyer Carl with Uta C. Merzback. *A History of Mathematics*. Wiley, New York: Wiley, 1989.

Brickhouse Thomas C. and Nicholas D. Smith, "Vlastos on the Elenchus." In *Oxford Studies in Ancient Philosophy Volume II*, edited by J. Annas, 185–95. New York: Oxford University Press, 1984.

Brentano, Franz. *Aristotle and His Worldview*. Edited and translated by R. George and R. M. Chisholm. Los Angeles: University of California Press, 1978.

Brown, Robert E. *Jonathan Edwards and the Bible*. Indianapolis: Indiana University Press, 2002.

Brownson, Orestes. "Presbyterianism and the Holy Scriptures." *Brownson Quarterly Review* (October 1846), http://orestesbrownson.com/index.php?id=256.

Brumbaugh, Robert S. *Plato's Mathematical Imagination: The Mathematical Passages in the Dialogues and Their Interpretation*. Bloomington, IN: Indiana University Press, 1968.

Buckley, Michael J. *At the Origins of Modern Atheism*. New Haven: Yale University Press, 1987.

Bundy, Alan, Mateja Jamnik and Andrew Fugard, "What is a Proof?" *Philosophical Transactions of the Royal Society A* 363 (2005): 2377–2391.

Burkert, Walter. *Lore and Science in Ancient Pythogoreanism*. Translated by Edwin L. Minar. Cambridge, MA: Harvard University Press, 1972.

Burnyeat, M. F. "Aristotle on Understanding Knowledge." In *Aristotle on Science: The Posterior Analytics Proceedings of the Eighth Symposium Aristotelicum Held in Padua From September 7 to 15, 1978*, edited by E. Berti, 97–139. Padova: Editrice Antenore, 1981.

———. "Platonism and Mathematics: A Prelude to Discussion." In *Mathematik und Metaphysik bei Aristoteles: Akten des X. Symposium Aristoleicum Sigriswil, 6.–12. September 1984*, edited by A. Graeser, 213–40. Bern und Stuttgart: Verlag Paul Haupt, 1987.

Byrne, Patrick. *Analysis and Science in Aristotle*. Albany, NY: State University of New York Press, 1997.

Carson, Emily. "Lock and Kant on Mathematical Knowledge." In *Intuition and the Axiomatic Method*, edited by E. Carson and R. Huber, 3–19. Dordrecht: Springer, 2006.

Carus, Paul. *The Foundations of Mathematics*. Open Court Publishing, 1908; repr. New York: Cosimo Inc., 2004.

Casey, Gerard. "An Explication of the De Hebdomadibus of Boethius in the Light of St. Thomas's Commentary." *The Thomist* 51 (1987): 419–34.

Chadwick, Henry. *Boethius The Consolations of Music, Logic, Theology, and Philosophy*. New York: Oxford, 1981.

Chang, Kyung-Choon. "Plato's Form of the Beautiful in the *Symposium* versus Aristotle's Unmoved Mover in the Metaphysics." *Classical Quarterly* 52 (2002): 431–46.

Cherniss, H. *Aristotle's Criticism of Presocratic Philosophy*. Johns Hopkins Press, 1935; repr., New York: Octagon Books, 1971.

———. "Plato as Mathematician." *The Review of Metaphysics* 4 (1951): 395–425.

Cleary, John J. *Aristotle and Mathematics: Aporetic Method in Cosmology and Metaphysics*. Philosophia Antiqua 67. Leiden: Brill, 1995.

———. "El papel de las matemáticas en la teología de Proclo." *Anuario Filosofico* 33 (2000): 67–85.

———. "Mathematics and Cosmology in Aristotle's Philosophical Development." In *Aristotle's Philosophical Development: Problems and Prospects*, edited by William Wians, 193–288. Lanham, MD: Rowman and Littlefield Publishers, Inc., 1996.

———. "Working Through Puzzles with Aristotle." In *The Crossroads of Norm and Nature: Essays on Aristotle's Ethics and Metaphysics*, edited by May Sim, 175–220. Lanham, MD: Rowan and Littlefield Publishers, Inc., 1995.

Code, Alan. "Metaphysics and Logic." In *Aristotle Today: Essays on Aristotle's Ideal of Science*, edited by M. Matthen, 127–49. Edmonton: Academic Printing and Publishing, 1987.

Cohen, Bernard. "Newton's Method and Newton's Style." In *Newton*, edited by I. B. Cohen and R. S. Westfall, New York: W. W. Norton and Company, 1995.

Cohen, Daniel J. *Equations from God: Pure Mathematics and Victorian Faith*. Baltimore: The John Hopkins University Press, 2007.

Coolidge, Julian Lowell. *A History of Geometrical Methods*. Oxford University Press, 1940; repr. New York: Dover Publications Inc., 1963.

Copleston, Frederick. *On the History of Philosophy*. New York: Barnes and Noble Books, 1979.

Corcoran, John. "A Mathematical Model of Aristotle's Syllogistic." *Archiv für Geschichte der Philosophie* 55 (1973): 191–219.

———. "Aristotle's Natural Deduction System." In *Ancient Logic and Its Modern Interpretations: Proceedings of the Buffalo Symposium on Modernist Interpretations of Ancient Logic, 21 and 22 April, 1972*, edited by John Corcoran, 85–131. Boston: D. Reidel Publishing Company, 1974.

Cornford, F. M. *Before and After Socrates*. New York: Cambridge University Press, 1932.

———. "Mathematics and Dialectic in the Republic VI.–VII. (I)." *Mind* 41 (1932): 37–52.

Craig, W. L. "Classical Apologetics." In *Five Views on Apologetics*, edited by S. Cowan, 25–54. Grand Rapids: Zondervan, 2000.

Crowe, Michael J. "Ten Misconceptions about Mathematics and Its History." In *History and Philosophy of Modern Mathematics*. Minnesota Studies in the Philosophy of Science Volume XI, edited by William Aspray and Philip Kitcher, 260–77. Minneapolis: University of Minnesota Press, 1988.

Curley, E. M. "Analysis in the Meditations: The Quest for Clear and Distinct Ideas." In *Essays on Descartes's Meditations*, edited by A. Rorty, 153–76. Los Angeles: Universtiy of California Press, 1986.

Davis, Stephen T. *The Debate about the Bible: Inerrancy Versus Infallibility*. Philadelphia: The Westminster Press, 1977.

Day, Jane M. "Introduction." In *Plato's Meno in Focus*, edited by J. M. Day, 1–34. New York: Routledge, 1994.

Dayton, Donald. "Evangelicalism without Fundamentalism." *Christian Century* (July 19–26, 1978): 710–13. Source: http://www.religion-online.org/showarticle.asp?title=1786.

———. "The Pietist Theological Critique of Biblical Inerrancy." In *Evangelicals and Scripture: Tradition, Authority and Hermeneutics*, edited by V. Bacote, L. C. Miguélez, and D. L. Okholm, 76–89. Downers Grove, IL: InterVarsity Press, 2004.

Dear, Peter. "Mersennes' Suggestion: Cartesian Meditation and the Mathematical Model of Knowledge in the Seventeenth Century." In *Descartes and His Contemporaries: Meditation, Objections, and Replies*, edited by R. Ariew and M. Grene, 44–62. Chicago: University of Chicago Press, 1995.

Dehn, Max. "Mathematics, 600 B.C.–600 A.D." In *Sherlock Holmes in Babylon and Other Tales of Mathematical History*, edited by Marlow Anderson, Victor Katz and Robin Wilson, 27–40. Washington, D. C.: The Mathematical Association of America, 2004.

Del Prete, Antonella. "Against Descartes: Marten Schoock's *De Scepticismo*." In *The Return of Scepticism from Hobbes and Descartes to Bayle*, ed. G. Paganini, 135–48. Boston: Kluwer Academic Publishers, 2003.

Demarco, C. Wesley. "Plato's Ghost: Consequences of Aristotelian Dialectic." In *The Crossroads of Norm and Nature: Essays on Aristotle's Ethics and Metaphysics*, edited by May Sim, 151–74. Lanham, MD: Rowan and Littlefield Publishers, Inc., 1995.

Derrida, Jacques. *Edmund Husserl's Origin of Geometry: An Introduction*. Translated by J. P. Leavey, Jr. Lincoln: University of Nebraska Press, 1989.

Descartes, Rene. *Discourse on Method and Related Writings*. Translated by D. Clarke. New York: Penguin Books, 1999.

———. *Geometry*. New York: Dover Publications, Inc. 1954.

———. *Meditations and Other Metaphysical Writings*. Translated by D. Clarke. New York: Penguin Books, 1998.

———. *Philosophical Writings of Descartes*. Translated by J. Cottingham, R. Stoothoff, and D. Murdoch. New York: Cambridge University Press, 1984.

Deslauriers, Marguerite. "Plato and Aristotle on Division and Definition." *Ancient Philosophy* 10 (1990): 203–19.

Dooley, Brendan. *The Social History of Skepticism: Experience and Doubt in Early Modern Culture*. Baltimore: The Johns Hopkins University Press, 1999.

Dunbar, David G. "The Biblical Canon." In *Hermeneutics, Authority and Canon*, edited by D. A. Carson and J. D. Woodbridge, 299–360. Grand Rapids: Zondervan, 1986.

Ehrman, Bart. *Misquoting Jesus: The Story Behind Who Changed the Bible and Why*. New York: HarperCollins, 2005.

———. *God's Problem: How the Bible Fails to Answer Our Most Important Question—Why We Suffer*. New York: HarperCollins, 2008.

Einarson, Benedict. "On Certain Mathematical Terms in Aristotle's Logic." *American Journal of Philology* 57 (1936): 33–44, 151–72.

Elden, Stuart. "The Place of Geometry: Heidegger's Mathematical Excursus on Aristotle." *Heythrop Journal* 42 (2001): 311–28.

Euclid, *The Thirteen Books of the Elements*. Volume 1. Translated by T. L. Heath. New York: Dover Publications, Inc., 1956.

Evangeliou, Christos. *Aristotle's Categories and Porphyry*. 2nd edition. New York: E. J. Brill, 1996.

Evans, Gillian R. "Boethian and Euclidean Axiomatic Method in the Theology of the Later Twelfth Century." *Archives Internationale d'Histoire des Sciences* 30 (1980): 36–52.

———. "*More Geometrico*: The Place of the Axiomatic Method in the Twelfth Century Commentaries on Boethius' Opuscula Sacra." *Archives Internationale d'Histoire des Sciences* 27 (101) (1977): 207–21.

———. *Old Arts and New Theology: The Beginnings of Theology as an Academic Discipline*. New York: Oxford University Press, 1980.

———. "The 'Sub-Euclidean' Geometry of the Earlier Middle Ages, up to the Mid-Twelfth Century." *Archive for History of Exact Sciences* 16 (1976–1977): 105–18.

Evans, J. D. G. *Aristotle's Concept of Dialectic*. New York: Cambridge University Press, 1977.

Eves, Howard. *An Introduction to the History of Mathematics*. 6th ed. New York: Saunders College Publishing, 1992.

———. *Great Moments in Mathematics Before 1650*. Washington, D. C.: Mathematical Association of America, 1982.

Fauvel, J. and J. Gray, editors. *The History of Mathematics: A Reader*. London and Milton Keynes: Macmillan and The Open University, 1987.

Ferejohn, Michael. *The Origins of Aristotelian Science*. New Haven, CT: Yale University Press, 1980.

Festugiere, A. J. *La revelation d'Hermes Trismégiste*. Paris, 1949.

Fideler, D., editor. *The Pythagorean Sourcebook and Library*. Translated by K. S. Guthrie. Grand Rapids: Phanes Press, 1988.

Filosofiska Institutionen. "Skepticism in Medieval and Renaissance Thought," 6 May 2005, Uppsala Universitet. Source: http://info.uu.se/konferens.nsf/id/2005-05 -06.skepticism.in.html. Accessed: June 10, 2008.

Fine, Gail. "Forms as Causes : Plato and Aristotle." In *Mathematik und Metaphysik bei Aristoteles: Akten des X. Symposium Aristoleicum Sigriswil, 6.–12. September 1984*, edited by A. Graeser, 69–112. Bern und Stuttgart: Verlag Paul Haupt, 1987.

———. "Inquiry in the Meno." In *The Cambridge Companion to Plato*, edited by R. Kraut, 200–226. New York: Cambridge University Press, 1992.

———. "Knowledge and True Belief in the *Meno*." In *Oxford Studies in Ancient Philosophy Volume XXVII*, edited by D. Sedley, 41–81. New York: Oxford University Press, 2004.

Fischer, Max W. *The Math of Ancient History: Integrating Mathematical Problem Solving Strategies With History*. Teacher's Choice Press, 2002.

Floridi, Luciano. "Mathematical Scepticism: A Sketch with Historian in Mind." In *The Skeptical Tradition around 1800: Skepticism in Philosophy, Science, & Society*, edited by Johan Van der Zande and R. H. Popkin, 41–60. Kluwer Academic Publishers. 1997, http://www.wolfson.ox.ac.uk/~floridi/pdf/msshf.pdf.

———. "Mathematical Scepticism: the Cartesian Approach." http://www.wolfson.ox.ac .uk/~floridi/ms.htm.

———. "Mathematical Scepticism: The Debate Between Hobbes and Wallis." In *Skepticism in Renaissance and Post-Renaissance Thought: New Interpretations*, edited by J. R. Maia Neto and R. H. Popkin, 143–84. Amherst, NY: Humanity Books, 2004.

Forder, Henry George. *The Foundations of Euclidean Geometry*. New York: Dover Publications Inc., 1958.

Fowler, D. H. *The Mathematics of Plato's Academy: A New Reconstruction*. New York: Oxford University Press, 1987.

Fowler, James W. *Stages of Faith: The Psychology of Human Development and the Quest for Meaning*. New York: HarperCollins, 1985.

Frame, John. *The Doctrine of the Knowledge of God*. Phillipsburg, NJ: Presbyterian and Reformed Publishing Company, 1989.

Franciosi, Filippo. "Some Remarks on the Controversy between Prof. Knorr and Prof. Szabo." In *Theory, Change, Ancient Axiomatics and Galileo's Methodology: Proceedings of the 1978 Pisa Conference on the History and Philosophy of Science Volume 1*, edited by Jaakko Hintikka, David Gruender, and Evandro Agazzi, 181–92. Boston: D. Reidel Publishing Company, 1981.

Frank, Dan. *Word and the World: Theology After the Sociology of Knowledge*. New York: Continuum International Publishing, 2007.

Fraser, Kyle. "Demonstrative Science and the Science of Being *qua* Being." In *Oxford Studies in Ancient Philosophy Volume XXII*, edited by D. Sedley, 43–82. New York: Oxford University Press, 2002.

Furley, David. "Aristotle the philosopher of nature." In *From Aristotle to Augustine*, Routledge History of Philosophy v. 2, edited by D. Furley, 9–39. London: Routledge, 1997.

Gadamer, Hans-Georg. *Dialogue and Dialectic: Eight Hermeneutical Studies on Plato*. Translated by P. Christopher Smith. New Haven: Yale University Press, 1980.

Gaukroger, Stephen. *Descartes' System of Natural Philosophy*. New York: Cambridge University Press, 2002.

Gaukroger, Stephen, editor. *Descartes' Philosophy, Mathematics and Physics*. Lanham: Rowman & Littlefield Publishing, Inc., 1980.

Gilbert, Neal W. *Renaissance Concepts of Method*. New York: Columbia University Press, 1963.

Gillespie, George. *A Treatise of Miscellany of Questions: Wherein Many Questions and Cases of Conscience Are Discussed and Resolved, For the Satisfaction of Those Who Want Nothing More, Then to Search for and Finde Out Precious Truths, in the Controversies of These Times*. Edinburgh, 1649.

Gilson, Etienne. *Being and Some Philosophers*. 2nd ed. Toronto: Pontifical Institute of Medieval Studies, 1952.

———. *History of Christian Philosophy in the Middle Ages*. New York: Random House, 1955.

———. *The Spirit of Mediaeval Philosophy*. Translated by A.H.C. Downes. University of Notre Dame Press, 1991.

Glima, Gyula. "De Bono: Boethius's De Hebdomadibus." http://www.fordham.edu/gsas/phil/klima/lectures.htm#Contents.

Gomez-Lobo, A. "Aristotle's First Philosophy and the Principles of Particular Disciplines." *Zeitschrift für philosophische Forschung* 32 (1978): 183–94.

———. "Aristotle's Hypothesis and the Euclidean Postulate.s" *The Review of Metaphysics* 30 (1976–1977): 430–39.

Gonzalez, Francisco J. *Dialectic and Dialogue: Plato's Practice of Philosophical Inquiry*. Evanston, IL: Northwestern University Press, 1998.

Gooch, Paul. "Irony and Insight in Plato's *Meno*." *Laval théologique et philosophique* 43 (1987): 189–204.

Gordon, T. David. "The Insufficiency of Scripture." Source: http://www.covopc.org/Papers/Insufficiency_of_Scripture.html.

Gotthelf, A. "First Principles in Aristotle's Parts of Animals." In *Philosophical Issues in Aristotle's Biology*, edited by A. Gotthelf and J. G. Lennox, 167–98. New York: Cambridge University Press, 1987.

Gotthelf, A. and J. G. Lennox, editors. *Philosophical Issues in Aristotle's Biology*. New York: Cambridge University Press, 1987.

Gould, S. H. "The Origins of Euclid's Axioms." *The Mathematical Gazette* 46 (1962): 269–90.

Grabiner, Judith. "Descartes and Problem-Solving." *Mathematics Magazine* 68 (1995): 81–97.

———. "Newton, Maclaurin, and the Authority of Mathematics." *American Mathematical Monthly* 111 (December 2004): 841–52.

Graham, D. W. *Aristotle's Two Systems*. New York: Oxford University Press, 1987.

Graham, Kenneth J. E. *The Performance of Conviction: Plainness and Rhetoric in the Early English Renaissance*. Ithaca, NY: Cornell University Press, 1994.

Greer, Rowan A. *Anglican Approaches to Scripture: From the Reformation to the Present.* New York: The Crossroad Publishing Company, 2006.

Gregory, Tullio. " 'Libertinisme Erudit' in Seventeenth Century France and Italy: The Critique of Ethics and Religion." *British Journal for the History of Philosophy* 6 (1998): 323–49.

Grenz, Stanley J. and John R. Franke, *Beyond Foundationalism: Shaping Theology in a Postmodern Context.* Louisville, KY: Westminster John Knox, 2001.

Grosholz, Emily. "Descartes' *Geometry* and the Classical Tradition." in *Revolution and Continuity: Essays in the History and Philosophy of Early Modern Science*, edited by Peter Barker and Roger Ariew, 183–96. Washington, D. C.: Catholic University of America Press, 1991.

Guggenheimer, Heinrich. "The Axioms of Betweenness in Euclid." *Dialectica* 31 (1977): 187–92.

Guillory, John. *Poetic Authority: Spenser, Milton, and Literary History.* New York: Columbia University Press, 1983.

Gulley, N. "Greek Geometrical Analysis." *Phronesis* 3 (1958): 1–14.

Gundry, Robert. "Post-Mortem: Death by Hardening of the Categories." *Books and Culture* (September/October 2006). Source: http://www.christianitytoday.com/bc/2006/005/3.8.html.

Guthrie, W. K. C. *History of Greek Philosophy Volume 1: The Earlier Presocratics and the Pythagoreans.* New York: Cambridge University Press, 1962.

———. "Pythagoras and Pythagoreanism." In *The Encyclopedia of Philosophy Volume 7*, edited by P. Edwards, 37–39. New York: Macmillan Publishing Co., Inc. and Free Press, 1967.

Hadot, Pierre. *Philosophy as a Way of Life: Spiritual Exercises from Socrates to Foucault*, edited by A. I. Davidson. Malder, MA: Blackwell, 1995.

———. *What is Ancient Philosophy?* Translated by Michael Chase. Cambridge, MA: Harvard University Press, 2002.

Hall, Douglas C. *The Trinity: An Analysis of St. Thomas Aquinas' Expositio of the De Trintate of Boethius.* New York: Brill, 1992.

Halper, E. "Some Problems in Aristotle's Mathematical Ontology." In *Proceedings of the Boston Area Colloquium on Ancient Philosophy Volume V 1989*, edited by J. J. Cleary and D. C. Shartin, 247–76. Lanham, MD: University Press of America, 1991.

Harari, Orna. *Knowledge and Demonstration: Aristotle's Posterior Analytics.* The New Synthese Historical Library 56. Boston: Kluwer Academic Publishers, 2004.

———. "Response to Wians." *Bryn Mawr Classical Review* (2005), http://ccat.sas.upenn.edu/bmcr/2005/2005-10-03.html.

Hartshorne, Robin. *Geometry: Euclid and Beyond.* New York: Springer, 2000.

Heath, Thomas L. *A History of Greek Mathematics Volume 1: From Thales to Euclid.* Clarendon Press, 1921; repr. New York: Dover Publications, Inc., 1981.

———. *A Manual of Greek Mathematics.* Oxford University Press, 1931; repr. New York: Dover Publications, Inc., 1963.

———. *Mathematics in Aristotle.* Sterling, VA: Thoemmes Press, 1998.

Heidel, W. A. "The Pythagoreans and Greek Mathematics." In *Studies in Presocratic Philosophy Volume I: The Beginnings of Philosophy*, edited by D. J. Furley and R. E. Allen, 330–81. New York: Humanities Press, 1970.

Heinaman, Robert. "Plato: Metaphysics and Epistemology." In *Routledge History of Philosophy Vol. I: From the Beginning to Plato*, edited by C. C. W. Taylor, 356–93. New York: Routledge, 1997.

Heirich, Max. "Change of Heart: A Test of Some Widely Held Theories About Religious Conversion." *The American Journal of Sociology* 83 (1977): 653–80.

Hersh, Ruben, editor. *18 Unconventional Essays on the Nature of Mathematics*. New York: Springer Science and Business Media, Inc., 2006.

Hilbert, David. *Foundations of Geometry*. 2nd edition. Translated by L. Unger. La Salle, IL: Open Court Publishing Company, 1971.

Hintikka, Jaakko. "Aristotelian Axiomatics and Geometrical Axiomatics." In *Theory, Change, Ancient Axiomatics and Galileo's Methodology: Proceedings of the 1978 Pisa Conference on the History and Philosophy of Science Volume 1*, edited by Jaakko Hintikka, David Gruender, and Evandro Agazzi, 133–44. Boston: D. Reidel Publishing Company, 1981.

———. "Commentary on Smith." In Aristotle: Critical Assessments, Volume 1, edited by L. P. Gerson, 20–28. New York: Routledge, 1999.

———. "On the Development of Aristotle's Ideas of Scientific Method and the Structure of Science." In *Aristotle's Philosophical Development: Problems and Prospects*, edited by William Wians, 83–104. Lanham, MD: Rowman and Littlefield Publishers, Inc., 1996.

———. "On the Ingredients of an Aristotelian Science." *Reports from the Institute of Philosophy University of Helsinki* 3 (1971): 1–17.

Hintikka, Jaakko and Unto Remes, *The Method of Analysis: Its Geometrical Origin and Its General Significance*. Boston Studies in the Philosophy of Science 25. Boston: D. Reidel Publishing Company, 1974.

Hobson, Theo. *The Rhetorical Word: Protestant Theology and the Rhetoric of Authority*. Burlington, VT: Ashgate Publishing Company, 2002.

Hofstadter, Douglas. *I Am a Strange Loop*. New York: Basic Books, 2007.

Hood, Jr., Ralph W., Peter C. Hill, and W. Paul Williamson, *The Psychology of Religious Fundamentalism*. New York: The Guilford Press, 2005.

Huffman, Carl. "Pythagoras," *Stanford Encyclopedia of Philosophy*. Source: http://plato.stanford.edu/entries/pythagoras/.

———. "The Philolaic Method: The Pythagoreanism Behind the *Philebus*." In *Essays in Greek Philosophy VI: Before Plato*, edited by A. Preus, 67–86. Albany: State University of New York Press, 2001.

———. "The Pythagorean Tradition." In *The Cambridge Companion to Early Greek Philosophy*, edited by A. A. Long, 66–87. New York: Cambridge University Press, 1999.

Husserl, Edmund. "On the Logic of Signs (Semiotic)." in *Early Writings in the Philosophy of Logic and Mathematics*. Translated by D. Willard. Boston: Kluwer Academic Publishers, 1994.

———. "Origins of Geometry" in *Edmund Husserl's Origin of Geometry: An Introduction* by Jacques Derrida, translated by J. P. Leavey, Jr, 155–80. Lincoln: University of Nebraska Press, 1989.

———. "Psychological Studies for Elementary Logic." In *Husserl: Shorter Works*, edited by P. McCormick and F. Elliston, 120–42. Notre Dame, IN: University of Notre Dame Press and Harvester Press, 1981.

———. "The Vienna Lecture." In *The Crisis of European Sciences and Transcendental Phenomenology: An Introduction to Phenomenological Philosophy*, translated by D. Carr, 269–300. Evanston, IL: Northwestern University Press, 1970.

Ivor, Thomas, editor. *Greek Mathematical Works: From Aristarchus to Pappus.* Loeb Classical Library. Cambridge, MA: Harvard University Press, 1968.

———. *Greek Mathematical Works: Thales to Euclid.* Loeb Classical Library. Cambridge, MA: Harvard University Press, 1990.

Janiak, Andrew. "Introduction." In *Newton: Philosophical Writings*, ed. A. Janiak, ix–xxxi. New York: Cambridge University Press, 2004.

Jardine, Nicholas. "Epistemology of the Sciences." In *The Cambridge History of Renaissance Philosophy*, edited by C. B. Scmitt, Q. Skinner, E. Kessler, and J. Kraye, 685–711. New York: Cambridge University Press, 1988.

Jesseph, Douglas. "Geometry, Theology, and Politics: Context and Consequences of the Hobbes-Wallis Dispute." Presented at the conference, *Wahrheit im Diskurs? Das agonale Moment in der öffentlichen Debatte* Potsdam, Germany, December 16–17, 2004. Source: http://www4.ncsu.edu/~dmjphi/Main/Papers/Geometry%20Theology %20Politics.pdf.

Jones, Charles V. "La influencia de Aristotoles en el fundamento de Los Elementos de Euclides." *Mathesis: filosofia e historia de las matematicas* 3 (1987): 375–87.

Joseph, George Gheverghese. *The Crest of the Peacock: Non-European Roots of Mathematics.* Princeton, NJ: Princeton University Press, 2000.

Kennedy, Rick. *Aristotelian and Cartesian Logic at Harvard: Morton's 'Logick System' and Brattle's 'Compendium of Logick.'* Boston: The Colonial Society of Massachusetts, 1995.

Kleiner, Israel. "Rigor and Proof in Mathematics: A Historical Perspective." *Mathematics Magazine* 64 (1991): 291–314.

Kline, Morris. *Mathematical Thought From Ancient to Modern Times.* (New York: Oxford University Press, 1972.

Knorr, Wilbur R. *The Ancient Traditions of Geometric Problems.* New York: Dover Publications, Inc., 1993.

———. "'Arithmêtikê stoicheiôsis': on Diophantus and Hero of Alexandria." *Historia Mathematica* 20 (2) (1993): 180–92.

———. "Infinity and Continuity: The Interaction of Mathematics and Philosophy in Antiquity." In *Infinity and Continuity in Ancient and Medieval Thought*, edited by N. Kretzmann, 87–145. Ithaca, NY: Cornell University Press, 1982.

———. "On the Early History of Axiomatics: A Reply to Some Criticisms." In *Change, Ancient Axiomatics and Galileo's Methodology: Proceedings of the 1978 Pisa Conference on the History and Philosophy of Science Volume 1.* Edited by Jaakko Hintikka, David Gruender, and Evandro Agazzi, 193–96. Boston: D. Reidel Publishing Company, 1981.

———. "On the Early History of Axiomatics: The Interaction of Mathematics and Philosophy in Greek Antiquity." In *Theory, Change, Ancient Axiomatics and Galileo's Methodology: Proceedings of the 1978 Pisa Conference on the History and Philosophy of Science Volume 1*, edited by Jaakko Hintikka, David Gruender, and Evandro Agazzi, 145–86. Boston: D. Reidel Publishing Company, 1981.

———. *The Evolution of the Euclidean Elements: A Study of the Theory of Incommensurable Magnitudes and Its Significance for Early Greek Geometry.* Boston: D. Reidel Publishing Company, 1975.

————. "What Euclid Meant: On the Use of Evidence in Studying Ancient Mathematics" In *Science and Philosophy in Classical Greece,* edited by A. C. Bowen and F. Rochberg-Halton, 119–63. New York: Garland Publishing Inc., 1991.

Koetsier, Teun. *Lakatos' Philosophy of Mathematics: A Historical Approach.* Studies in the History and Philosophy of Mathematics Volume 3. New York: North-Holland, 1991.

Kullman, Wolfgang. "Die Funktion der mathematischen Beispiele in Aristoteles' Analytica Posteriora." In *Aristotle on Science: The Posterior Analytics Proceedings of the Eighth Symposium Aristotelicum Held in Padua From September 7 to 15, 1978,* edited by E. Berti, 245–70. Padova: Editrice Antenore, 1981.

Kutrovátz, Gábor. "Philosophical Origins in Mathematics? Árpád Szabó Revisited." Paper given at the 18th Novermbertagung on the History of Mathematics, Frankfort, November, 2002, hps.elte.hu/~kutrovatz/frankfur.htm.

Lakatos, Imre. *Mathematics, Science and Epistemology.* Philosophical Papers Vol. 2. Edited by J. Worrall and G. Currie. New York: Cambridge University Press, 1978.

Langton, Stacy. "Review of Euclid: The Creation of Mathematics by Benno Artmann." In *Read This! The MAA Online Review Column,* http://www.maa.org/reviews/artmann.html.

Lasserre, Francois. *The Birth of Mathematics in the Age of Plato.* Larchmont, NJ: American Research Council, 1964.

Lear, Jonathan. *Aristotle: the Desire to Understand.* Cambridge: Cambridge University Press, 1988.

Lee, H. D. P. "Geometrical Method and Aristotle's Account of First Principles." *Classical Quarterly* 29 (1935): 113–23.

Leibniz, G. W. *Philosophical Essays,* edited by R. Ariew and D. Garber. Indianapolis, IN: Hackett Publishing Company, Inc., 1989.

Lennon, Thomas M. "Jansenism and the *Crise Pyrrohonienne,*" *Journal of the History of Ideas* 38 (2006): 299–313.

Lennox, J. G. "Divide and Explain: the *Posterior Analytics* in Practice." In *Philosophical Issues in Aristotle's Biology,* edited by A. Gotthelf and J. G. Lennox, 90–119. New York: Cambridge University Press, 1987.

Leslie, John Beck. *The Method of Descartes: A Study of the Regulae.* New York: Oxford University Press, 1952.

Leszl, Walter. "Aristotle's Logical Works and His Conception of Logic." *Topoi* 23 (2004): 71–100.

————. "Mathematics, Axiomatization and the Hypothesis." In *Aristotle on Science: The Posterior Analytics Proceedings of the Eighth Symposium Aristotelicum Held in Padua From September 7 to 15, 1978,* edited by E. Berti, 271–328. Padova: Editrice Antenore, 1981.

Lloyd, G. E. R. *Early Science: Thales to Aristotle.* New York: W. W. Norton & Company, 1970.

————. "The Theories and Practices of Demonstration in Aristotle." In *Proceedings of the Boston Area Colloquium on Ancient Philosophy Volume VI 1990,* edited by J. J. Cleary and D. C. Shartin, 371–401. Lanham, MD: University Press of America, 1992.

Lo Bello, Anthony. *Gerard of Cremona's Translation of the Commentary of al-Nayrizi on Book I of Euclid's Elements of Geometry with an Introductory Account of the Twenty-Two Early Extant Arabic Manuscripts of the Elements.* Ancient Mediterranean and Medieval Texts and Contexts; Medieval Philosophy, Mathematics, and Science 2. Boston: Brill, 2003.

————. *The Commentary of al-Nayrizi on Book I of Euclid's Elements of Geometry with an Introduction on the Transmission of Euclid's Elements in the Middle Ages*. Ancient Mediterranean and Medieval Texts and Contexts; Medieval Philosophy, Mathematics, and Science 1. Boston: Brill, 2003.

————. *The Commentary of Albertus Magnus on Book I of Euclid's Elements of Geometry*. Ancient Mediterranean and Medieval Texts and Contexts; Medieval Philosophy, Mathematics, and Science 3. Boston: Brill, 2003.

Lonergan, Bernard. *Method in Theology*. Toronto: University of Toronto Press, 1971.

Loomis, David E. "Euclid: Rhetoric in Mathematics." *Philosophia Mathematica* 5 (2) (1990): 56–72.

Losee, John. *A Historical Introduction to the Philosophy of Science*. 3rd ed. New York: Oxford University Press. 1993.

Lowry, J. M. P. *The Logical Principles of Proclus' Stoicheiosis theologike' as Systematic Ground of the Cosmos*. Amsterdam: Rodopi, 1980.

Lucas, J. R. *The Conceptual Roots of Mathematics: An Essay on the Philosophy of Mathematics*. New York: Routledge, 2000.

Lukacs, Ladislaus and Giuseppe Cosentino. *Church, Culture and Curriculum: Theology and Mathematics in the Jesuit* Ratio Studiorum. Translated and edited by F. A. Homann. Philadelphia: Saint Joseph's University Press, 1999.

Luzzatto, Steffano. "Is Philosophy Detrimental to Mathematics Education?" *Philosophia Mathematica* 6 (2) (1991): 65–72.

MacDonald, Scott. "Augustine's Christian-Platonist Account of Goodness." *The New Scholasticism* 63 (1989): 485–509.

————. "Boethius's Claim that All Substances Are Good." *Archiv für Geschichte der Philosophie* 70 (1988): 245–79.

————. "Gilbert Poitiers's Metaphysics of Goodness." In *Die Metaphysik und das Gute: Aufsatze zu ihrem Verhaltnis in Antike und Mittelalter: Jan A. Aertsen zu Ehren*. Recherches de Theologie et Philosophie medievals 2, edited by W. Goris, 57–77. Leuven: Peeters, 1999.

————. "The Metaphysics of Goodness and the Doctrine of Transcendentals." In *Being and Goodness: The Concept of the Good in Metaphysics and Philosophical Theology*, edited by Scott MacDonald, 31–55. Ithaca, NY: Cornell, 1991.

————. "The Relation between Being and Goodness." In *Being and Goodness: The Concept of the Good in Metaphysics and Philosophical Theology*, edited by Scott MacDonald, 1–28. Ithaca, NY: Cornell University Press, 1991.

MacDonald, Scott, editor. *Being and Goodness: The Concept of the Good in Metaphysics and Philosophical Theology*. Ithaca, NY: Cornell University Press, 1991.

Magnani, Lorenze. *Philosophy and Geometry: Theoretical and Historical Issues*. Boston: Kluwer Academic Publishers, 2001.

Mahoney, M. "Another Look at Greek Geometrical Analysis." *Archive for History of Exact Sciences* 5 (1968): 318–48.

Mahoney, Michael. "The Mathematical Realm of Nature." In *The Cambridge History of Seventeenth-Century Philosophy*, edited by. D.Garber and M. Ayers, 702–58. New York: Cambridge University Press, 1998.

Mancosu, Paolo. "Aristotelian Logic and Euclidean Mathematics: Seventeenth century developments of the 'Quaestio de Certitudine Mathematicarum.'" *Studies in History and Philosophy of Science* 23 (1992): 241–65.

Marchi, Peggy. "The Method of Analysis in Mathematics." In *Scientific Discovery, Logic and Rationality: Proceedings of the 1978 Guy L. Leonard Memorial Conference in Philosophy, University of Nevada, Reno*, edited by T. Nickles, 159–72. Boston: D. Reidel Publishing Company, 1980.

Marenbon, John. *Boethius*. New York: Oxford University Press, 2003.

Marshall, John. *A Short History of Greek Philosophy*. London: Percival and Co., 1891.

Martin, John N. "Proclus and the Neoplatonic Syllogistic." *Journal of Philosophical Logic* 30 (2001): 187–240.

Mascord, Keith A. *Alvin Plantinga and Christian Apologetics*. Paternoster, 2006.

Masi, Michael. *Boethian Number Theory: A Translation of the De Institutione Arithmetica*. Amsterdam: Rodopi, 1983.

Masi, Michael, editor, *Boethius and the Liberal Arts: A Collection of Essays*. Peter Lang Publishing Inc., 1982.

Maziarz, Edward A. and Thomas Greenwood. *Greek Mathematical Philosophy: The Development of Mathematics and Philosophy*. New York: Barnes and Nobles Books, 1968.

McInerny, Ralph. *Boethius and Aquinas*. Washington, D.C.: The Catholic University of America Press, 1990.

———. "Saint Thomas on *De hebdomadibus*." In *Being and Goodness: The Concept of the Good in Metaphysics and Philosophical Theology*, edited by Scott MacDonald, 74–97. Ithaca, NY: Cornell University Press, 1991.

McKirahan, Richard. "Aristotle's metaphysics from the Perspective of the Posterior Analytics." In *Proceedings of the Boston Area Colloquium on Ancient Philosophy Volume XI 1995*, edited by J. J. Cleary and W. Wians, 275–97. Lanham, MD: University Press of America, 1997.

———. *Principles and Proofs: Aristotle's Theory of Demonstrative Science*. Princeton: Princeton University Press, 1992.

McGowan, A. T. B. *The Divine Spiration of Scripture: Challenging Evangelical Perspectives*. Nottingham: Apollos, 2007.

Medvedev, F. A. "On the Role of Axiomatic Method in the Development of Ancient Mathematics." In *Theory, Change, Ancient Axiomatics and Galileo's Methodology: Proceedings of the 1978 Pisa Conference on the History and Philosophy of Science Volume 1*, edited by Jaakko Hintikka, David Gruender, and Evandro Agazzi, 223–25. Boston: D. Reidel Publishing Company, 1981.

Mejer, Jørgen. "Eudemus and the History of Science." In *Eudemus of Rhodes*. Rutgers University Studies in Classical Humanities XI, edited by. I. Bodnar and W. W. Fortenbaugh, 243–61. New Brunswick: Transaction Publishers, 2002.

Mendell, Henry. "Making Sense of Aristotelian Demonstration." In *Oxford Studies in Ancient Philosophy Volume XVI*, edited by C. C. W. Taylor, 161–265. New York: Oxford University Press, 1998.

Metzger, Bruce M. *The Canon of the New Testament: Its Origin, Development and Significance*. New York: Oxford University Press, 1987.

Mittelstrass, Jürgen. "The Philosopher's Conception of 'Mathesis Universalis' from Descartes to Leibniz." *Annals of Science* 36 (1979): 593–610.

Modrak, Deborah K. "Aristotle on the Difference between Mathematics and Physics and First Philosophy." *Apeiron* 22 (1989): 121–39.

————. "Aristotle's Epistemology: One or Many Theories?" In *Aristotle's Philosophical Development: Problems and Prospects,* edited by W. Wians, 151–70. Lanham, MD: Rowman and Littlefield Publishers, Inc., 1996.

De Montaigne, Michel. "Apology for Raymond Sebond." In *The Complete Works of Montaigne.* Translated by D. M. Frame. Stanford, CA: Stanford University Press, 1958.

Moravcsik, Julius. "Plato on Numbers and Mathematics." In *Ancient and Medieval Traditions in the Exact Sciences : Essays in Memory of Wilbur Knorr,* edited by P. Suppes, J. M. Moravcsik, and H. Mendell, 177–95. Stanford, CA: Center for the Study of Language and Information, 2001.

Moreland, J. P. *Universals.* Montreal: McGill-Queen's, 2001.

Most, Glenn W. "Philosophy and Religion." In *The Cambridge Companion to Greek and Roman Philosophy,* edited by D. Sedley, 300–322. New York: Cambridge University Press, 2003.

Mueller, Ian. "Aristotle and the Quadrature of the Circle." In *Infinity and Continuity in Ancient and Medieval Thought,* edited by N. Kretzmann, 146–64. Ithaca, NY: Cornell University Press, 1982.

————. "Aristotle on Geometrical Objects." In *Articles on Aristotle: 3. Metaphysics,* edited by J. Barnes, M. Schofield, and R. Sorabji, 36–107. London: Gerald Duckworth & Company Limited, 1979.

————. "Euclid's Elements and the Axiomatic Method." *The British Journal for the Philosophy of Science* 20 (1969): 289–309.

————. "Greek Arithmetic, Geometry and Harmonics: Thales to Plato." In *Routledge History of Philosophy Vol. I: From the Beginning to Plato,* edited by C. C. W. Taylor, 271–322. New York: Routledge, 1997.

————. "Greek Mathematics and Greek Logic." In *Ancient Logic and Its Modern Interpretations: Proceedings of the Buffalo Symposium on Modernist Interpretations of Ancient Logic, 21 and 22 April, 1972,* edited by J. Corcoran, 35–70. Boston: D. Reidel Publishing Company, 1974.

————. "Mathematical Method and Philosophical Truth." In *The Cambridge Companion to Plato,* edited by R. Kraut, 170–99. New York: Cambridge University Press, 1992.

————. "Mathematics and the Divine in Plato." In *Mathematics and the Divine: A Historical Study,* edited by T. Koetsier and L. Bergmans, 99–122. New York: Elsevier, 2005.

————. "On the Notion of a Mathematical Starting Point in Plato, Aristotle, and Euclid." In *Science and Philosophy in Classical Greece,* edited by A. C. Bowen and F. Rochberg-Halton, 59–97. New York: Garland Publishing Inc., 1991.

————. *Philosophy of Mathematics and Deductive Structure in Euclid's Elements.* Cambridge, MA: The MIT Press, 1981.

————. "Platonism and the Study of Nature (*Phaedo* 95eff.)." In *Method in Ancient Philosophy,* edited by Jyl Gentzler, 67–89. New York: Oxford University Press, 1994.

————. "Remarks on Euclid's *Elements* 1,32 and the Parallel Postulate." *Science in Context* 16.3 (2003): 297–97.

————. "Review of *The Method of Analysis: Its Geometrical Origin and Its General Significance* by Jaakko Hintikka and Unto Remes." *Journal of Philosophy* 73 (1976): 158–62.

Mueller, Ian, editor. *PERI TWN MAQHMATWN.* Edmonton: Academic Printing and Publishing, 1991.

Muller, Richard A. "Inspired by God—Pure in All Ages': The Doctrine of Scripture in the Westminster Confession." In *Scripture and Worship: Biblical Interpretation and the Directory for Worship*, edited by R. A. Muller and R. S. Ward, 31–58. Phillipsburg, NJ: Presbyterian and Reformed Publishing, 2007.

———. *Post-Reformation Reformed Dogmatics: The Rise and Development of Reformed Orthodoxy, ca. 1520 to ca. 1725. Volume Two: Holy Scripture, The Cognitive Foundation of Theology*. 2nd ed. Grand Rapids: Baker, 2003.

Muller, R. A. and R. S. Ward, editors. *Scripture and Worship: Biblical Interpretation and the Directory for Worship*. Phillipsburg, NJ: Presbyterian and Reformed Publishing, 2007.

Nagel, Ernest and James R. Newman. *Gödel's Proof*. Revised edition. New York: New York University Press, 2001.

Netz, Riviel. "The Pythagoreans." In *Mathematics and the Divine: A Historical Study*, edited by T. Koetsier and L. Bergmans, 77–98. New York: Elsevier, 2005.

———. *The Shaping of Deduction in Greek Mathematics: A Study in Cognitive History*. New York: Cambridge University Press, 2003.

———. "Why Did Greek Mathematicians *Publish* Their Analysis?" In *Ancient and Medieval Traditions in the Exact Sciences: Essays in Memory of Wilbur Knorr*, edited by P. Suppes, J..M. Moravcsik, and H. Mendell, 139–57. Stanford, CA: Center for the Study of Language and Information, 2001.

Neugebauer, O. *The Exact Sciences in Antiquity*. 2nd ed. Brown University, 1957; repr. New York: Dover Publications, Inc., 1969.

Newton, Isaac. *Principia*. Philadelphia: Running Press Book Publishers, 2002.

Nicomachus of Gerasa, *Introduction to Arithmetic*. Translated by M L. D'Ooge. Annapolis: The St. John's University Press, 1960.

Nijenhuis, J. "'Ens' Described as "Being or Existent." *American Catholic Philosophical Quarterly* 68 (1994): 1–14.

———. "Existence vs. Being: An All-Important Matter of Terminology." *American Catholic Philosophical Quarterly* 69 (1995): 89–95

Nikulin, Dmitri. *Matter, Imagination and Geometry: Ontology, Natural Philosophy and Mathematics in Plotinus, Proclus, and Descartes*. Ashgate Publishing, 2002.

———. "Physica More Geometrico Demonstrata: Natural Philosophy in Proclus and Aristotle." In *Proceedings of the Boston Area Colloquium in Ancient Philosophy Volume XVIII, 2002*, edited by J. J. Cleary and G. M. Gurtler, 183–209. Boston: Brill, 2003.

O'Connor J. J. and E. F. Robertson, "Squaring the Circle." http://www-history.mcs.st -andrews.ac.uk/HistTopics/Squaring_the_circle.html.

Olivo, Gilles. "L'évidence en règle: Descartes, Husserl et la question de la mathesis universalis." *Études Philosophiques* (1996): 189–221.

———. "La sagesse des principes: la *mathesis universalis* dans les *Principiae philosophiae* de Descartes." In *Lire Descartes aujourd'hui*, edited by Olivier Depré and Danielle Lories, 69–84. Louvain-Paris: Éditions Peters, 1997.

O'Meara, Dominic J. *Pythagoras Revived: Mathematics and Philosophy in Late Antiquity*. New York: Oxford University Press, 1991.

de Landázuri, Carlos Ortiz. "Mathesis universalis en Proclo de las aporias cosmologicas al universo euclideo." *Anuario Filosófico* 33 (2000): 229–57.

Otte M. and M. Panza, editors. *Analysis and Synthesis in Mathematics: History and Philosophy*. Springer-Verlag, 2001.

Owens, Joseph. *The Doctrine of Being in the Aristotelian* Metaphysics: *A Study in the Greek Background of Mediaeval Thought.* 3rd ed. Toronto: Pontifical Institute of Mediaeval Studies, 1978.

Panier R. and T. D. Sullivan, "Aquinas on 'Exists.'" *American Catholic Philosophical Quarterly* 67 (1993): 157–65.

———. "Being, Existence and the Future of Thomistic Studies: A Reply to Professor Nijenhuis" *American Catholic Philosophical Quarterly* 69 (1995): 83–88.

Pappas, Theoni. *The Joy of Mathematics: Discovering Mathematics All Around You.* San Carlos, CA: Wide World Publishing, 1989.

Parsons, Charles. *Mathematics in Philosophy: Selected Essays.* Ithaca, NY: Cornell University Press, 2005.

Parvu Alexandrina and Ilie Parvu. "The Postulate Problem in the Works of Aristotle, Euclid and Proclus." *Revue romaine de philosophie et logique* 24 (1980): 333–44.

Patch, H. *The Tradition of Boethius: A Study of his Importance in Medieval Culture.* New York: Oxford University Press, 1935.

Perl, Eric. 'Hierarchy and Participation in Dionysius the Areopagite and Greek Neoplatonism.' *American Catholic Philosophical Quarterly* 68 (1994): 15–30.

Perreiah, A. R. "Aristotle's Axiomatic Science: Peripatetic Notation or Pedagogical Plan?" *History and Philosophy of Logic* 14 (1) (1993): 87–99.

Pessin, Sarah. "Hebdomads: Boethius Meets the Neopythagoreans." *Journal of the History of Philosophy* 37 (1999): 29–48.

Philip, J. A. *Pythagoras and Early Pythagoreanism.* Toronto: University of Toronto Press, 1966.

———. "The Biographical Tradition-Pythagoras" *Transactions and Proceedings of the Philological Association* 90 (1959): 185–94.

Plato. *Protagoras and Meno.* Translated by W. K. C. Guthrie. New York: Penguin Putnam, Inc., 1956.

———. *Republic II, Books VI-X.* Loeb Classical Library. Translated by P. Shorey. Cambridge: MA: Harvard University Press, 1970.

———. *The Last Days of Socrates* (containing the *Phaedo*). Translated by H. Tredennick. New York: Viking Penguin, Inc., 1954.

———. *The Republic.* Translated by R. W. Sterling and W. C. Scott. New York: W. W. Norton & Company, Inc., 1985.

Pinnock, Clark. *The Scripture Principle: Reclaiming the Full Authority of the Bible.* 2nd edition. Grand Rapids: Baker Books, 2006.

Politis, Vasilis. "Aristotle on *Aporia* and Searching in Metaphysics." In *Proceedings of the Boston Area Colloquium on Ancient Philosophy Volume XVIII 2002,* edited by J. J. Cleary and G. M. Gurtler, 145–74. Lanham, MD: University Press of America, 2003.

Popkin, Richard H. *The History of Scepticism from Erasmus to Spinoza.* Berkeley and Los Angeles: University of California Press, 1979.

Popkin, R. H. and J. R. Maia Neto, editors. *Skepticism: An Anthology.* Amherst, NY: Prometheus Books, 2007.

Popovich, M. V. "Concerning the Ancient Greek Ideal of Theoretical Thought" In *Theory, Change, Ancient Axiomatics and Galileo's Methodology: Proceedings of the 1978 Pisa Conference on the History and Philosophy of Science Volume 1,* edited by Jaakko Hintikka, David Gruender, and Evandro Agazzi, 113–24. Boston: D. Reidel Publishing Company, 1981.

Preus, Robert. *The Inspiration of Scripture: A Study of the Theology of the 17th Century Lutheran Dogmaticians.* 2nd ed. Oliver and Boyd: Edinburgh, 1957.

Proclus. *A Commentary on the First Book of Euclid's Elements.* Translated by G. R. Morrow. Princeton: Princeton University Press, 1992.

———. *The Elements of Theology.* 2nd ed. Translated by E. R. Dodds. New York: Oxford University Press, 1963.

Pycior, Helena M. *Symbols, Impossible Numbers and Geometric Entanglements: British Algebra through the Commentaries on Newton's Universal Arithmetick.* New York: Cambridge University Press, 1997.

Quint, David. *Origin and Originality in Renaissance Literature: Versions of the Source.* New Haven: Yale University Press, 1983.

Raven, J. E. *Pythagoreans and Eleatics: An Account of the Interaction between the Two Opposed Schools during the Fifth and Early Fourth Centuries B.C.* Amsterdam: Adolf M. Hakkert, 1966.

Reale, Giovanni. "Fundamentos, Estructura Dinamico-Relacional Y Caracteres Esenciales De La Metafisica de Plotino." *Anuario Filosofico*, 22 (2000): 163–91.

Reed, David. *Figures of Thought: Mathematics and Mathematical Texts.* New York: Routledge, 1995.

Remmert, V.R. "Galileo, God and Mathematics." In *Mathematics and the Divine: A Historical Study*, edited by T. Koetsier and L. Bergmans, 347–60. Elsevier, 2005.

Robinson, R. "Analysis in Greek Geometry." *Mind* 45 (1936): 464–73.

Rogers, G. A. J. "The Basis of Belief: Philosophy, Science and Religion in Seventeenth-Century England." *History of European Ideas* 6 (1985): 19–39

Rogers, Jack. *Scripture in the Westminster Confessions: A Problem of Historical Interpretation for American Presbyterianism.* Grand Rapids: Eerdmans, 1967.

Rorty, Amelie Oksenberg, editor. *Essays on Descartes' Meditations.* University of California Press, 1986.

Ross, David. *Aristotle.* 6th ed. New York: Routledge, 1995.

Rota, Gian-Carlo. "Complicating Mathematics." In *Discrete Thoughts: Essays on Mathematics, Science and Philosophy*, edited by P. Renz, 153–55. Boston: Birkhäuser, 1992.

Rowe, Christopher. "Explanation in *Phaedo* 99C6–102A8." In *Oxford Studies in Ancient Philosophy Volume XI*, edited by C. C. W. Taylor, 49–69. New York: Oxford University Press, 1993.

Russell, Paul. "Skepticism and Natural Religion in Hume's Treatise." *Journal of the History of Ideas* 49 (1988): 247–65

Russo, Lucio. "The Definitions of Fundamental Geometric Entities Contained in Book 1 of Euclid's Element." *Archive for History of Exact Sciences* 52 (1998): 195–219.

Rutt, Norman E. "The Sources of Euclid." *National Mathematics Magazine* 11 (1937): 374–81.

de Santillana, George and Walter Pitts. "Philolaos in Limbo, or: What Ever Happened to Pythagoreans?" *Isis* 42 (1951): 112–20.

Saracino, M. "Hobbes, Shakespeare and the Temptation to Skepticism," *Hobbes Studies* 9 (1996): 36–50

Sasaki, Chikara. *Descartes's Mathematical Thought.* Boston Studies in the Philosophy of Science 237. *Boston: Kluwer Academic Publishers,* 2003.

Schofield, Malcolm. "The Presocratics." In *The Cambridge Companion to Greek and Roman Philosophy*, edited by D. Sedley, 42–72. New York: Cambridge University Press, 2003.

Scholder, Klaus. *The Birth of Modern Critical Theology: Origins and Problems of Biblical Criticism in the Seventeenth Century*. Translated by J. Bowden. Philadelphia: Trinity Press International, 1990.

Schreiber, Scott G. *Aristotle on False Reasoning: Language and the World in the* Sophistical Refutations. Albany: State University of New York Press, 2003.

Schrimpf, Gangolf. *Die Axiomenschrift des Boethius (De hebdomadibus) als philosophisches Lehrbuch des Mittelalters*. Studien zur Problemgeschichte der antiken und mittelalterlichen Philosophie 2. New York: Köln, 1966.

Schuster, John A. "What Shall We Do with Cartesian Method? Reclaiming Descartes for the History of Science." In *Essays on the Philosophy and Science of Rene Descartes*, edited by S. Voss, 195–223. New York: Oxford University Press, 1993.

Scott, G. A., editor. *Does Socrates Have a Method? Rethinking the Elenchus in Plato's Dialogues and Beyond*. University Park, PA: Pennsylvania State University Press, 2002.

Secada, Jorge. *Cartesian Metaphysics: The Scholastic Origins of Modern Philosophy*. New York: Cambridge University Press, 2000.

Seidenberg, A. "Did Euclid's Elements, Book 1, Develop Geometry Axiomatically?" *Archive for History of Exact Sciences* 14 (1974–1975): 263–95.

Serene, Eilene. "Demonstrative Science." In *The Cambridge History of Later Medieval Philosophy*, edited by N. Kretzmann, A. Kenny, and J. Pinborg, 496–517. New York: Cambridge University Press, 1982.

Shaw, Allen A. "A Pre-Euclidean Fragment of the *Elements*." *National Mathematics Magazine* 13 (1938): 76–82.

Shaw, Robert. "An Exposition of the Westminster Confession of Faith (1845)." http://www.reformed.org/documents/shaw/.

Shoenfield, Joseph R. *Mathematical Logic*. Reading, MA: Addison-Wesley Publishing Company, 1967.

Sim, May, editor. *The Crossroads of Norm and Nature: Essays on Aristotle's Ethics and Metaphysics*. Lanham, MD: Rowman & Littlefield, 1995.

Siorvanes, Lucas. *Proclus: Neo-Platonic Philosophy and Science*. New Haven, CT: Yale University Press, 1997.

Smith, Peter. *An Introduction to Gödel's Theorems*. (New York: Cambridge University Press, 2007).

Smith, Robin. "Aristotle as Proof Theorist." *Philosophia Naturalis* 27 (1984): 590–97.

———. "Aristotle on the Uses of Dialectic." *Synthese* 96 (1993): 335–58.

———. "Dialectic and Method in Aristotle." In *From Puzzles to Principles? Essays on Aristotle's Dialectic*, edited by May Sim, 39–56. Lexington Books, 1999.

———. "Dialectic and the Syllogism." *Ancient Philosophy* 14 (1994): 133–51.

———. "The Axiomatic Method and Aristotle's Logical Methodology." *Southwest Philosophical Studies* 8 (1982): 49–59.

———. "The Mathematical Origins of Aristotle's Syllogistic." *Archive for History of Exact Sciences* 19 (1978): 201–10.

———. "What Use is Aristotle's Organon?" In *Proceedings of the Boston Area Colloquium on Ancient Philosophy Volume IX 1993*, edited by J. J. Cleary and W. Wians, 261–85. Lanham, MD: University Press of America, 1995.

Snider, Alvin. *Origin and Authority in Seventeenth-Century England: Bacon, Milton, Butler.* Toronto: University of Toronto Press, 1994.

Southgate, B. C. "'A Philosophical Divinity': Thomas White and an Aspect of Mid-Seventeenth Century Science and Religion." *History of European Ideas* 8 (1987): 45–59.

Steel, Carlos. "'The Greatest Thing to Learn is the Good': On the Claims of Ethics and Metaphysics to Be the First Philosophy." In *Die Metaphysik und das Gute: Aufsatze zu ihrem Verhaltnis in Antike und Mittelalter: Jan A. Aertsen zu Ehren.* Recherches de Theologie et Philosophie medievals 2, edited by W. Goris, 1–25. Leuven: Peeters, 1999.

Stein, Howard. "'*Logos*, Logic and *Logistiké*' Some Philosophical Remarks on Nineteenth-Century Transformation of Mathematics." In *History and Philosophy of Modern Mathematics.* Minnesota Studies in the Philosophy of Science. Volume XI, edited by W. Aspray and P. Kitcher, 238–59. Minneapolis: University of Minnesota Press, 1988.

Stekeler-Weithofer, Pirmin. "On the Concept of Proof in Elementary Geometry." In *Proof and Knowledge in Mathematics*, edited by M. Detlefsen, 135–57. New York: Routledge, 1992.

Stenius, Erik. "Foundations of Mathematics: Ancient Greek and Modern" *Dialectica* 32 (1978): 255–90.

Stout, Jeffrey. *The Flight from Authority: Religion, Morality and the Quest for Autonomy.* Notre Dame, IN: University of Notre Dame Press, 1981.

Striker, Gisela. "Aristotle and the Uses of Logic." In *Method in Ancient Philosophy*, edited by Jyl Gentzler, 209–26. New York: Oxford University Press, 1994.

Strong, Edward W. *Procedures and Metaphysics: A Study in the Philosophy of Mathematical-Physical Science in the Sixteenth and Seventeenth Centuries.* Berkeley, CA: University of California Press, 1936.

Stump, Eleonore and Norman Kretzmann. "Being and Goodness." In *Being and Goodness: The Concept of the Good in Metaphysics and Philosophical Theology*, edited by Scott MacDonald, 93–128. Ithaca, NY: Cornell University Press, 1991.

Suppes, Patrick. "Limitations of the Axiomatic Method in Ancient Greek Mathematical Sciences." In *Theory, Change, Ancient Axiomatics and Galileo's Methodology: Proceedings of the 1978 Pisa Conference on the History and Philosophy of Science Volume 1*, edited by Jaakko Hintikka, David Gruender, and Evandro Agazzi, 197–214. Boston: D. Reidel Publishing Company, 1981.

Suppes, Patrick, Julius M. Moravcsik, and Henry Mendell, editors. *Ancient and Medieval Traditions in the Exact Sciences : Essays in Memory of Wilbur Knorr.* Center for the Study of Language and Information, 2001.

Sweeney, Eileen. "Literary Forms of Medieval Philosophy." *Stanford Encyclopedia of Philosophy* http://plato.stanford.edu/entries/medieval-literary/.

Sweeney, Leo. "Are Plotinus and Albertus Magnus Neoplatonists?" In *Graceful Reason: Essays in Ancient and Medieval Philosophy Present do Joseph Owens, CCR on the Occasion of His Seventy-Fifth Birthday and the Fiftieth Anniversary of His Ordination*, edited by L. P Gerson, 177–202. Toronto: Pontifical Institute of Mediaeval Studies, 1983.

Szabó, A. *The Beginnings of Greek Mathematics.* Boston: D. Reidel Publishing Company, 1978.

———. "Greek Dialectic and Euclid's Axiomatics. " In *Problems of the Philosophy of Mathematics*, edited by I. Lakatos, 1–8. Amsterdam: North-Holland Publishing Company, 1967.

———. "The Transformation of Mathematics into Deductive Science and the Beginning of Its Foundation on Definitions and Axioms." *Scripta Mathematica* 27 (1964): 27–48, 113–39.

———. "Working Backwards and Proving by Synthesis." In *The Method of Analysis: Its Geometrical Origin and Its General Significance.* Boston Studies in the Philosophy of Science 25, edited by Jaakko Hintikka and Unto Remes, 118–29. Boston: D. Reidel Publishing Company, 1974.

Tait, William W. *The Provenance of Pure Reason: Essays in the Philosophy of Mathematics and Its History.* New York: Oxford University Press, 2005.

Tarski, Alfred. *Introduction to Logic and to the Methodology of Deductive Sciences.* Translated by Olaf Helmer. Oxford University Press, 1946; repr. New York: Dover Publications, Inc., 1995.

———. *Logic, Semantics, Metamathematics.* 2nd ed. Translated by J. H. Woodger; Edited by J. Corcoran. Indianapolis: Hackett Publishing Company, Inc., 1983.

———. "What is Elementary Geometry?" In *The Axiomatic Method with Special Reference to Geometry and Physics: Proceedings of an International Symposium held at the University of California, Berkeley, December 26, 1957–January 4, 1958*, edited by L. Henkin, P. Suppes, and A. Tarski, 16–29. Amsterdam: North-Holland Publishing Company, 1959.

Thatcher, Adrian. *The Savage Text: The Use and Abuse of the Bible.* Malden, MA: Blackwell, 2008.

Thomas, Ivor, editor. *Greek Mathematical Works: From Aristarchus to Pappus.* Loeb Classical Library. Cambridge, MA: Harvard University Press, 1968.

———. *Greek Mathematical Works: Thales to Euclid.* Loeb Classical Library. Cambridge, MA: Harvard University Press, 1990.

Tucker, Neely. "The Book of Bart." *Washington Post* (March 5, 2006). Source: http://www .washingtonpost.com/wp-dyn/content/article/2006/03/04/AR2006030401369 _2.html.

Tummers, P. M. J. E. "The Commentary of Albert on Euclid's Elements of Geometry." In *Albertus Magnus and the Sciences. Commemorative Essays 1980*, edited by J. A. Weisheipl, 479–99. Toronto: Pontifical Institute of Medieval Studies, 1980.

Tuplin, C. J. and T. E. Rihll, editors. *Science and Mathematics in Ancient Greek Culture.* New York: Oxford University Press, 2002.

Vallicella, William F. *A Paradigm Theory of Existence: Onto-Theology Vindicated.* Philosophical Studies Series 89. Norwell, MA: Kluwer Academic Publishers, 2002.

van de Beek, A. "Being Convinced: On the Foundations of the Christian Canon." In *Canonization and Decanonization*, edited by A. van der Kooj and K. Van der Toom, 331–50. Leiden, Brill, 1998.

van der Waerden, B. L. *Science Awakening: Egyptian, Babylonian and Greek Mathematics.* Translated by A. Dresden. New York: John Wiley & Sons, Inc., 1963.

Van Till, Howard. "How Firm a Foundation? A Response to Justin L. Barrett's 'Is the Spell Really Broken?'" *Theology and Science* 6 (2008): 341–48.

Te Velde, Rudi. "The Good According to Thomas Aquinas." In *Die Metaphysik und das Gute: Aufsatze zu ihrem Verhaltnis in Antike und Mittelalter: Jan A. Aertsen zu Ehren.* Recherches de Theologie et Philosophie medievals 2., edited by W. Goris, 79–103. Leuven: Peeters, 1999.

Vickers, Jason E. "Canonical Theism and the Primacy of Ontology: An Essay concerning Human Understanding in Trinitarian Perspective." In *Canonical Theism: A Proposal for Theology and the Church*, edited by W. J. Abraham, J. E. Vickers, and N. B van Kirk, 156–74.Grand Rapids: Eerdmans, 2008.

Vlastos, Gregory. "Elenchus and Mathematics: A Turning-Point in Plato's Philosophical Development." *The American Journal of Philology* 109 (1988): 362–96.

———. "Raven's Pythagoreans and Eleatics." In *Studies in Greek Philosophy Volume I: The Presocratics*, edited by D. W. Graham, 180–88. Princeton: Princeton University Press, 1993.

———. "Theology and Philosophy in Early Greek Thought." In *Studies in Greek Philosophy Volume I: The Presocratics*, edited by D. W. Graham, 3–31. Princeton: Princeton University Press, 1993.

von Campenhausen, Hans. *The Formation of the Christian Bible*. Minneapolis: Fortress Press, 1972.

von Fritz, Kurt. "The Discovery of Incommensurability by Hippasus of Metapontum." In *Studies in Presocratic Philosophy Volume I: The Beginnings of Philosophy*, edited by D. J. Furley and R. E. Allen, 382–412. New York: Humanities Press, 1970.

Wagner, Robert J. "Euclid's Intended Interpretation of Superposition." *Historia Mathematica* 10 (1983): 63–70.

Wallace, Daniel. "The Gospel According to Bart." Source: http://www.bible.org/page.php?page_id=4000.

Wallace, E. C. and S. F. West. *Roads to Geometry*. Englewood Cliffs, NJ: Prentice Hall, 1992.

Wallace, W. A. *Galileo's Logic of Discovery and Proof: The Background, Content, and Use of His Appropriated Treatises on Aristotle's Posterior Analytics*. Boston Studies in the Philosophy of Science 137. Boston: Kluwer Academic Publishers, 1992.

———. "The Certitude of Science in Late Medieval and Renaissance Thought." *History of Philosophy Quarterly* 3 (1986): 281–91.

Warfield, B. B. *The Westminster Assembly and Its Work*. New York: Oxford University Press, 1931.

Webster, John. *Holy Scripture: A Dogmatic Sketch*. New York: Cambridge, 2003.

Wedberg, Andres. *Plato's Philosophy of Mathematics*. Stockholm: Almqvist & Wiksell, 1955.

Wedin, Michael V. "The Scope of Non-Contradiction: A Note on Aristotle's 'Elenctic' Proof in *Metaphysics* Gamma 4." *Apeiron* 32 (1999): 231–42.

Weingartner, Paul. "The Ideal of the Mathematization of All Sciences and of "More Geometrico" in Descartes and Leibniz." In *Nature mathematized. Historical and philosophical Case Studies in Classical Modern Natural Philosophy*, edited by W. R. Shea, 151–95. Boston: Kluwer Academic Publishers, 1983.

Weisstein, Eric W. "Lune." From MathWorld—A Wolfram Web Resource, http://mathworld.wolfram.com/Lune.html.

White, Alan W., editor. *Essays in Humanistic Mathematics*. Washington, D. C.: The Mathematics Association of America, 1993.

White, N. "The Origins of Aristotle's Essentialism." *The Review of Metaphysics* 26 (1972): 57–85.

Whitehouse, Harvey. *Modes of Religiosity: A Cognitive Theory of Religious Transmission*. Walnut Creek, CA: AltaMira Press, 2004.

Wians, William. "Aristotle, Demonstration and Teaching." *Ancient Philosophy* 9 (1989): 245–53.

———. "Commentary on Lloyd." In *Proceedings of the Boston Area Colloquium on Ancient Philosophy Volume VI 1990*, edited by J. J. Cleary and D. C. Shartin, 402–12. Lanham, MD: University Press of America, 1992.

———. "Review of Orna Harari, *Knowledge and Demonstration: Aristotle's Posterior Analytics.*" *Bryn Mawr Classical Review.* (2005), http://ccat.sas.upenn.edu/bmcr/2005/2005-09-37.html

———. "Scientific Examples in Posterior Analytics." In *Aristotle's Philosophical Development: Problems and Prospects*, edited by W. Wians, 131–50. Lanham, MD: Rowman and Littlefield Publishers, Inc., 1996.

Wians, William, editor. *Aristotle's Philosophical Development: Problems and Prospects.* Lanham, MD: Rowman and Littlefield Publishers, Inc., 1996.

Wilkinson, Will. "Aristotle on Dialectic and Demonstration." http://enlightenment.supersaturated.com/essays/text/willwilkinson/aristotledialectic.html.

Williams, C. J. "Good and Necessary Consequence in the Westminster Confession." In *The Faith Once Delivered: Essays in Honor of Dr. Wayne R. Spear*, edited by A. T. Selvaggio, 171–90. Phillipsburg, NJ: Presbyterian and Reformed Publishing, 2007.

Wolfsdorf, David. "The Method εξ υποθεσεως at *Meno* 86e1–87d8." *Phronesis* 53 (2008): 35–64.

Wolter, Allan B. *The Transcendentals and Their Function in the Metaphysics of Duns Scotus.* St. Bonaventure, NY: The Franciscan Institute, 1946.

Wynn, Mark R. *Emotional Experience and Religious Understanding: Integrating Perception, Conception and Feeling.* New York: Cambridge University Press, 2005.

Zhmud, Leonid. "Pythagoras as Mathematician." *Historia Mathematica* 16 (1989): 249–68.

* 9 7 8 1 4 9 8 2 5 2 9 5 9 *